Smartie

by
Steve Graham

Grosvenor House
Publishing Limited

This book is published by
Grosvenor House Publishing Ltd
Link House
140 The Broadway, Tolworth, Surrey, KT6 7HT.
www.grosvenorhousepublishing.co.uk

A CIP record for this book
is available from the British Library

ISBN 978-1-83975-617-7

Dedication

This book is dedicated to the memory
of Gillian Smart and is written with love
for my wife Carol, my son's David and Scott,
Stepson's Gary and Richie and our grandchildren,
Thomas Graham, Ava Graham, Edward Lynn
and Harriet Lynn.

CONTENTS

FOREWORD

I was delighted to hear that someone was writing a history of Seaton Burn Cricket Club based around the record number of centuries of David Smart.

Having played in the league for more than 30 years I got to know David Smart very well and always found him to be an excellent batsman and a man who has been a friend for most of those years.

When Steve started to research the book he asked me for some information and, luckily, I had access to all the historical files compiled by Jack Chapman which gave details of the records of many of the leading players in The TSL.

A lot of hard work has gone into the research for the book and it will be of interest to many former TSL players who will have been on the receiving end of many of the centuries described there.

There is also information about many of the opposition in the games described so you may find yourself appearing in some of the articles.

I hope the book is a huge success and that it will encourage many of you to consider writing a history of your own club because we are already 20 years past the final games in The TSL and we need to keep those memories alive of great competition played in friendly rivalry.

Peter Carroll Blaydon CC

PREFACE

This book is about the cricket and cricketer's over a period of time who played in the Tyneside Senior League. It is based on the memories and centuries of one of the best player's who graced the league in that time, and who, fortunately for me, also kept a number of scorebooks!

How and why it came about is best explained below.

The author was a keen amateur cricketer in his teen and early adult years. I played all my cricket for my local team, Seaton Burn Cricket Club in The Tyneside Senior League. I developed into a good second team fast bowler and useful batsman. I was an outstanding gully fielder if I immodestly say so myself!

If I played a full season I would probably score one fifty, fast bowling was my passion and the reason I played cricket. In short I was a decent second team cricketer for the period I played with an occasional good day in the first team.

I enjoyed my cricket but through a combination of work and a repeated knee problem I stopped playing in the early-mid nineties.

I have hardly been near local cricket since I stopped playing but during the recent pandemic I went to every Seaton Burn home game with my camera.

During these visits I reconnected with a number of former players from back in the day. Through talking to them I realised that there were virtually no records or photographs from this time period.

There were probably old score books lying around various locations which no-one would bother to download to the internet and some fantastic cricket and life memories would fade away as the combatants themselves pass away.

One of those I spoke to was David Smart, better known to all, as "Smartie."

Once the season finished and the pandemic continued I had a knee replacement at the end of September. During my six days in hospital I reflected on what a shame it was that all that local cricket knowledge was being slowly lost forever. I have one team photo from my playing days, that's from around 15 years playing, even Smartie, for all his runs and records, has just one action shot.

I had also realised from talking to Smartie and his son Ian, Stewart and Graeme Nixon, John Dixon, Graeme Dakers and Ray Cardwell just how good some of these local cricketers were, and how competitive the cricket was in The Tyneside Senior League during the time we played.

I started looking for a base to record some of these memories and quickly realised that Smartie was one of those top local cricketers of that time, and that the 23 League hundreds he scored from the first, in July 1979, till the last in August 2003, would make a nice time frame to cover.

I also realised, as did Smartie, that no-one of sound mind would want to read a book just about Smartie, so that I would like to try and recall some of those excellent local cricketers, some of those top class overseas professionals and some of the characters who played at this level.

Many of those mentioned will be grandads like myself, our kids and grandkids will know "Grandad/Dad played a bit of cricket," but I thought it would be nice for them to see in writing a bit more about that cricket.

Before you start reading the main body of the book, I would like to point out that when aggregate runs or wickets are written, that this would be the minimum that particular player got, records were often incomplete for a variety of reasons, not least because local papers stopped printing the full cricket scorecards when the football season started!

I should probably also clarify that I'm not related to Bill Graham!

CHAPTER 1

THE VILLAGE

Seaton Burn is a village in North Tyneside, six miles north of Newcastle City Centre. The Old Great North Road, The A1, runs through the heart of the village.

In every sense it's a former mining village and community. Seaton Burn Colliery opened in 1844, closing in 1965.

At it's peak in 1921 it employed 1311 people.

In 1953 Brenkley Drift Mine opened nearby and it eventually replaced Seaton Burn Colliery, including taking over some of it's buildings.

During the 1984-85 Miner's strike, such was the size and location of Brenkley Colliery that the "flying pickets" couldn't find the place and the colliery stayed open the Thursday and Friday of the week the strike started before Union meetings over the subsequent weekend ensured it fell in line with "most" of the rest of country and came out on strike.

Brenkley Colliery closed in December 1985, at the time it employed 639 men in total, 550 working underground, including the author, and a further 89 on the surface.

At the time of the closure the village had three pubs, The Moor House, The Six Mile Bridge Inn and The Drift Inn. The Drift, formerly known as The Miners Arms, was also known locally as "The Trap," presumably because of it's ability to ensnare miners who would call in for "a drink" and finds themselves still there hours later!

As well as the pubs the village also had a Social Club, Seaton Burn Working Men's Club.

Today, 2020, the Social Club has been demolished and replaced by sheltered accomodation. The Six Mile is now a very good Indian Restaurant. The Moor House alone remains.

The Drift Inn was demolished and the site remains an unused, partially overgrown car park. Over the years the Drift was a spiritual home for the cricket club, I'm sure many visiting teams and players have enjoyed a post match pint or three in there.

A few of the old colliery surface buildings remain and are now assorted modern day businesses and a business park stands where the main Brenkley Colliery Yard was.

The entrance to the Colliery Yard was almost directly across the old Great North Road from the access to the welfare and thereby, the cricket club.

CHAPTER 2

THE CRICKET CLUB

Seaton Burn Cricket Club was formed in 1873. It's history is very poorly documented. The fact that they played at Seaton Burn Miners Welfare for a long as anyone could remember would suggest it was originally paid for by a wealthy mineowner, for the benefit of their workers, or, it was paid for by the workers themselves.

On Wednesday 24th July 1907 the newly built cricket pavilion was presented to the cricket club by the colliery company.

The current version was built in 1955.

It's upkeep in later year's was paid for by deductions from Miners Pay to C.I.S.W.O, The Coal Industry Social and Welfare Organisation.

The land, technically, was owned by the National Coal Board (N.C.B)which was formed in 1947 to run the nations coal industry. With the decimation of that coal industry that followed the 1984-85 Miner's Strike, the N.C.B was dissolved in 1987.

My understanding is that Seaton Burn Miner's Welfare was given under covenent to North Tyneside Council to run as a leisure facility. I believe part of that covenent is that there is no change of use of the land allowed. It remains the home of Seaton Burn Cricket Club to this day, although "Miner's" has been dropped from the title of the welfare.

In terms of life on the cricket field there is almost nothing to denote any success at all! There was a lot of talk of the club having a very good team in the late sixties, there were an occasional cup final here and there in the eighties and nineties, I even played in one myself, but for almost 150 years of cricket, not a lot of trophies!

In fairness to the current crop of players both first and second team's won promotion in the 2019 season!

One of the main things that made life difficult for the Club was the lack of their own bar. Folklore says the "welfare" used to have it's own bar until certain licensing irregularities were discovered one Sunday morning, sometime in the early 70's, and the license was revoked. The lack of a bar meant the club didn't have the funds to hire a professional for a long time.

During the period covered in this book the cricket club was fortunate to enjoy the support of a succession of licensees at The Drift Inn. Sandra Graham, Brandy Robinson and Darren Carr would provide prizes and pints in support of quiz evenings, race nights, even barbeques, a belated thank you to all three!

Darren became landlord of the "Drift" late in 1992. Having played cricket for The DHSS from 1988 it was a natural fit that he would play for Seaton Burn. Incredibly, in 2004, in his first game back after suffering a brain haemorrhage, he scored 100 not out for the seconds against Percy Main. He would add a second hundred in 2005, 111 against Lanchester for the seconds, caught at third man! He was still playing for the club during the 2020 Pandemic Season.

His son, Ryan, would play both junior and senior cricket at Seaton Burn and also represent Northumberland as a junior.

The club did produce one or two notable player's over the years, albeit not necessarily in the cricketing world.

Footballer and England International Andy Sinton played junior and a liitle senior cricket at Seaton Burn. I recall opening the batting for the juniors with him and also playing for the second team with him. He was a talented batsman. He played a handful of games for the first team before he left the area at 16 to sign for Cambridge United F.C.

Within a few months of going he was playing first team football in the "old" second division. He would go on to play for Brentford, QPR, Sheffield Wednesday and Tottenham Hotspur. He would play 12 full Internationals for England. Andy's brother, Graeme, played cricket for the club for many years and his dad, Ken, was a regular spectator at the cricket field.

Probably the best and most well known cricketer the club helped produce was John Graham. John was one of two sons of Bill Graham.

Bill made his first team debut in 1961 whilst still a pupil at Gosforth Grammar School. He made an immediate impact as a batsman, going on to score centuries in 1963 and 1964. It's worth noting that centuries were much rarer in these days too.

Bill was a talented football player too, so much so that his football took him away from cricket. He was centre forward for Aberdeen in 1964 and despite scoring a hat trick in the last game of the season he moved to Queen of the South in 1965. He would go on to play for South Shields for a number of years.

On 3rd January 1970 he played for Shields in the 3rd round of the F.A Cup away against Queens Park Rangers. The QPR side had Terry Venables and Rodney Marsh playing so the 4-1 score wasn' too much of a surprise but getting this far in the competition would have been a tremendous achievement.

When his soccer career was over, he was still a good enough cricketer to score another century in 1974 and Smartie is convinced there is a fourth century in Bill's career that the statisticians have missed.

At the time of writing Bill is one of only fifteen batsman good enough to have scored over 10,000 runs in the TSL and N & TSL. Smartie recalls that despite only taking up bowling when his batting tailed off a bit, he developed into a very good left arm spinner, taking all 9 Shotley Bridge wickets that fell in a match in 1984.

He had a number of roles at the club over the years, including first team captain and he became club secretary in 1978.

Cade Brown recalls when he was to come to the club as a teenage professional from Australia how he received a lovely hand written letter from Bill, welcoming him to the club. Cade describes him as a "man who I admired for his humour and competitive spirit."

He would go on to become Team Manager of Northumberland CC, during which time he guided them to an appearance at Lords in 2004 in the Final of the MCCA Knockout Trophy.

Bill's eldest son Mark, was scorer for a number of seasons as a youngster and a good few of the scorebooks I used to compile this book were in his handwriting. Only an occasional cricketer before he went to university, I do recall him scoring a fifty for the second team.

Younger son John, played junior, second team and first team cricket at Seaton Burn. He was a right handed batsman and useful occasional medium pace bowler. He scored 2614 runs for Seaton Burn.

In 1995, aged 17, he scored 912 League runs for the club, including one century, an unbeaten 104 against Greenside plus eight half centuries.

After playing for Durham Academy, unfortunately a period when he was struck with both illness and injury, he became better known to the local cricketing world when he moved three miles down the road from Seaton Burn to South Northumberland Cricket Club in the year 2000.

John played Under 19 cricket for England, including a tour abroad, and has represented both Durham and Northumberland Counties.

At South North he was captain for many years and won many Premier League Titles and cups. In 2006 he captained the side which won The Cockspur Cup, a national competition at Lord's. He now has over 10,000 North East Premier League runs and although he relinquished the captaincy in 2016, he has continued to score runs.

The other well known local cricketer who started at Seaton Burn was Kevin Corby. Kevin was a truly outstanding wicketkeeper. He would go on to have trials with Northants, Warwickshire and Glamorgan. Sadly the first two games of those trials were washed out, leaving him with only one real trial.

Even now if his name crops up on social media, someone will always put a comment on saying he was the best wicketkeeper they ever saw or ever played with or against. He started as a young man at Seaton Burn in 1974 aged 15, as a wicketkeeper and promising batsman. He played one game for the second team, at South Moor, and then was in the first team the following week.

Remembering his Seaton Burn days, Kevin states that "Over the years at Seaton Burn I played with some inspiring cricketers, David Smart, Bill Wilkinson, Bill Taylor, Bill Graham and many more, I learnt a lot from them."

Bill Graham, Seaton Burn captain at the time, was to say in the local media of the 17 year old Kevin Corby, "I can see Kevin emerging as a really top batsman."

He left Seaton Burn for Tynedale following the 1977 season. He would remain there for nine seasons. The club went through a purple patch during those years, winning many cups and league titles.

Whilst there Kevin himself says "I had the honour of playing with some great professionals, Alex Johnson, Kelvin Williams, Courtney Walsh and Stewart Gillespie."

He made his debut for Northumberland Minor Counties against Lancashire at Jesmond in 1977. He played for Northumberland from 1977 until 1991, making 55 Minor Counties appearances and 9 MCCA Knockout Matches. He played 4 List A matches, the first against Middlesex in the Natwest Trophy in 1984.

During these years with Northumberland Corby was regularly keeping wicket to quality international bowlers such as Mushtaq Mohammad, Wasim Raja, Chris Old and many others.

In 1984 he played for the Minor Counties against a touring Kenya side.

1982-Kevin Sharp of Yorkshire is stumped by Kevin Corby of Northumberland

In 1987 Corby moved to County Club where he played for five seasons before returning to Seaton Burn. He scored at least six centuries for County Club, including a century in three consecutive innings.

Corby also played in some of the Callers Pegasus Festival matches held at Jesmond. They started out on 6th August 1981 and ran until 1983, being replaced in 1984 until 1990 with an England side taking on the Rest of the World.

Kevin describes the highlight being selected for the Rest of the World side against England in 1988 following an injury to Jeff Dujon. The scorecard of the day shows that Allan Border, Steve Waugh, Imran Khan and Dennis Lillee were among those also playing for the side that day! The England side was led by Graham Gooch and included Robin Smith, Phil Defreitas, Neil Foster and Gladstone Small!

I can recall going as a spectator to these games and whilst I can't remember the details, Kevin's wicketkeeping didn't look out of place in the very exalted company he was keeping!

Corby moved back to Seaton Burn around 1992, taking on the captaincy and also becoming Chairman. To remain competitive the club then took the decision to engage a professional, fast bowler Alan Francis, who was signed from Kirkley.

Following the success of Francis, Corby also played with professionals, Cade Brown and Jamie Sullivan from Australia, and West Indian, Leroy Lazama. He states "all did the club proud."

Brown describes Corby as "the best stumper I have ever seen or played with. He was one hell of a guy. He was my captain, my mate, my mentor and a guiding light through three seasons I was there. His keeping was like nothing I had ever seen before. Limited footwork but a pair of hands that were made for the role, the ball made the softest sound when it hit his gloves. He was faultless when standing back to the quicks but it was his work standing up to the stumps which left me in awe. Leg side stumpings off Alan Francis would often drag us back into a contest and Kevin knew he could win us a game from nowhere through doing something special.

His batting was great to watch. He used to take the attack to the bowlers under all circumstances and was before his time. I still scratch my head as to why he didn't play not just a little bit of first class cricket, but a lot. He also didn't mind a pint!"

Corby scored at least 4 centuries in his second Seaton Burn career, there is no record of how many career victims he had behind the stumps, probably too many to count!

Think of the 17 year old Kevin Corby leaving Seaton Burn and joining the Durham Academy instead of Tynedale. Everyone who ever saw him keep wicket is of the opinion he was good enough to play first class cricket. Who knows what he could have achieved if the opportunity had been there which is available to the best of today's youngsters.

Kevin had followed his grandfather Les to become a player for Seaton Burn, it was from his grandfather that Kevin got his love of cricket. His own father also Les, and mother Ethel, were great supporters of Kevin's career, as was his wife Julie, all attending as many games as possible.

I had a chat with Julie about Kevin's cricket career. She said at one point, their son Neil was still a baby and the couple living at Cramlington, they had a family discussion with Kevin's parents about the possibility of a first class career for Kevin.

Such was her support for his career she agreed that should the opportunity arrive, the family would move to wherever necessary and live in a caravan to give Kevin the best chance to make it.

Neil was to follow in his fathers footsteps as a wicketkeeper at Seaton Burn, starting there as a junior in the 1990's. He worked his way through the second team to the first team, playing Northumberland Junior Cricket along the way. He moved to South Northumberland in 2004, going on to establish himself as first team wicketkeeper and helping the club to win the Premier League title five times.

The highlight of Neil's time there was winning the 2006 Cockspur Cup Final at Lords when "South North" beat Bromley. Part of the prize was to play in a cricket festival in Barbados!

Neil Corby also played in the winning T20 National Knockout Cup Side in 2008. This game took place at The Swalec Stadium in Cardiff, Wales and was televised live by Sky Television.

In 2010 he moved to County Club as a wicketkeeper batsman and played there until 2016. He spent seven months in 2011/12 at Claremont Nederland in Perth, Australia playing cricket.

In 2017 he moved to Swalwell, winning the league in the first two seasons he was there.

Richard Allan was another who represented his country. Richie was deaf from birth. He never allowed this to hold him back, on or off the field, and he was well known throughout the Tyneside Senior League. He was a left handed opening batsman and right arm swing bowler.

In 1991 he had trials and was selected for the British Deaf Cricket Team to tour Australia in 1992.

He was required to find £750 towards the cost of the trip. The whole of the cricket club rallied around him, Gary Stephenson leading the way, and eventually a total of £1547.30p was raised on his behalf.

This paid for his trip plus another player to go and what was left he was given to buy himself some new gear. He left to go on tour on 26th December 1991 and returned on 3rd February 1992.

In the first ever Deaf Cricket Match between the two countries played on 6th January 1992 at The W.A.C.A, he has the distinction of being the first wicket to fall, LBW for 9.

Although the Australians won five nil Richie played in all of the test matches and had a top score of 41.

Sunday 28th July 1991 Richie Allan going out to bat
in the match to raise the funds to send him to Australia

CHAPTER 3

THE LEAGUE

The Tyneside Senior League was formed in 1900 and remained intact through until it merged with the Northumberland League in 1999. It operated through the war years.

In 1933 the league was predominantly Northumberland based teams with several teams from Durham. In 1934 the Northumberland teams officially broke away leaving the Tyneside Senior League to fend for itself.

The Tyneside Senior League covered by this book, featured fourteen teams, only two of whom were based north of the River Tyne, Seaton Burn and Wallsend. The demise of one of those clubs, Wallsend, is well illustrated in this book. Wallsend were replaced by Felling Cricket Club.

Each team played the 13 other teams home and away, maximum 26 league games in total. The points system was 4 or 5 points for a win, depending if the opposition were bowled out or not, 1 or 0 points for a loss using the same criteria, if you lost and were all out, no points, if you lost and had even one wicket in tact, you got a point.

It would be remiss when writing about the Tyneside Senior League not to mention Don Robson and Bob Jackson. Both men were heavily involved with the league before they set about the task of bringing first class status to Durham. Robson became League Chairman in 1970 and Jackson the League Secretary for many years.

Robson first got involved with cricket during a conversation in Winlaton with Peter Carroll. He had played some cricket for Blaydon at this point. Greenside at the time was a colliery or "pit" village and Carroll mentioned that they were struggling to find enough players on the Saturday because of the "pit" holidays.

Robson turned out and so began a long term relationship with Greenside CC.

He quickly became Club Chairman and was the driving force behind a bar being installed in the clubhouse and then the appointment of a Club Professional.

On the field, Greenside won the league in 1966, shared the title with Shotley Bridge in 1967 and then won it the next seven years in a row.

The ground was purchased from the NCB in 1967 for £750. It was subsequently fenced and then the field levelled, the latter being a major task!

A new scorebox was next, followed in 1972 by a new pavillion!

One of his major contributions to the league was the formation of junior leagues.

Roles with the Durham Cricket Board, Durham County Council and Chairman of the National Cricket Council all followed.

Smartie recalls talking to Don Robson one day, walking round the boundary at a cricket match somewhere as local cricketers do, and they were discussing society in general. It was some time during the eighties, against the back drop of the Miner's Strike, Thatcherism and riots in London.

He had said to Smartie "I'm really pleased I'm involved with cricket." Naturally Smartie had asked him "Why?" The reply stuck with Smartie even all these years later "Because you find that there are very, very few people who play cricket, who are not good people."

When Don Robson died in 2016, aged 82, he was a C.B.E. Durham was a first class cricket county and it's pavillion was named after him.

Bob Jackson was a Lintz man. He started as a junior becoming a second team regular, making only an occasional appearance for the first team.

Lintz had been members of The North West Durham League, Jackson had been Secretary since 1962.

In 1970 they became members of The Tyneside Senior League.

One night Don Robson met with Lintz Chairman, Bill Carradice, he told him the League had need of a Secretary.

"My Son-In-Law is good" said Carradice.

Appointment duly made, Robson would later go on to describe Jackson as "the perfect administrator," mind you he was quick to add "Getting Bob was a good move, cos' we got his wife Maureen as well!"

Jackson was to go on to become Durham Cricket Association Secretary, a Durham CCC Director, a Director of The ECB and Deputy Chairman of the Regional Assembly. In 2011 he was awarded an M.B.E for voluntary services to North East Cricket.

Durham were made a first class county in 1992.

Incredible to think that two humble men who had their roots in Tyneside Senior League cricket would go on to make such an impact on the wider cricketing world.

CHAPTER 4

OPENING THE INNINGS

David Smart was born in November 1951. His mother was Dorothy and his father Joe. He was always going to be known as Smartie!

Joe had a reputation as a gent, never known to swear, he was club treasurer at Seaton Burn for many years and he was also well known for his love of cricket. He was always one to encourage the youngsters.

At the time Joe played the club had a relatively strong first team and he played most of his cricket in the second team, as a middle order batsman. He passed his love of cricket on to his only son, David, and he recalls spending a lot of time at the cricket field watching his father play and credits his own love of the game to his father.

Ray Cardwell recalls aged 10 or 11, playing cricket with Smartie in the school yard at lunchtime. Ray says that the rule was if you hit a six you were out.

He remembers himself and his fellow school mates trying to hit sixes, despite the consequences, all except one, one kid who was practising playing straight and ended up not out........Smartie!

Smartie's made his debut in Senior cricket in 1967, with Seaton Burn Second Team against Greenside. He played one game for the first team that season, scoring 7 against South Moor.

He was playing first team cricket regularly by the start of the 1969 season.

His first senior half century came in 1971, in a second team game against Vickers when he hit 79 not out. At the time Vickers was regarded as one of the best batting tracks in the League.

Ray Cardwell also played in that game, scoring 70 odd himself, he recalls outscoring Smartie when the pair were at the crease together. Remembering those much earlier schoolboy days

16

Ray liked to boast to Smartie that he had outscored him, albeit Ray modestly admits, "probably for the only time!"

Ray also points out that Smartie had opened the batting, Ray went in three or four, although he outscored Smartie during the innings, just like the school yard, Smartie was not out, Ray wasn't!

This was also to become a regular occurence when Smartie scored big runs in the League, he had three scores over 150, all of which were unbeaten, as were 15 of the 23 League hundreds he scored.

His maiden senior 50 was quickly followed just two innings later with another, 58 not out against South Moor Second Team.

With the last league game of the 1972 season, Smartie got his maiden first team fifty, 52, against Wallsend. He would score 29 half centuries between this one and the game in July 1979 against Shotley Bridge when he scored his first hundred.

SBCC 1973

Back Row- Ray Cardwell, Stewart Nixon, David Smart, John Macguire, Dennis Gibson, Brian Ord
Front Row- David Graham, Billy Taylor, Bobby Dodds, Billy Wilkinson, Bill Graham

I recall bowling to him in the nets, watching him from the sidelines and also occasionally being the batsman at the other end. He always played so straight, looking to get on the front foot.

At over six feet tall and powerfully built he liked to get to the pitch of the ball and hit it in the "v" or through the covers. From memory, every six I saw him hit, and there were a few, were always straight.

It wasn't as if he didn't have the cut, the pull or the hook in his armoury because he certainly did, I think he realised where his strengths lay and looked to utilise those strengths, scoring off the front foot whenever possible.

He was also "world class" at counting to six and finding the gaps in the field to take a single off the last ball of the over!

I think there are a couple of things which should also be remembered.

Only one or two clubs had covers, Seaton Burn not being one of them, so effectively you were almost always batting on uncovered wickets.

Furthermore, it would have only been the very latter years of his career that helmets became common amongst local league cricketers. As you read the book, I hope you get the sense of how quick some of the bowlers of this time were!

The last thing to raise would be the practise regime of the day.

Seaton Burn would have indoor nets probably from late February until the week before the season started. Weather permitting, we would try and get one outdoor session in before the season started.

Once the season was underway we would have an outdoor net on a Tuesday evening. It was done in such a way that the order you arrived in, was the order you batted in. Also, how long you got depended on how many people had turned up, 10 to 12 minutes would be a great session, 8 or 9 would be more normal.

Once the season was underway we would often play cup matches on a Tuesday so there was often no practise that week!

Think about it, uncovered pitches, no helmets, quality fast bowling and very limited practise. Good luck scoring runs.

CHAPTER 5

THE MAIDEN CENTURY-
SHOTLEY BRIDGE

On Saturday 14th July 1979 Seaton Burn played a home league fixture against Shotley Bridge at Seaton Burn Miners Welfare.

Shotley Bridge around this time were an excellent side. They would go on to win the league this year and the following year and then again in 1984.

In 1979 they had three players in the league batting averages, professional Steve Atkinson would finish this season top of the league batting averages with 1171 runs at an average of 65.06. Davie Collingwood with 512 runs at an average of 24.38 and Jack Chapman with 247 runs at 20.58 would also feature.

Collingwood was missing from today's fixture. Paul Nesbit remembers him well, describing him as "The first team opening bat from the early 1960's to the late 1980's when he dropped down into the second team for three seasons. During this time he scored 20,000 runs in first team league and cup cricket. This is the second most aggregate runs scored by a Shotley player, beaten only by his son, Peter. Dave was never a big hitter, but he was an intelligent right handed batsman who valued his wicket and had a great defence.

His style was workmanlike, finding gaps and accumulating runs in single's, two's and three's. That said, his timing was excellent, cutting, driving straight and through the covers and playing balls off his toes, always along the ground.

Over his career he had many opening partners, the one with Steve Atkinson from 1979 to 1981 was one of the most fruitful and enjoyable."

Smartie recalls that Collingwood was "like lightning between the wickets, he liked to play off the front foot but could play all round the wicket. He was a really nice fella off the pitch."

He is also known as being the father of England cricket legend Paul!

Stuart Wilkinson would top the league bowling averages with 59 wickets at 9.69 each. Lee Pollard with 55 wickets at 13.76 would also feature in the league bowling averages.

Both Wilkinson and Pollard were also missing this game today.

Smartie's memories of Stuart Wilkinson are mainly about the pace. He recalls "a right arm fast bowler, before overseas pro's came into the league there was Bill Jones, Ian Wishart and "Wilkie" who were the three quickest in the local leagues. If you played any of these three, plus Bob Cook, you knew you were in for a testing afternoon because of their pace. "Wilkie" also had that rare ability to swing the ball at great pace. He was a quiet man on and off the field but a true "legend of north east cricket."

Smartie recalls one game in particular against Wilkinson at Seaton Burn, although not for the reason you might expect!

As he walked to the wicket to bat, the umpire, Jock Houghton, said to him

"Wilkie's going to bowl you first ball today Smartie!"

Houghton was a real character, originally from Cornwall, he played his cricket at Leadgate. He was known as Jock because he always wore a tartan cap. I fondly recall him from my own cricket days, always good natured, cheeky with it and the above comment completely in keeping with the man.

Wilkinson duly bowled the first ball and Smartie with it!

Houghton immediatley broke into loud laughter, as he passed him at square leg on the way back to the pavillion Smartie, also laughing, pretended to kick Houghton in the rear and turned the air blue, making Houghton's laughter even worse.

The umpire at the other end asked what had been said, as did Charlie Stephenson, Smartie told them and the Shotley lads found it hilariously funny too!

At this time of today's game Smartie would have been 28 years old and have been regarded by opposition as the main batting threat in the Seaton Burn side. He had scored 29 first team half centuries up to this point with a top score of 87 not out.

The scorer for the match was Bill Taylor. Bill was a Seaton Burn stalwart, even now, over 40 years later, he is still seen almost every Saturday afternoon during the season, doing at least one "lap" of the Seaton Burn outfield. He played for Seaton Burn first of all as a 14 year old boy.

He was a stylish right hand batsman, particularly strong off his back foot, especially when playing the cut shot. He was also a very good off spinner, and it was this that got him selected for the league side in 1983, aged 50!

The game was a Wilkinson Cup match against the North East Durham League, it took place on 5th June at Coles Crane Ground. He bowled well with figures of 10-3-16-2. Despite this, and 31 from fellow Seaton Burn player, Bill Graham, it wasn't quite enough as they lost by 7 runs.

His role in todays events shall reveal itself at tea!

Shotley Bridge wicketkeeper/batsman Paul Nesbit has provided some memories of those who played on the day.

This was Nesbit's second first team game back after a cartilage operation. A good footballer he had sustained the injury at the end of the 1978/79 season while playing for Annfield Plain in The Wearside League. After a small number of games in the second team he had returned to the first team just prior to this game with Seaton Burn.

He had started his cricket career as a junior wicketkeeper/batsman at Shotley in 1967. In his first game in senior cricket he captured six victims, although he credits that to the "great leg spinner, Michael Beveridge."

Progress was straight into the second team but they already had a regular keeper in George Nash, so the more mobile Nesbit was mainly used in the outfield.

At the end of that season, Jack Milburn, father of England Legend Colin, asked Shotley if they would let Nesbit move across to Burnopfield to keep wicket for their first team. Everything was done properly in those days and the move was amicably agreed.

That started a long first team career with Burnopfield until 1974, then he rejoined Shotley in 1975.

Although a wicketkeeper/batsman he would spend the 1979 season, this season, in the field as he recovered from the knee operation. Barry Hicks would keep wicket instead.

Nesbit would also have a spell as captain. During this period the team won the Tyneside Senior League in 1984. He recalls that "Wasim Raja, the Pakistan International Leg Spinner was professional that season and that when bowling he did not just make batsmen look foolish but also the wicketkeeper more times than he cares to remember!"

During the late 1980's Nesbit would share wicketkeeper duties with Barry Hicks, as Shotley sought to utilise his fielding abilities. He was a capable fielder, with great hands and relatively quick across the grounds, his throwing however could go anywhere except the wicketkeeper's gloves!

As a batsman, Nesbit describes himself as "having good eyes which helped me overcome a lack of technique. I was however, a master of the sweep!"

Whilst still registered and playing for Shotley third team in 2015 and 2016 he also played for Burnopfield second eleven.

Nesbit had the honour of playing for Leeds University in 1972 and 1973 and the Tyneside Senior League representative side in 1976.

He has spent the last decade playing for the Durham and Northumberland Over 60's side and records show that he accumulated over 22,000 runs in all forms of cricket.

Seaton Burn batted first and Smartie opened the batting with Gary Stephenson. Gary, a right handed batsman and often, in later life, a wicketkeeper, was in his late teen's at this time.

The opening bowlers for Shotley were Keith Emerson and Alan Raine. Emerson would normally be supporting Stuart Wilkinson with the new ball, but in this game Shotley were without him and Lee Pollard.

Emerson had rejoined Shotley from Langley Park in 1977, having previously played for three seasons for Shotley at the beginning of the decade. During his seven years at Shotley he would take just short of 500 wickets.

Whilst at Langley Park he had also played for Langley Park Ramshead in a seven a side competition. After losing the 1975 final they would go one better a year later, winning the final in Corfu!

Nesbit describes Emerson as "right arm medium quick, this brought him 58 league and cup wickets during the 79 season, although the previous season had seen him have his best season at Shotley with 78 wickets in all competitions."

Nesbit remembers Raine as "still a young cricketer at this time. He had come up through the junior ranks. He was a particularly good second team bowler but someone who never made the transition into the first eleven."

Smartie recalls that Raine would have been "Just a young lad at this time, that said, he moved the ball about quite a bit."

Both were seen off wicketless to be replaced by Steve Atkinson and Keith Oxley.

Atkinson had been engaged as club professional this season, based mainly on his batting ability. On arrival at the club he had managed to persuade Barry Hicks, the club captain, that he was also a bowler.

It was not until the subsequent two seasons that his bowling talent really shone through. In his three seasons as professional and an additional five games in 1982, he developed into a more than capable in-swing bowler, capable of surprising pace and taking a total of 288 league and cup wickets.

That said it was his batting which had earned his reputation and in his 147 innings over three seasons he scored 5838 runs at an average of 52.

This would be Oxley's only first team game of the season. He had started as a junior in 1954 and played nearly 40 years for the club, playing almost all of his cricket in the second eleven. He captained the second eleven from 1973 to 1979.

Almost every junior who progressed through the club during these years had the benefit of Oxley's support, helping to develop before being blooded in the first eleven. Alan Raine who had opened the bowling today was a good example of this.

It must have been tough going as after bowling nine overs Emerson had bowled four maidens and given away just six runs!

Smartie and Stephenson put on an opening stand of 78 before Stephenson was bowled by the third ball of Oxley's second over for 24.

This brought the left handed Billy Wilkinson to the crease. "Pep" or "Peppers" as he was known throughout the league. Smartie was too young to see Billy batting at his prime but recalls that "he had been good enough to have built a good reputation as a batsman. At this stage of his career, he could still hit the ball hard and regularly, though he wasn't too keen on a quick single!"

A second wicket stand of 31 before Wilkinson was bowled by Raine for 15.

Bill Graham was batting at four. Another left hander, Smartie and Bill had opened many times together over the years. Smartie recalls that "Bill always kept himself very fit and we ran well together, I can only recall one run out between us during the many occasions we batted together. Bill never threw his wicket away, he wasn't a flamboyant batsman but he was a good player through the covers and off his legs if the ball was pitched up. He was not a hooker or puller as a batsman and would simply get out of the way and let the ball go if it was short and at his body."

A short lived partnership of 11 followed, Graham being caught by Alan Milburn off the bowling of Atkinson for 1.

Seaton Burn 120 for 3.

Barry Smithson, a former Shotley Bridge player, came in at five. In later years I played a lot of second team cricket with Barry, he was a lovely, lovely man, always encouraging, very mild mannered. As a cricketer he was a right handed batsman who liked to put bat to ball.

Ray Cardwell, who captained Barry for a number of years in the second team, describes how he always sought Barry's advice on incoming batsman, because of Barry's memory of individuals and how they liked to play, remembering their strengths "he's a driver, he's good off his legs, he likes to pull or hook."

After another partnership of 11, Smithson was caught and bowled by Raine for 4. Seaton Burn had slipped from 109 for 1 to 131 for 4 and the innings was in the balance.

Malcolm Ashforth came in at 5. He had started as a junior at County Club, where his father, also Malcolm, had played. He played a lot of Sunday cricket for a team called "Vikings". They were loosely based out of County Club but only played away fixtures.

He was a very upright batsman, right handed, he liked to hit the ball straight and could certainly hit it hard. His son, Keith, still plays for Seaton Burn, just short of his 50th birthday, and his grandson, Lewis would also play for the club.

Keith was like his father in respect of where he liked to hit the ball, straight and hard, he also had the best arm in the outfield that I ever saw!

An unbroken stand of 48 ensured that the innings didn't fall away.

A competitive total of 179 for 4 was reached from the allotted 45 overs.

Ashforth was 22 not out, including three boundaries.

Smartie was 99 not out!

Raine was the pick of the bowlers with 12-1-46-2. Oxley had 4-1-17-1, Atkinson 11-0-58-1 and Emmerson 18-4-45-0.

Seaton Burn's scorebox, back in the day, and is still there today, is on the first floor of the pavillion. It was a very basic scoreboard, metal tins with painted numbers hung on nails. Total, wickets, overs bowled and first inning scored being the only things on show.

No luxuries here, such as batsman's individual score. If a batsman got 50, or on the very rare occasion's a 100, the scorer would stand up, stick their head out of the scorebox window and shout across to the field "Batsman's 50" or "Batsman's 100."

So some batsman used to count their runs as they got them.

Smartie was one of those batsman.

With two balls to go in the innings, the batsman had conferred in the middle of the wicket, Smartie saying to Malcolm, "I'm on ninety nine, there's two balls left, I'm going to try and push a single, you can try and hit the next one for six for all I care!"

A single was duly taken......no reaction from the scorebox, or anywhere else for that matter.

As he walked off the field at the end of the over, Steve Atkinson, who Smartie knew well through playing for the league side, said to him

"Did you think you had a hundred there?"

Smartie replied "I know I did, cos' I count!"

Atkinson responded with "How the hell do you manage that?"

Smartie replied "I've counted since I was a kid!"

I'm pretty sure Cambridge Graduate Atkinson could count too but you know what he meant!

41 years later I have checked, and re-checked the scorebook.......Bill Taylor, as a good scorer should, had periodically made small notes at certain times in the course of Smartie's innings, 20, 30, 50, 66, 77 and 93.

At sixty, Smartie had hit a six, then a single, the mark of 66 could be interpreted as being above either the six or the single. The next note was with the score at 77.......it was actually 78!

No raised bat, no applause from team mates but somehow in keeping completely with village cricket!

As was the way of club cricket, both captains would check the scorebook at tea. Alan Milburn's son, Neil, then a young lad, had been scoring for the day and discovered the discrepency. It was pointed out to Kenny Day and the matter was corrected, Smartie had his first ton!

Later on in life Neil Milburn would play second team cricket at Seaton Burn, he was a great character and teammate and useful opening batsman, albeit a clumsy fielder at best!

Shotley Bridge opened the batting with Steve Atkinson and John Chapman. Chapman was known to all as Jack.

Paul Nesbit is fulsome in his praise for the abilities of Steve Atkinson, describing him as "the most complete local batsman ever to play at Shotley Bridge in the last 50 years, even when compared with the visiting overseas professional's, there were few who were his equal.

His base was a solid defence, that then erupted into playing shots to every part of the ground.

He was a tall strong batsman who played through the covers off the back foot with such power, hitting lofted drives to the fuller balls.

Although not a natural sweeper, he would pull and hook with ferocity. He was a natural athlete, when the bowling was tight he always looked for the quick single and looked to turn the singles into two's, the two's into three's."

In Smartie's opinion Steve Atkinson was a truly outstanding cricketer. He was Shotley's professional this season. On June 30th 1973, in the 1st round of the 60 over a side Gillette Cup, Durham became the first Minor Counties side to beat a first class county in a competitive match. Atkinson opened the batting for Durham that day, scoring 14. His fellow Shotley player, Stuart Wilkinson bowled a certain Geoffrey Boycott that day too. Yorkshire had four England players in their team as Durham made history!

Atkinson would score over a thousand runs this season, including three centuries, with a best of 127. He later moved to Holland and subsequently Hong Kong for work, Shotley and Durham both lost a great player.

There is a twist in the tale. It seems Hong Kong Cricket were benefactors of Steve Atkinson's move. Years later his son, Jamie, would go on to captain their national side in 2014 in their first global tournament, the World T20 in Bangladesh. He was a right handed batsman and wicketkeeper.

Jack Chapman initially got into Leslie's first team in 1955 and subsequently captained them for ten seasons. As they declined in the early 70's Chapman knew he would have to leave to maintain a decent standard of cricket. In 1973 Chapman scored more than a quarter of the entire first teams runs, despite this they did not win a match. He finished the season with 518 runs with a highest score of 83. Leslie's disbanded. Chapman was the highest run scorer in their history with 6257 runs and he also took 50 wickets for them.

Blaydon were the new choice of club for Chapman. He states he had a "wretched" first season, not helped by twisting his knee when running with fellow opener Dave Richardson. Chapman says that Richardson was renowned for his running, running him out no less than six times that season!

He moved to Shotley Bridge in 1978, staying there for three seasons, including winning the TSL in 1978 and 1979 as well as numerous cups.

This season for Shotley he made the league averages, with 247 runs from 12 completed innings at 20.58.

He again returned to Blaydon for the 1981 season.

Chapman would play second team and then third team cricket for Blaydon until his retirement in 1999.

When Blaydon were approaching their Centenary Year, 1991, Chapman wrote and produced a book, 100 Years of Blaydon CC. He went on to write two more cricket books "Cream Teas and Nutty Slack" and "Cream Teas and Canny Crack."

When Blaydon started in The North East Premier League he would produce a game programme for them.

Jack Chapman scored over 7,000 runs in The Tyneside Senior League, he also served for many years as Statistics Secretary and was made a Life Member for services to the League.

Courtesy of Peter Carroll, many of the statistics and records I have used have originated from Jack Chapman.

Mike Smith and Billy Wilkinson opened the bowling for Seaton Burn. Mike Smith was my chemistry teacher at Seaton Burn High School and a solid Yorkshireman! He must have been a pretty good teacher as I got the equivalent of an "O" Level in Chemistry!

A right arm fast bowler, he was very capable at this level. Smartie describes him as being "a very good bowler, very accurate, a Yorkshireman who liked to give nothing away, including runs!

Smith was also ultra competitive, not in an aggressive way but that he was always determined to give his all and he left nothing out there when he was done."

This season he took 26 wickets at an average of 26.84.

In 1977 Smith had a good enough year to make the league averages, taking 53 wickets at 16.70 each.

Smartie remembers Billy Wilkinson as "a right arm, slow/ medium bowler. He liked to bowl "up the bank" at Seaton Burn. He had a round arm action bowling away swingers to the right handed batsman. The thing is, he could also bowl an excellent, well disguised off break, the one that comes back into the right hander, and he was good enough and wily enough to bowl one an over!"

He finished the season with 28 wickets at an average of 22.60 each. He caused many batsmen problems over the years and bowled more than one side out!

In 1984, Billy had 49 wickets at an average of 14.65 each and 42 the following season at 20.19 each.

Some tight bowling by the Seaton Burn openers culminated with Smith taking the first wicket in the seventh over, Chapman, out for 1, caught Smart, with the score at 11.

Paul Nesbit came in at three and the pair made good progress, taking the score to 70 before change bowler Smart had Atkinson caught by Billy Wilkinson for 39.

Smartie was a right arm medium paced swing bowler. He finished this season with 21 wickets at 30.66 each. In the 1972 league season he had bowled 162.5 overs, taking 25 wickets at 23.08, with a best of 3 for 19 against Greenside. In 1974 he took a career best 4 for 13 against Shotley Bridge.

In total he took at least 136 wickets in the Tyneside Senior League "A" Division, with a season high of 28 at 20.50 in 1975.

Smartie recalls "It wasn't a concious decision to stop bowling, but I had only really bowled to help the team out, as the team's bowling attack got stronger, and I started scoring more runs, my bowling tailed off."

Charlie Stephenson came in at four. Smartie recalls that he was "a very, very good cricketer at this level. A left handed bat, equally good off the front or back foot, just as comfortable stroking the ball through the covers as he was pulling the ball through the on side. He could play all round the wicket and had a very solid defensive technique to compliment everything else."

Smartie would open the batting regularly for the league side over the years with Stephenson and enjoyed watching him bat.

A further 24 was added before Nesbit was caught and bowled by Billy Wilkinson for 37.

Shotley Bridge 94 for 3.

Barry Hicks batted at five.

The league effectively started keeping records in 1972. In 1975, against Seaton Burn, Hicks had scored 176, which was then a league record for an individual score.

This game was Smartie's first as Seaton Burn captain so he remembers the game and Hicks in particular. He describes Hicks as "a character, an absolutely cracking bloke, his technique was to just hit it, he could play defensively but when he went for it he gave it everything he possibly could. If he fired and it was his day, he was a matchwinner, he was a very, very quick scorer. He was captain of Shotley for a number of years, including I think this year. I'm pretty sure he was captain of the league side I played in on a number of occasions too. He was another player who I used to like to watch bat.

In respect of the highest individual score, this was the first time of three occasions I was on the field when the record was broken.

I also played on August 20 1987 when Clyde Butts broke the record at Seaton Burn whilst playing for Blaydon. In a game restricted to 30 overs a side because of rain, Butts hit 187 not out from 106 balls. The innings included 8 sixes and 24 fours. Butts and James Howstan added 237 for the second wicket, a record for both the wicket and the highest ever partnership at the time in the Tyneside Senior League.

The third time I was on the field when that record was broken when I broke it myself against Burnopfield in 1984."

Seaton Burn didn't have to wait too long for the next wicket, Smartie bowling Stephenson for 17 with the score now 102 for 4.

Keith Emmerson was next in, batting at six.

However a short partnership of just 9 runs was not what Shotley required as Hicks was caught behind by Murray Baker for 7 off the bowling of Smartie. Baker was a good "keeper," taking 14 catches and 4 stumpings in this season.

John Stokoe batted at seven. He would also play for Greenside during his career, including one match in July 1985 when Smartie scored another hundred.

Nesbit recalls that Stokoe was "an excellent fielder, extremely quick over the ground and with the longest throw around in local cricket. He did not have too many opportunities to bat in this side and even fewer opportunities to bowl. He was happy to take the 8/9/10 spot which strengthened the tail in games where Shotley required further batting depth."

His first 14 scoring shots were all singles as he and Emerson took a methodical approach to chasing down the score. The pair added 25 for the sixth wicket when Emerson was ran out for 21.

Shotley now 136 for 6.

Alan Milburn was in at eight. He had played first team cricket from 1958 through to 1978 and had been drafted into today's team through other's unavailability. Throughout a long and distinguished career he had batted throughout the order, he was most comfortable though when he was opening the innings. After this game he played few games for the first team, as he spent the next 15 years helping the seconds out.

He has been an ever present at the club since he first started playing and as senior groundsman, he is still playing a major part, 63 years after he first turned up.

He added four of a partnership of eight before being caught Smart off the bowling of the now returned Mike Smith, as Shotley slid to 144 for 7.

The game was now finely balanced.

Kenny Day was batting nine. He had joined Shotley Bridge from Leadgate in 1972 with his good friends Lol Daly and Tony Westgarth. He was a good bat who showed his true potential in later seasons when he moved back to open the batting with David Collingwood.

Paul Nesbit says "There are many stories of Ken, but most of his fans recognise his best innings was in a cup tie at Leadgate in the early 1980's. At the age of 46, and batting in glasses with no helmet, he scored 47 facing West Indian quick Dennis Hewitt. The faster Hewitt bowled, the further Ken hooked and pulled him. Always the welcoming face of Shotley Bridge, Ken was sadly missed when he passed away in 2015."

Day and Stokoe added 29 for the eighth wicket which fell at 173 when Stokoe was caught behind by Murray Baker off the bowling of Smith for 20.

Shotley at 173 for 8, needed 7 to win, with two wickets remaining. Bowlers Keith Oxley at ten, and Alan Raine at 11, were the next two batsmen.

Unfortunately for them, with only one more run added, first Oxley was ran out for a duck and then Raine followed suit, also run out for a duck!

Kenny Day was stranded on 14 not out.

Shotley Bridge 174 all out.

Mike Smith had 3-27, Billy Wilkinson 1-69 and Smartie 3-64.

Seaton Burn had won by just five runs with seven balls to go of the 45 overs. This would be the only game of the season where Shotley failed to pick up at least a point.

Seaton Burn

D. Smart	Not	Out	100
G. Stephenson		B K. Oxley	24
W. Wilkinson		B A. Raine	15
W. Graham	C A. Milburn	B S. Atkinson	1
B. Smithson	C & B	A. Raine	4
M. Ashforth	Not	Out	22
Extras			13
Total			179-4 Wkts

K. Emmerson 0-45 A. Raine 2-46   S. Atkinson 1-58 K. Oxley 1-17

Shotley Bridge

S. Atkinson	C W. Wilkinson	B D. Smart	39
J. Chapman	C D. Smart	B M. Smith	1
P. Nesbit	C & B	W. Wilkinson	37
C. Stephenson		B D. Smart	17
B. Hicks	C M. Baker	B D. Smart	7
K. Emmerson	Run	Out	21
J. Stokoe	C M. Baker	B M. Smith	20
A. Milburn	C D. Smart	B M. Smith	4
K. Day	Not	Out	14
K. Oxley	Run	Out	0
A. Raine	Run	Out	0
Extras			14
Total			174-All Out

M. Smith 3-27   W. Wilkinson 1-69 D. Smart 3-64

The 1979 League table makes grim reading if you were connected to Seaton Burn!

All teams played 26 games and there were two ties.

	WON 5PTS	WON 4PTS	LOST 1PT	LOST 0PTS	Drawn	Tied	PTS
Shotley Bridge	7	12	2	1	4	0	89
Consett	3	14	3	0	5	1	81 1/2
Reyrolle	7	7	4	3	5	0	72
Greenside	6	7	4	4	5	0	67
Lintz	8	3	3	6	5	1	62 1/2
Swalwell	8	3	3	5	7	0	62
Blaydon	6	4	7	4	5	0	58
Wallsend	7	2	6	7	4	0	53
Burnopfield	2	7	3	6	7	1	50 1/2
Sacriston	4	3	8	6	5	0	45
South Moor	4	4	6	9	3	0	45
Ryton	4	3	6	8	4	1	44 1/2
Annfield Plain	3	3	7	6	7	0	41
Seaton Burn	3	1	11	7	4	0	34

The League averages this year were sketchy to say the least, a lot of games weren't picked up anywhere so if it says a batsman had "x" amount of runs that should be taken as a minimium, likewise with the bowling figures and wickets taken.

League Batting Averages 1979

	Runs	High Score	Comp Inns	Average
S. Atkinson (Shotley Bridge)	1171	127	18	65.06
Q. Omar (Sacriston)	987	127	19	51.95
J. Mccabe (Blaydon)	722	104	15	48.13
I. Stoneman (Burnopfield)	330	105no	9	36.67
G. Baker (Lintz)	293	62no	8	36.63
G. Hunter (Consett)	583	107	18	32.39
N. Turner (Reyrolle)	303	68	12	25.25
D. Collingwood (Shotley Bridge)	512	61	21	24.38
R. Stokoe (Consett)	526	68	22	23.91
D. Smart (Seaton Burn)	505	100no	22	22.96
D. Minnikin (Ryton)	533	64	24	22.21
J. Chapman (Shotley Bridge)	247	58	12	20.58
E. Largue (Lintz)	274	48	14	19.57

League Bowling Averages 1979

	Runs	Wkts	Average
S. Wilkinson (Shotley Bridge)	569	59	9.64
S. Gamble (Swalwell)	532	53	10.04
D. Parnaby (Reyrolle)	774	72	10.75
N. Pickering (Swalwell)	336	30	11.20
R. Bainbridge (Lintz)	880	75	11.70
A. Smith (Greenside)	772	59	13.09
R. Cook (Lintz)	886	66	13.42
N. Turner (Reyrolle)	232	17	13.65
L. Pollard (Shotley Bridge)	757	55	13.76
C. Depeiza (South Moor)	1227	86	13.94
I. Wishart (Greenside)	509	30	16.97
J. Mccabe (Blaydon)	559	31	18.09

CHAPTER 6

"MAKE A NAME FOR YOURSELF"

On Saturday 23rd June 1984 Seaton Burn played a home league fixture against Burnopfield Cricket Club.

Burnopfield would finish sixth in the league this season, with Neil Hewison sixth in the league bowling averages with 52 wickets at 13.02 each.

Throughout the 80's and 90's Burnopfield always put out an experienced and competitive side. The side they selected on this date was no exception. A bowling attack which was certainly capable of rolling you over cheaply and a very, very solid top six.

Smartie had one season, a poor one by his own admission, at Benwell in 1982. He was captain of Seaton Burn for the first time for the 1984 season. He was renowned as a bat first captain, using the principal "if the wickets no good at the start, it won't be any better after 45 overs." As an opening bat and captain, he also wanted to take the fight to the opposition.

As Smartie went out to bat, Billy Wilkinson said to him "The Sunday Sun Photographer is here today, go and score a ton and make a name for yourself."

The bowling was opened by Neil Hewison and Dave Sweeney. Hewison was a left armer, Sweeney a right. Both were experienced cricketers at this level and regulars in the end of season league averages.

When he had scored seven, Neil Hewison, bowling "up the bank," bowled one short, outside off stump, Smartie cut it, straight to Tommy Nichols at gully. He says he didn't middle it and although it was hit straight to Nichols hands, he feels that Nichols probably thought it was coming at him a lot harder than it really was.

Nichols was by all accounts an excellent fielder with great hands. The cricket gods were smiling on David Smart, it was one of the few catches Nichols would ever put down!

Years later, when their paths would occasionally cross, including one day Smartie remembers well at Newcastle Racecourse, they would always remind each other of the day Tommy dropped Smartie on 7!

An opening stand of 68 with Gary Stephenson before Stephenson was out for 12.

Smartie remembers Stephenson as "being good enough on his day to play and perform at this level, he just didn't have enough of those days, largely through a lack of cricket caused by work."

He was a right handed batsman, he would have been aged about 23 at the time of this game. He was an experienced first team opener, playing at the right level. A bubbly character, great fundraiser and servant of the club. If the club had a race night, quiz night or barbeque, you could guarantee Gary would be involved in the organising of it somewhere.

I can recall a brilliant 50 he scored against Henry Twizell and Swalwell. This game was the opening game of the season and marked Twizell's debut as Swalwell's professional. Stephenson stood up to everything Twizell threw at him, I do believe this included the word "cowboy" at one point, as he hooked and pulled his way to his half century. His cricket career was severely hampered within a few years of this game as he went onto continental shifts and would play one weekend and then miss the next.

He was bowled by Alan Beck.

Beck was a medium paced bowler who was skilful enough to swing and cut the ball.

Bill Graham came in first wicket down and the partnership was 16, he was out for a duck, also bowled by Beck.

Bill was an excellent all-rounder. A left handed batsman, who had three hundred's to his name, he was a very competent bat, he was also a very good slip fielder and left arm spin bowler. Later this season, on 7th July, he had figures of 16-1-56-9 against Shotley Bridge, unfortunately for Bill, the ninth wicket fell with the last ball of the last over, so he had no opportunity to take all ten!

Davie Gibson came in at number 4, this partnership was worth 65, Gibson contributed 13 before he was LBW to Collins.

He would have been around 21 at the time of this game. He was another all-rounder, an excellent left handed bat, he also had a hundred to his credit later in his career. He was a very elegant bat, lovely to watch, using timing and technique rather than force. As a right arm fast bowler he had a smooth run up and a graceful action, he was however a handful, moving the ball off the seam and sharp enough to pose even the best opening batsman problems. He took 43 wickets this season at an average of 18.65. He was also a brilliant cover fielder. He was one of those lads who was good at whichever sport he turned his hand too.

Sean Smith batted at 5. This partnership added 27. Smith scored a single before he was bowled by Davison. He would have been in his late teens at this time and very much still finding his way into senior cricket. He was a right handed bat, he went on to score plenty of runs in senior cricket, although largely at second team level, but he certainly had good days in the first eleven.

Billy Wilkinson batted at 6.

This partnership was worth 32. Billy scored 5 before he was caught by Peart off the bowling of Hewison. A very popular and well respected cricketer throughout the league. A hard hitting left handed batsman but probably better remembered as a right arm swing bowler.

I personally owe Billy a lot. He gave me a reference when I successfully applied to join Northumbria Police in 1987. I read that reference many years later and would like to thank Billy for it, it helped change my life.

Sadly Billy died in January of 2018.

Davie Watson batted at 7. Davie was an established senior cricketer at this time. This partnership added 48, with Watson finishing on 10 not out.

He was a right handed batsman and right handed slow medium bowler. As a bat he would look to plant his front foot and hit hard and straight, as a bowler he looked for accuracy. He played a lot of second team cricket where he was captain for a number of seasons and a regular contributor, as well as being a tremendous competitor. He was renowned for wanting "one more over" when he was bowling and took the ribbing that followed in good spirit.

After he finished playing, he would go on to umpire in the league for many years. Davie was another who has since passed away, cancer taking him in July 2020.

One of the striking things about this innings as a whole was that extras, with 16, was the next top scorer after Smartie! The other thing that struck me was how well Burnopfield must have bowled to the other batsman. It was a decent batting line up Seaton Burn put out that day, all those who batted, were, on their day, capable of scoring runs at this level, but the next top score was 13.

A total of 258 for 5 from 45 overs, Dave Sweeney recalls that the Burnopfield lads thought it was a "decent score, but not insurmountable."

When you look at the bowling figures, they were very much in line with what you would expect, five an over or so from five of the bowlers, with Tim Collins 5-3-16-1 being the pick of them.

Smartie batting with fielder Paul Davison and wicketkeeper
Freddie Hood watching on as he powers his way to 201 not out

Dave Sweeney has kindly provided pen pictures of his team mates and a memory or two from that day.

When Burnopfield batted, the innings was opened by Andy Peart and Malcolm Brown. Two excellent opening batsmen who over the years scored thousands of runs. On 30th April 1988 they set the then league record for a first wicket partnership of 289 against Reyrolle, with Andy Peart scoring an incredible 210 not out and Brown 79.

Peart was a stylish left handed batsman who made batting look effortless, in an era when the league had a number of excellent left handed opening bats, such as Gordon Hunter, Robert Stokoe, Ian Somerville and Charlie Stephenson amongst others. Andy could also bowl effective medium pace "wobblers" and was good enough to represent Durham County B Team.

Malcolm Brown was a more gritty opener who loved to pull and hook. He was an excellent fielder and occasional off spin bowler. He had made his first team debut on 18th June 1966, aged 12!

By 1971 he had secured a regular first team place and in 1973 he scored 865 League runs at an average of 43.20.

During this season he also scored centuries in consecutive weeks, 104 away at Reyrolle on 11th August, his first century for the club, and 171 not out at home to Wallsend the following week.

A truly exceptional cover point fielder, quick off the mark and across the ground, no wonder he was invited to act as 12th man for Durham County! He was good enough to play one season as a professional, at Ushaw Moor, and also played for Gateshead Fell.

They had a steady start, 21 for the first wicket before Peart was bowled for 6 by Ray Cardwell.

Ray Cardwell was in the last and longest of three spells with Seaton Burn. He was a steady medium/fast right handed bowler and a decent right handed middle order batsman.

Each spell away impacted on his cricket as he didn't play any outside the area. He originally left the area in 1974 aged 24, to work in Middlesbrough. He returned to the Newcastle area in 1977 or 78.

He finished top of the first team bowling averages in 1978 with a very creditable 25 wickets at just 12.56 from 80.2 overs.

On 24th June 1979 Cardwell had a knock of 68 for the first team against Burnopfield, showing his potential as a true all rounder.

He moved again in 1980, to Scotland this time, returning to the North East in 1982.

When he returned from Scotland he would go on to become Club Treasurer and did a stint as second team captain. He remained Treasurer until 2011. He was an unselfish cricketer. He knows he could have batted higher, scored more runs, bowled more and taken more wickets, but he was the ultimate club man and therefore ideal second team captain, who often put others before himself to ensure he had 11 players next week! As a captain he was always willing to listen to people and I, for one, enjoyed playing under his leadership.

The second wicket between Brown and Neil Hewison put on 82, before Hewison was caught by Ray Cardwell off the bowling of Billy Wilkinson for 47.

Neil Hewison was a talented and very highly rated cricketer in the North East. A determined, stylish and often destructive right handed batsman. He would score at least ten centuries in his career, with a best score of 143, and is credited with over 10,000 league runs.

Neil was also an excellent quick bowler who could trouble the best around. As a testament to his bowling ability he took 52 wickets this season at an average of 13.02 to finish fifth in the league bowling averages. He took over 500 TSL wickets.

On 21st August 1976 he took the first 9 South Moor wickets to fall, then bowled the tenth with a no-ball. His bowling partner then nipped in and took the last wicket, leaving Neil with 9-33. He later turned his hand to wicket keeping!

Neil also played in the Durham Senior League for Chester Le Street, and as both an amateur and a professional at Burnopfield and Whickham.

His son Chris, who started his club career at Burnopfield, went on to play representative cricket for England at age level groups, having a brief flirtation with Nottinghamshire and then becoming one of the best batsmen the North East Premier League and the Northumberland and Tyneside Leagues have ever seen.

The third wicket fell just one run later as opening batsman Brown was caught by Smartie off the bowling of Billy Wilkinson for 46. His innings had included 6 fours.

This meant two new batsman were at the crease, Freddie Hood and Tommy Nichols.

Hood was a naturally gifted, eccentric and often unorthadox powerful batsman. He kept wicket in this game but was not a regular wicketkeeper.

Sweeney says "I recall a game when we required 5 to win off the last over with Fred on strike. He calmly played the first four balls back to the bowler leaving us in the changing room tearing our hair out. The fifth ball was bowled which Fred deposited over the boundary for six! Game won! To this day Fred still can't understand why we were all fretting in the changing room!

Tommy Nichols had one of the best eyes I have ever seen in local cricket. An unorthadox batsman who liked to shuffle down the wicket and deposit the bowler over mid wicket, straight or play the late cut!

There are many stories to tell about Tommy, one that sticks in my mind, was a game against Felling. Tommy was having a great day, smashing the ball to all parts, when Chris Pleasants, the Felling Captain, turned to his professional, Indian Test Player and World Cup Winner, Madan Lal, to come back to bowl.

Madan turned away and refused to come back to bowl for fear of getting the "Tommy" treatment!

I can also recall a cup tie against Bishop Auckland when Tommy was batting against West Indian fast bowler Tony Gray. Gray was over six foot six inches tall and played five test matches and twenty five one day internationals for his country.

When Gray asked Tommy why he wasn't wearing a helmet, Tommy replied "he had never faced anyone quick enough!"

The next few overs made for some very interesting cricket watching!

Nichols is credited with scoring over 10,000 TSL runs, with 2 centuries, including a best of 137 not out. He had started his career at Swalwell in 1967, joining Burnopfield in 1975. He scored in excess of 600 League runs in 1989, 1990 and 1994.

He was an excellent gully fielder and the best captain I played under."

These two added 58 for the fourth wicket, taking the score to 162 before the next wicket fell when Hood was caught by Gary Stephenson off the left arm spin of Bill Graham for 40. His innings had included 5 fours and 2 sixes.

At this point there were around 11 overs left and 96 runs were still needed, I can imagine just prior to this wicket falling one or two nervous lads amongst the Seaton Burn players, especially when Freddie Hood was putting bat to ball.

The next over saw Davie Gibson take two wickets in four balls, first out was Tommy Nichols, bowled for 16, then Alan Beck, bowled for a duck.

Beck was an experienced cricketer who was a good accumulator of runs, excellent fielder and a more than useful medium pace bowler who could swing and cut the ball. He later served as groundsman for many years at Burnopfield, Swalwell and Newcastle City.

162 for 3 had become 166 for 6 in the space of ten balls.

Davie Gibson's next over was a wicket maiden, Micky Small being bowled for 4.

Small was a very experienced cricketer. A tall, upright, straight hitting right handed batsman, normally batting at 5 or 6. He was also a superb slip fielder, "Buckets" to his friends and an excellent left hand swing bowler.

He had started his club cricket at Clara Vale then Ryton, before he moved to Burnopfield in 1969. He scored his first 50 for the club in 1970, 55 not out against Leslie's in July and registered a hat trick the same year against League Champions in waiting, Greenside!

1971 was another excellent year but it was 1972 that established his reputation as a top all rounder. He scored 747 runs at an average of 21.30 and took an incredible 103 wickets in the season, 63 of them in the league. This included his then personal best of 7 for 22 against Seaton Burn.

He was, and still is, a permanent fixture at the club as Treasurer. He played for Langley Park for a year as professional and a short period of time at Gateshead Fell with his good friend, Malcolm Brown.

The game then petered out, another maiden over from Davie Gibson, then Bill Graham had Paul Davison caught by Davie Gibson for 4. Davison was a good steady batsman and medium pace bowler. He did not get to play as much cricket as he would have liked due to work commitments.

When Davie Gibson bowled Tim Collins in the next over for 5, making the score 183 for 9, that was the end of the wickets.

Collins came to senior cricket a little later than most. He was an excellent local rugby player and most of his time had been devoted to that. He could however be a very effective cricketer with his medium paced bowling and belligerent, powerful, left handed batting. He later played cricket for Ryton too.

Davie Gibson's second spell of 5-3-6-4 effectively ended the game as a contest. In those days the scoring system meant that if a team wasn't "all out" they would score a point, with the winners awarded four points.

Dave Sweeney scored 7 not out batting at number 10 and Bill Peveller was 1 not out batting at number 11 to ensure their point for Burnopfield.

With no offence intended from Dave Sweeney, Bill was not a regular first team cricketer, and, as was common practise for a lot of teams in the day, was drafted in to make up the numbers!

Sweeney was a right arm fast bowler and a hard hitting right handed batsman. Smartie recalls that he was "a tall lad, he could always extract extra bounce from a wicket." He had a safe pair of hands in the field and a good throwing arm in the outfield. He played for a number of local league sides over the years, including two spells at North Durham 1970-75 and 1985-88, four years at Chester-Le-Street 1976-79, a year at Greenside in 1980 and two stints at Burnopfield, 1981-84 and 1989 until the present day where he is currently Chairman.

During the second stint at Burnopfield, in 1990, Sweeney was good enough to finish 13th in the League bowling averages with

51 wickets at 19.88 each. In 1991 he took a further 67 league wickets at an average of 22.10 each.

In addition to league cricket Sweeney also represented Durham University from 1975-77, Durham County at Under 19 and Under 21 level, where he was also Captain, the Durham Senior League at Under 25 level and, perhaps most impressively, Durham/Northumberland over 60's!

His best bowling figures were 8-32 against Lintz firsts and his highest batting score was 129 not out against Ponteland seconds.

Dave Sweeney took three hat tricks in his career, the first for Chester Le Street first team against North Durham, the next for Burnopfield firsts against Whitburn and the third for Burnopfield seconds against Consett.

Dave Sweeney describes this game as follows

"A memorable afternoons cricket, almost solely due to a magnificent innings of 201 not out from the legendary David Smart.

The reason I remember this game so well was that I happened to be one of the Burnopfield opening bowlers that day!

Indeed as Seaton Burn began the last over of their innings, David Smart was on strike on 197.

So he had six balls to face from me in order to aquire the three runs necessary to reach his double ton.

In those days I was a bowler of reasonable pace and despite Smartie's onslaught, my figures up to this point weren't too bad, 0-51 from 11 overs.

As the scorebook shows, he failed to score a run from the first three balls of the over. Ball four he managed to clip away for two runs, leaving two deliveries to score the one run to reach the magical two hundred.

I bowled the fifth ball, no run!

One run from one ball required.....at this point our captain, Tommy Nichols, came to have a word. Seaton Burn and Burnopfield lads had always got on well, we decided to push the field back slightly, so that if Smartie got bat on ball, he could jog through for his single and also his 200.

I duly bowled the last ball of the over which David clipped off his legs and the cheeky so and so ran two!

A magnificent innings from Smartie!"

Seaton Burn won the game by 69 runs.

The 201 not out by Smartie was possibly the second recorded double hundred scored in north east cricket, there was believed to be another scored in 1933!

It was scored against an experienced, competitive, Burnopfield team who were certainly no push overs.

With thanks to the scorer of the day, Brian Ridley.

The innings had started at 2.33 pm and was concluded at 5.07pm. Two hours and thirty four minutes. His 50 came off 32 balls in 28 minutes, 100 off 75 balls in 73 minutes, 150 of 111 balls in 117 minutes and contained 23 fours and 7 sixes.

It's worth remembering to, that Seaton Burn is one of the bigger outfields in local cricket, not too many easy boundaries!

This innings proved a watershed moment for David Smart, up until this point he had scored a single hundred, five years earlier against Shotley Bridge. He had however, scored 14 half centuries in the intervening period, with a high score of 93, so it was clearly coming!

In 1984 alone he would score a further five centuries, two of them unbeaten in a double weekend, when teams played a league game on a Saturday and then another the next day on the Sunday.

He also scored three hundreds in three successive weeks, from 25th August to 8th September. He also scored seven half centuries this season, two of which were unbeaten, the highest score of which was 91 not out!

His average at it's peak in 1984 was 72.15, before dropping to a season finale of 70.19!

In total he scored 1474 league runs that season, a Tyneside Senior League Record. The two players below him in the league averages were Pakistan test player, Wasim Raja, 912 runs at an average of 70.15, and West Indian test player Clyde Butts, 1089 runs at an average of 57.32.

League Secretary Bob Jackson said at the time in local media "Joe died a couple of years ago and it is a pity for David that his dad was not here to see him have such a tremendous season. He would have been proud of him."

Smartie did point out to me that he did get to bat 26 times this season, with only one game of Seaton Burn's league fixtures being effected by the weather.

Over a period of 10 years, including this year, Smartie played in 232 out of 260 games. He missed five games through holidays, (I know I couldn't believe it either!) and one through illness. So 22 games lost to the British Summer in a ten year period.

During the course of the researching this project I had many conversations with Smartie. I was surprised at how much thought he put into his batting. He said that if he got out for under 30 it was probably a "win" for the bowler and they had got him out, anything over that he feels was down to an error by himself!

As stated earlier he also used to count his runs as he went, he says that this helped him concentrate.

I also asked him what changed for him as a cricketer in 1984. His answer had nothing to do with cricket. He simply said he got married! He said marrying Gillian gave him a contentment away from cricket, he was one of those who lived and breathed cricket, to the point of obsession, but that getting married simply cleared his mind for him and that meant when he played the longer form of the game in particular, he was simply in a better headspace to concentrate on the task in hand.

Seaton Burn

D. Smart	Not	Out	201
G. Stephenson		B A. Beck	12
W. Graham		B A. Beck	0
D. Gibson		LBW B T. Collins	13
S. Smith		B P. Davison	1
W. Wilkinson	C A. Peart	B N. Hewison	5
D. Watson	Not	Out	10
Extras			16
Total			258-5 Wkts

N. Hewison 1-63   D. Sweeney 0-55   M. Small 0-38   A. Beck 2-47
T. Collins 1-16   P. Davison 1-23

Burnopfield

A. Peart		B R. Cardwell	6
M. Brown	C D. Smart	B W. Wilkinson	46
N. Hewison	C R. Cardwell	B W. Wilkinson	47
F. Hood	C G. Stephenson	B W. Graham	40
T. Nichols		B D. Gibson	16
M. Small		B D. Gibson	4
A. Beck		B D. Gibson	0
P. Davison	C D. Gibson	B W. Graham	4
T. Collins		B D. Gibson	5
D. Sweeney	Not	Out	7
W. Peveller	Not	Out	1
Extras			13
Total			189-9 Wkts

D. Gibson   R. Cardwell   W. Wilkinson   W. Graham
  4-51   1-31   2-57   2-37

CHAPTER 7

"DOUBLE WEEKEND"

Over the course of a season, it was the practise in the Tyneside Senior League at this time to play four double weekends, that is you played a league game on the Saturday and another on the Sunday. They would play one of the double weekends over a Saturday and a Bank Holiday Monday.

On Saturday 14th July 1984 Seaton Burn played a league fixture at Reyrolle.

Reyrolle had originally started out as a works team, they were known world wide for their production of electrical switchgear for the mining industry. I'm pretty sure I worked on some of their gear when I was an apprentice. Their true name is Reyrolle, no "S" on the end but many people, including former players refer to them as Reyrolles with the "S." You will therefore see both versions of the spelling in the book as I interchange depending on the source of the information.

Reyrolle would finish fourth in the league this season and had two batsmen, Norman Turner and Malcolm Bell would be in the top twelve league batting averages and one bowler, Tony Smare, in the top eight bowling averages. Turner would score 657 runs at an average of 32.85 this season and Bell would score 586 runs at an average of 29.30. Fortunately Bell missed this fixture. Smare took 76 wickets at an average of 14.55 this season.

Chris Cox has kindly provided some information regarding the Reyrolle players. Cox himself was skipper of the side for part of the 70's and all of the 80's. He opened the bowling throughout that period. He was tall and slim with an upright action who bowled at good pace, often for long periods of time. He was a seam bowler who intelligently varied his pace and position on the delivery crease.

Cox had first played for Reyrolle in 1970. He registered his 400th league wicket in 1976 when he bowled Harry Statt in a match against South Moor. It is unclear how many career wickets he finished with.

Smartie and Gary Stephenson opened the batting for Seaton Burn.

Tony Smare and Chris Cox opened the bowling for Reyrolle.

Smartie faced the first over and played out a maiden to Tony Smare. Smare, originally from Gateshead Fell, was club professional this season.

Smartie recalls Smare as being "a decent bowler with a bit of pace about him and a decent bat too."

Cox describes Smare as "an all rounder, however it was as a bowler that he where he would make his main contribution to the team. He was decidedly quick, he could bowl all day but was often used by the skipper in short spells. He moved the ball both in the air and off the wicket. When requested he could bowl a 3 or 4 over spell of hostile, spiteful, very quick deliveries."

The Seaton Burn innings then started badly, Gary Stephenson was caught by Johnson off the bowling of Chris Cox for a duck from the first ball of the second over without a run having been scored.

Richie Allan came in at three and hit the first ball he faced for four. Richie was well known around the league as he was one of the few deaf cricketers playing first team cricket at the time. He was also very popular with team mates and opposition alike. A talented left handed bat and useful right arm medium pace swing bowler. He was an excellent fielder in the covers, with a strong arm.

Unfortunately for Richie this wasn't to be his day, despite the promising start, from the fourth ball he faced he was caught by Michael Collins, again off the bowling of Cox.

Seaton Burn were 4 for 2 after one over and five balls.

After another dot ball to Davie Gibson, Chris Cox had the impressive figures of 1-0-4-2.

Smartie got off the mark with the second ball of Smare's next over being hit for six and he took successive four's from the fourth and fifth balls of the over and he was away.

The third wicket stand between Smartie and Davie Gibson was worth 87, Davie, another left hander, scoring a steady 20 before being caught by Jim Crammon off the bowling of Norman Turner in the 22nd over.

Turner was a fine all rounder, as a bowler he bowled a nagging length of a short run. Smartie describes his bowling as being similar to Billy Wilkinson's, slow /medium, away swingers which could be difficult to score off. He took at least 513 TSL wickets at an average of 15.59. He was a regular in the league representative side, on 20th May 1984 he took 4 for 14 from ten overs for that side in a Wilkinson Cup match against The Darlington District League.

Chris Cox recalls Turner as "the first change bowler for much of the period he played. He was small but aggressive, he was mainly known for his football prowess but he was also a gifted all round cricketer. He bowled only off a few paces, mainly out swingers which swung very late, few were comfortable against him."

Turner then hit a purple patch, from the 22nd over, his sixth of the spell, he removed Davie Gibson, then took the wicket of Sean Smith, batting at five, for a duck caught by Tennet, having added 18 for the fourth wicket. He then removed Phil Myers, stumped by Jim Crammon, also for a duck, batting at 5.

Myers was late in life to play cricket, probably in his late teens when he took the game up, and not much older today. He was a right handed bat who used to like to strike the ball straight and often, although he could be limited in defence. On his day he was a very clean hitter and very destructive.

Turner had bowled a spell of 5-1-9-3 and Seaton Burn's innings was now hanging in the balance at 113 for 5.

Billy Wilkinson came to bat at seven. Billy was a left handed bat who wasn't fond of too many quick singles at this stage of his career! He opened his account with a six and hit another later on, along with a couple of fours in a much needed 32, in a partnership of 66 for the sixth wicket. Billy was out caught Collins off the bowling of Cox, who had returned for a second spell.

179 for 6 after 40 overs quickly became 184 for 7 as Seaton Burn chased quick runs before the end of their 45 overs and Ray Cardwell was bowled by Smare, who was also in his second spell, for a single.

One run later Dave Watson, batting at nine, was caught by Pritchard off the bowling of Cox for a duck.

This brought Graeme Sinton to the crease, with two overs and one ball left. Graeme was a talented right handed batsman, another who was popular in the dressing room and who had a great outlook on cricket and life in general. His cricket career was unfortunately blighted by the continental shift patterns he always worked, he would play one weekend, then miss the next. He was talented enough to play a lot more first team cricket, but very difficult to maintain any kind of consistency at this level with a work pattern like that.

In typical "Sinta's" style, Graeme hit the last two balls of the innings for four to finish 9 not out.

Billy Taylor was the unused number eleven for Seaton Burn. A very useful bat in his day, he did have a century to his name earlier in his career, and he was still a useful off spinner. Billy was another veteran, well respected throughout the league, who had been a match winner in his day with bat or ball.

Seaton Burn had reached a creditable 207 for 8 wickets off their allotted 45 overs. The three bowlers used all had respectable bowling figures in line with such a score. Smare 16-1-63-1, Cox 16-3-72-4 and Turner 13-2-62-3.

Smartie was 131 Not Out. His innings contained 12 fours and 7 sixes. He had reached his fifty off fifty five deliveries and his century off a hundred and sixty three balls.

Jimmy Crammon and Gerard Smare opened the batting for Reyrolle. Crammon was also a reliable left handed opening bat. A police officer by profession he was over six feet tall and had a powerful physique. He was normally a middle order batsman.

Cox recalls that "his main resource to the team was his fielding. He was quick with a very good arm and consequently often fielded away from the wicket. That was sad because he was the best catcher in the gully or point that I have ever seen."

Cox recalls Gerard Smare as "a talented, stylish batsman, who unfortunately, because of availability issues, wasn't free to play every week."

Davie Gibson and Ray Cardwell opened the bowling for Seaton Burn.

These two very quickly put on 28 for the first wicket off just four overs and four balls, before Crammon was caught and bowled by Davie Gibson for 11.

This brought Norman Turner to the crease, he would finish tenth in league batting averages this year with 657 runs at an average of 32.85. He originally started his career at Leslie's, when they folded he moved along the road to Reyrolle for the 1973 season. He scored at least 7437 TSL runs, including three centuries with a best of 126. Smartie describes Turner as being "small in stature" but a very compact and competant batsman.

Cox remembers Turner as "a magnificent right handed batsman, he normally batted 3 or 4."

After three overs for twenty, Ray Cardwell was removed from the attack and replaced by Billy Wilkinson.

His first over went for 17, including successive fours and a six from Turner, as the Reyrolle batsman showed their intention to try and chase the runs down.

Davie Gibson took his second wicket with the fourth ball of the next over, the ninth, with the score on 63, he had Gerard Smare caught by Gary Stephenson for 33.

With the first ball of his second over Wilkinson bowled Michael Collins for a single.

Cox recalls that Collins was "another young player who had impressed at both junior and second team level but offered few good opportunities to impress in the first team."

Game on, 64 for 3 after just 9.1 overs.

This brought Jeff Gutteridge to the crease.

Cox descibes Gutteridge as "the future. A young guy who batted and bowled but who did not get as many opportunities as his abilities suggested. We have all been there. In 1984 the hope was that he stayed, picking up good practise from the senior players of the day."

Turner and Gutteridge added 60 for the fourth wicket in eight overs. Billy Wilkinson's fourth over had finished with three successive boundaries from Turner and Richie Allan's medium pace swing had replaced him and Billy Taylor's off spin had replaced Davie Gibson.

Taylor faired no better than Billy Wilkinson, his two overs costing nineteen, and Allan's third ball went for six!

The third ball of Allan's second over bowled Gutteridge for 27. His innings had included two four's and two sixes.

Opening bowler and right handed batsman Tony Smare came in to bat at six. Cox earlier described him as "an accumulator of runs," he adds "that he seemed to accumulate those runs very quickly."

He added 25 for the sixth wicket, Smare contributing 10 before Billy Taylor caught him off the bowling of Davie Gibson.

149 for 5 wickets off 26.1 overs, game still nicely in the balance.

Brian Errington was batting seven. Cox recalls him as someone who had "an outstanding first team career as a right hand batsman and quite brilliant fielder, especially close to the wicket. Later in his career he concentrated on bringing players through the second eleven. At this time games in the first eleven normally coincided with player shortage due to illness, work commitments or holidays."

A partnership of 33 in just over 7 overs for the sixth wicket before Errington was bowled by Richie Allan for 19 in the 34th over.

D. Johnson came in at eight and with Turner slowing down a little at the other end, these two batted sensibly and despite only two boundaries in the next seven overs, Reyrolle won the game comfortably, the scores being level when Johnson hit one of those two boundaries to win by four wickets with four overs to spare.

Turner was 92 not out, an innings which had included nine four's and a six. Johnson was 15 not out.

The unused batsmen would have included Maurice Price and Alan Whitfield.

Price was Club Secretary. A dogged late order right handed bat and another one who excelled in the field. He was quick across the ground with a good arm and a fantastic catcher, so much so Chris Cox "cannot remember seeing him drop one." He was the ultimate team man, often sacrificing his batting position to a younger player who had just joined the first team ranks.

Alan Whitfield joined the first team from Durham University. He was a gifted all round cricketer. A quick bowler who normally joined the attack as 3rd or 4th bowler. He mainly moved the ball in the air. A polished right hand batsman who could bat from 3 to 8 depending on circumstances.

Davie Gibson was the pick off the Seaton Burn bowlers with 19-2-75-3 and Richie Allan had a decent 13-1-52-2.

This was the first time out of twenty three league hundreds, when Smartie would score a century and finish on the losing side. All credit to Reyrolle, Turner in particular, almost all contributed with the bat and they paced their innings well.

Seaton Burn

D. Smart	Not	Out	131
G. Stephenson	C D. Johnson	B C. Cox	0
R. Allan	C M. Collins	B C. Cox	4
D. Gibson	C J. Crammon	B N. Turner	20
S. Smith	C Tennet	B N. Turner	0
P. Myers	St J. Crammon	B N. Turner	0
W. Wilkinson	C M. Collins	B C. Cox	32
R. Cardwell		B A. Smare	1
D. Watson	C Pritchard	B C. Cox	0
G. Sinton	Not	Out	9
Extras			10
Total			207-8 Wkts

A. Smare 1-63   C. Cox 4-72   N. Turner 3-62

Reyrolle

J. Crammon	C & B	D. Gibson	11
G. Smare	C G. Stephenson	B D. Gibson	33
N. Turner	Not	Out	92
M. Collins		B W. Wilkinson	1
J. Gutteridge		B R. Allan	27
A. Smare	C W. Taylor	B D. Gibson	10
B. Errington		B R. Allan	19
D. Johnson	Not	Out	15
Extras			3
Total			211-6 Wkts

D. Gibson 3-75   R. Cardwell 0-20   W. Wilkinson 1-42   W. Taylor 0-19
R. Allan 2-52

The following day, Sunday 15th July Seaton Burn played another league fixture, an away game against Wallsend.

Wallsend would finish bottom of the league this year, not winning a game and this season marked their last in the Tyneside Senior League.

Smartie would score unbeaten hundreds in both games this season against them and they fielded two very different sides in each game.

Craig Johnson has played for and been associated with Wallsend for over 40 years, first joining the club as an eleven year old. He has kindly provided information on the Wallsend players.

He also played with Smartie for a couple of seasons at Kirkley in the twilight of Smartie's career. He describes Smartie as "a cracking player, even then, later in his playing days."

Seaton Burn batted first and, very much like the previous day, things didn't start well. Smartie and Gary Stephenson opened the innings once again. The bowling was opened by Gary Walton and Ernie Brown.

Walton was a right arm fast bowler, he had genuine pace and could be a real handful when he got it right. He would have been the youngest member of this team, in his early 20's. Smartie remembers him as "a useful performer and a "bit nippy" for pace."

Brown was a right arm, medium pacer.

A single from the first ball of the opening over from Smartie off Walton and a maiden from Brown. Walton had Gary Stephenson LBW with the first ball of his second over for a duck. Gary's second duck in two days, funny game cricket, one opener scoring successive hundreds, one copping a pair!

One for one very quicky became one for two when Walton bowled Richie Allan first ball!

Davie Gibson came in at four and the third wicket put on 140. Gibson contributing 56, with nine boundaries, before being LBW to Brown.

Gibson was an elegant left hander, he was a stylish batsman who was a pleasure to watch when in form. He was good enough to represent the league under 25 side as an all rounder. Sadly he stopped playing cricket a few years before he reached thirty so no-on knows how good he really could have been.

Sean Smith was batting at five, a partnership of 14 before he too was LBW to Brown.

Another partnership of 14 with Billy Wilkinson for the fifth wicket before Billy was caught by Joe Mulgrove off the bowling of Brown for 9. Typically of Billy, the 9 included two fours!

At 169 for 5 off 32.3 overs the innings could have gone either way.

Fortunately wicketkeeper Murray Baker, batting unusually high at 7, came in and played a nice little innings. Baker was a larger than life character, it seems wicket keeping attracts the eccentric more than other cricket positions. He was a very good wicket keeper and could put bat to ball on occasion.

Baker had a high score of 47 not out this season, against Blaydon. That innings had included four four's and three sixes against a bowling attack which included West Indian Test Spinner Clyde Butts!

The innings finished on 243 for 5 after the allotted 45 overs.

Murray Baker was 19 not out. Of the four bowlers used by Wallsend, only two took a wicket, Walton finished with 13-2-51-2 and Brown with 22-4-104-3. Joshi had 6-0-38-0 and Mulgrove 4-0-22-0

Smartie finished on 125 Not Out. The innings contained 11 fours and 6 sixes. His 50 had come of 65 balls and the 100 off 105.

Wallsend's batsman found life a struggle from the start. Ernie Brown was bowled first ball of the innings by Davie Gibson.

His opening partner Billy Henderson and N.Joshi put on 20 for the second wicket. Henderson was an opening right arm swing bowler who normally batted in the lower middle order. An accident at Wallsend Shipyards ended his playing days.

Gibson then took his second wicket as he had Joshi caught by Sean Smith for 13. Smith had a very safe pair of hands, in addition to being a good outfielder.

Ray Cardwell then took 3 wickets in 8 balls without a run being added as 20 for 2 became 20 for 5.

Opener, Henderson was caught by Davie Gibson for six.

George Dunn was then caught by Gary Stephenson for a duck. Dunn was one of two club stalwarts who kept the club alive during transition from the Tyneside Senior League to the Northumberland County League. He was an excellent right arm spin bowler with a lovely smooth action and a fantastic loop on his deliveries. He had many offers and opportunities to play at a higher level but was a gentleman on and off the field and stayed loyal to Wallsend. He also played his cricket in the right way. He would bat in the middle to lower order and had some flamboyant shots. He was a porter at Rake Lane Hospital.

Morris Bowman was then also caught Gibson off Cardwell, also for a duck. Bowman was a right handed batsman, normally an opener, he was a bus driver by trade.

The sixth wicket partnership between Terry Pears and Micky Jackson put on 24.

Pears was a flame haired, usually opening, left handed batsman. He was a very elegant batsman and very correct in his play. He was famed for making "singles out of two's," this became a dressing room phrase "that's a TP walking one!" especially when the non striker wanted two! Pears always had a story to tell.

Micky Jackson was club captain. He was the other club stalwart who, along with George Dunn, carried the club for so long. He was an excellent leader and respected by all. A right handed, middle order batsman, he could pull the ball like Ricky Ponting!

He would always say, just after having made runs, "Your only as good as your last innings!" Sadly he died in the late 1990's.

The stand was ended when Pears was bowled by Gibson for 7.

Batsman eight Bob Pyke added a single before he was bowled by Cardwell. Pyke was a right handed bat, he was a hard man to get out and would generally bat in the top three.

Jackson alone resisted the bowling of Gibson and Cardwell as first Billy Tubman went for 5, bowled Gibson, 56 for 8, then Gary Walton for 4, bowled Gibson and finally Joe Mulgrove for a duck also bowled Gibson.

Mulgrove was a right arm swing bowler, often first change after the opening bowlers. He was hard to get away and was particularly effective with the wicketkeeper standing up to the stumps and the field set to save the single. He worked in an abbatoir.

Wallsend were 66 all out in 21 overs.

Gibson taking 3 wickets in 12 balls, all bowled, to finish off the innings.

Jackson was unbeaten on 28 not out, with four boundaries.

Davie Gibson finished with figures of 11-5-25-6 and Ray Cardwell with figures of 10-2-39-4.

Seaton Burn had won by 177 runs.

Seaton Burn

D. Smart	Not	Out	125
G. Stephenson		LBW B G. Walton	0
R. Allan		B G. Walton	0
D. Gibson		LBW B E. Brown	56
S. Smith		LBW B E. Brown	6
W. Wilkinson	C J. Mulgrove	B E. Brown	9
M. Baker	Not	Out	19
Extras			28
Total			243-5 Wkts
G. Walton	E. Brown	N. Joshi	J. Mulgrove
2-51	3-104	0-38	0-22

Wallsend

E. Brown	C S. Smith	B D. Gibson	0
W. Henderson	C D. Gibson	B R. Cardwell	6
N. Joshi	C S. Smith	B D. Gibson	13
G. Dunn	C G. Stephenson	B R. Cardwell	0
M. Bowman	C D. Gibson	B R. Cardwell	0
T. Pears		B D. Gibson	7
M. Jackson	Not	Out	28
R. Pyke		B R. Cardwell	1
W. Tubman		B D. Gibson	5
G. Walton		B D. Gibson	4
J. Mulgrove		B D. Gibson	0
Extras			2
Total			66-All Out

D. Gibson 6-25   R. Cardwell 4-39

In the double weekend of 14/15th July, Smartie had batted for 90 overs. He had scored 256 runs and not been out over the two days.

He had hit 23 four's and 13 six's.

For these two centuries in a weekend he was "The Sunday Sun Sportspack Cricketer of the Month" for June 1984

June 1984 Sunday Sun Cricketer of the Month

CHAPTER 8

THE HAT TRICK

On Saturday 25th August 1984 Seaton Burn played a home league fixture against Ryton.

Ryton finished 11th, out of 14 teams, in the league that year. Stuart Stanton featured in the league batting averages with 510 runs at 23.18 each and professional Ian Wishart finished sixth in the league bowling averages with 68 wickets at 14.40 each, fortunately Wishart missed this game!

Stuart Stanton, known to all as "Stuey," has kindly provided infomation on his team mates and a memory or two from the day.

Stanton made his debut as a junior in 1966 and played his last senior match in 2012. He started off as a medium/fast bowler but gradually morphed into a batsman who could bowl when needed. He scored over 500 runs in three consecutive years in the 1980's, as well as a couple of centuries.

In 1977 in a game against Wallsend, Stanton and Tommy Thompson scored a then league record of 172 for the third wicket partnership. This record stood until 1985 when it was beaten by a stand of 222 by Bobby Coulson and John Littleton for Felling against Ryton.

He was captain of Ryton for this fixture and despite missing a couple of big players in Tommy Thompson and Ian Wishart, Stanton recalls that he fancied their chances that day, largely dependent on getting out Smartie cheaply.

He remembers Smartie being "a big frame, strong off the front foot, and a fierce competitor, he was the one we needed.

Geoff Young had highlighted what we thought was an area of weakness in his game and to be fair Ryton had generally managed to prevent Smartie from spoiling the game!"

Seaton Burn batted first.

Once again Smartie opened the innings, this time with Peter Ford as Gary Stephenson was unavailable.

Peter Ford was a lovely bloke, quietly spoken, very polite, never heard him say a bad word about anyone or anything. A very steady reliable batsman, who opened regularly for the second team and for whom he often contributed twenties and thirties, without ever getting the fifties he deserved.

The Ryton bowling attack was opened by Vince Collier. He was known as "The Halty Express." He had genuine pace and came off one of the longest run ups any of us will have seen. He used to travel in from Haltwhistle by train to Ryton on match days. He had several successful seasons at Ryton as a strike bowler. He was good for bar profits, and on occasion, that is where he slept having missed the last train home!

Smartie hit two boundaries in his opening over.

Geoff Young took the second over and with his second ball he bowled Peter Ford for a duck. Young was a right arm medium pace bowler who looked to seam the ball or get a bit of swing. He gave many years of service to Ryton, aquiring an indepth knowledge of oppositions strength and weaknesses and was a well known character around the League. Stanton says there was always uncertainty about Young's exact age, though he states it was "common knowledge that he was in the year above W.G.Grace at school!"

This brought in the left handed Bill Graham at three. Bill was a tenacious batsman at this point in his career, never giving his wicket away, getting his head down and "sticking in" as the saying goes. He had a highest score this season of 74 not out against Annfield Plain.

They took the score to 57 off 12.2 overs, a steady partnership of 49 before Graham was bowled by Collier for 14.

Graeme Sinton came in at four, he was no slouch with the bat and not out of his depth at this level. He and Smartie added 59 for the third wicket, Sinton scoring 13, before he was bowled by change bowler, Michael Madine.

Stanton recalls that Madine would have been 19 years old at this time and wouldn't have much first team cricket behind him to this point. A right arm medium fast bowler who did have some potential. Work commitments took him elsewhere after three or four seasons.

116 for 3 off 21.2 overs.

Sean Smith was batting five and a stand of 33 was added for the fourth wicket, Smith scoring 12. He was caught by Stuart Stanton off the bowling of the other change bowler, Neil Scott.

Neil was the son of another well known local cricketer, Don Scott. He was regarded as an all rounder, as a bowler he was right arm medium pace, generally keeping a good line and length and looking to make it hard for the batsman to score.

Phil Myers came in at six, another steady stand, this time of 35. This time however it was Smartie who was out, for 128, when he was bowled by another change bowler, Johnny Walker.

Walker was a more than capable off spin bowler. He had two or three seasons at Ryton before returning to Blaydon. He didn't look to turn the ball sharply, but just enough to beat the batsman with changes of pace and flight. A regular wicket taker who was keen to avail himself of any opportunities of the "turf"- horse racing that is, his other passion!

This lead to a flurry of wickets as the score fell from 184 for 4 to 188 for 8 as Walker took 3 wickets in 5 balls and Stuart Stanton nipped in with another.

After Smartie, next to go was Ray Cardwell, bowled by Walker for 1, then Myers caught Stanton bowled Walker for 12.

Dave Watson had come in at 8 but he had hardly taken guard before Dave Clark, batting at 9 was caught by Young off the bowling of Stanton for a duck.

Stanton describes himself as "a medium pace seam up bowler, at his best when the wickets were green and damp!"

Clark was, no offence intended, a second team cricketer, a lovely lad, but out of his depth as a cricketer at this level.

John Scott came in at ten, he would have been around 19 at this time and was a good right arm, fast/medium bowler. He took plenty of wickets over his career, largely at second team level. He was never much of a batsman at this level but did occasionally have his day with the bat.

Scott and Watson steadied things down a little, taking the score to 201 when Watson was bowled by Stanton for 14.

This brought Rob Parkin to the crease. Rob was a right arm fast bowler. Operating off a relatively short run, he could generate plenty of pace with a fast arm action. He could also get the ball to rear unexpectedly off a length every now and then and was certainly a handful on his day. As a batsman Rob would look to hit hard and generally straight.....today was not his day, caught by Havery off the bowling of Stanton with 4 balls left in the innings.

Scott was left 13 not out, a decent knock for a number ten in the circumstances he came in at!

Seaton Burn 217 all out in 44.2 overs.

Smarties score of 128 contained 13 fours & 5 sixes.

His 50 was scored off 73 balls.

Six Seaton Burn batsmen, apart from Smartie, got into their teens and made a contribution.

All six of the Ryton bowlers used took at least one wicket, with Stuart Stanton 7.2-0-19-3 and Johnny Walker 7-0-30-3 being the pick of them.

The scorecard also shows that Stanton took a couple of catches, even years later he recalls that "he clung on to a couple of good catches in this game."

Ryton opened the batting with John Morley and Davy Armstrong.

Morley was a left handed batsman who had joined the club from Gateshead Fell. He was particularly strong on the leg side and a hard hitter on his day. Those familiar with Gateshead Fell may recall his brothers, Dave and Keith. Like many a left hander he did have a penchant for wafting outside his off stump and that was to lead to his downfall today. He was a very good slip fielder.

Armstrong was a Ryton stalwart. He played many years of second team cricket for the club. A right handed opening bat he liked to play off the back foot, particularly through the off side. He is described as being "not the best runner between the wickets and indecision did lead to him or his partner being run out on a good few occasions!" Unfortunately he died at the relatively young age of 63 in September 2014 after a lengthy spell of illness.

The Seaton Burn bowling attack contained some inexperience at this level, John Scott and Rob Parkin both under 20, likely to do most if not all of the bowling. That said, they would be supported by the experience of Bill Graham and Ray Cardwell.

Scott and Cardwell opened the bowling, both right handed, medium/fast bowlers and Scott got a breakthrough with the fourth ball of his second over, having Morley caught by Bill Graham for 6.

Ryton were 13 for 1.

This brought Derek Mcconnell to the crease. He was a talented wicketkeeper/batsman who had very good technique and shaped well. Well enough in fact for Warwickshire to ask him to come down for trials.

Both Seaton Burn opening bowlers had short opening spells, Cardwell going for 17 runs in just 3 overs and Scott a more creditable 5-1-16-1.

Bill Graham had been first change, replacing Cardwell.

The second wicket took the score to 40 before Armstrong was run out for 18.

Rob Parkin replaced Scott.

Stuart Stanton batted at four. He describes himself as a right handed, tall, upright batsman with a high backlift. He was particularly strong off the front foot, scoring many runs with drives on both sides of the wicket.

In a steady third wicket partnership with Mcconnell they took the score to 75 before Mcconnell was caught by Shaun Smith off the bowling of Rob Parkin.

David Minnikin came in at five. Minnikin was known to all as "Charlie". He rose through the juniors at Ryton. A tall, right handed batsman who possessed good technique and could play all around the wicket, he could also strike the ball a long way. He had several seasons scoring over 500 runs with Ryton and Blaydon.

Parkin also got the next wicket, with the score at 90 he bowled Minnikin for 9.

Although Bill Graham was proving expensive, with the score still 90, he bowled Stanton for 30 in the next over.

Ryton now 90 for 5 in the 20th over.

With those two quick wickets that meant two new batsman were at the crease, Neil Scott batting at six, and Paul Havery batting at seven.

Neil Scott had a good batting technique and relished the opportunity to play a few shots, today being a prime example.

Paul Havery, though largely a second team player, was aggressive in his batting and quick between the stumps. A good fielder, he was also a good local footballer and therefore in much demand.

These two, counterattacked and quickly took the score to 139 before the sixth wicket fell, Havery being caught by Phil Myers off the bowling of Parkin. He had got off the mark with a six and his innings had included a four and three sixes!

This brought Geoff Young to the crease batting at eight. Young was a genuine all rounder, a right handed batsman, he was known to score runs quickly at times and he could hit the ball a long way, a fact Madan Lal had once found out at Felling. Equally he had the game to defend resolutely if the occasion called for it.

I recall playing in a second team game a few years later when Geoff Young hammered us all round Ryton, we had them in a bit of bother if I remember it right, until Geoff set about us. I bowled him for 96 in the last couple of overs of the innings as he went for his century.

He too got off the mark with a six but, after a brief partnership of 11, he too was caught by Myers off the bowling of Parkin.

Ray Cardwell now replaced Bill Graham.

Vince Collier came in to bat at nine. He was a resolute right handed batsman who could hang around in difficult circumstances, often until he ran out of partners.

A short partnership of just six, was ended when Smartie caught Scott, again off the bowling of Parkin, and giving the youngster his fifth wicket, for 29. His innings had included four four's and a six.

The score was now 156 for 8.

Johnny Walker, who was a solid looking batsman and looked to play down the line came in at number ten and scored 8 out of a partnership of 10, before he was bowled by Cardwell. 166 for 9.

Last man was Michael Madine. He had good forward defensive technique but had to curb his natural instinct to have a go. He added a single out of a partnership of 11, before, he, quite fittingly, was also bowled by Parkin.

The recently turned 18 year old Parkin had returned figures of 14-2-40-6, and arguably had turned the game for Seaton Burn. The other bowlers, Scott, Cardwell and Graham had all taken a wicket each and the winning margin was 40 runs.

Seaton Burn			
D. Smart		B J. Walker	128
P. Ford		B G. Young	0
W. Graham		B V. Collier	14
G. Sinton		B M. Madine	13
S. Smith	C S. Stanton	B N. Scott	12
P. Myers	C S. Stanton	B J. Walker	12
R. Cardwell		B J. Walker	1
D. Watson		B S. Stanton	14
D. Clark	C G. Young	B S. Stanton	0
J. Scott	Not	Out	13
R. Parkin	C P. Havery	B S. Stanton	0
Extras			10
Total			217-All Out

V. Collier 1-53 G. Young 1-38 N. Scott 1-33 M. Madine 1-34
S. Stanton 3-19 J. Walker 3-30

Ryton			
J. Morley	C W. Graham	B J. Scott	6
D. Armstrong	Run	Out	18
D. Mcconnell	C S. Smith	B R. Parkin	15
S. Stanton		B W. Graham	30
D. Minnikin		B R. Parkin	9
N. Scott	C D. Smart	B R. Parkin	29
P. Havery	C P. Myers	B R. Parkin	27
G. Young	C P. Myers	B R. Parkin	8
V. Collier	Not	Out	8
J. Walker		B R. Cardwell	8
M. Madine		B R. Parkin	1
Extras			18
Total			177-All Out

J. Scott 1-16 R. Cardwell 1-37 W. Graham 1-66 R. Parkin 6-40

On Saturday 1st September 1984 Seaton Burn played an away league fixture at Greenside. Greenside would finish ninth in the league this season, Shaun Stokoe finished fourth in the league batting averages, with 948 runs at an average of 52.67, with a highest score of 150 and a further two centuries.

Seaton Burn again found themselves batting first. Smartie had another opening partner, the left handed Davie Gibson.

Paul Carrick bowled the first over of the day.

Carrick, who would establish himself as one of the Leagues best all rounders in later years, has provided some memories of his team mates of the day.

Carrick did recognise, even at an early age, the importance of Smartie's wicket, that if they couldn't get him early, 45, and later 50 overs, could be a long afternoon!

He also remembers that Seaton Burn were regarded as a good bunch of lads who played the game in the right way.

He states that both teams had a top batsman, Shaun Stokoe for Greenside, Smartie for Seaton Burn. I would add that, perhaps not in 1984 but certainly not too many years later, both sides had a capable all rounder in their side, Carrick himself for Greenside and Davie Gibson for Seaton Burn.

Smartie describes a "young" Paul Carrick as "a really good bowler, one who could swing the ball either way and generate pace off the wicket."

The week before he scored his 201 Smartie remembers being bowled by Carrick for eight.

In respect of himself, Paul says he was "a decent cricketer who got everything he possibly could out of the ability he had, that he gave his all, every time he played."

I think Paul was being modest, I can remember playing against him, he was regularly a thorn in our side. Right arm fast/medium paced, he took 50 wickets twice in a season in the TSL, with a best haul of 67 in 1992. This year also saw his career best bowling figures of 9-62. He ended his career credited with 646 wickets. One of the centuries he did score was 118 against Seaton Burn.

Carrick has been involved in cricket all his adult life. As well as a player he was a players agent for a few years, only giving it up when a new "sports visa" moved the goalposts. This business though gave him cricket contacts all over the world, many of whom were ex players who would go on to become coaches. In recent years he has run coaching clinics in India, giving young players the opportunity to learn how to play and bowl spin. These days he is a coach at Gateshead Fell.

Michael Fearon took the second over. Fearon was six foot four inches tall, medium paced, who could extract extra bounce from the wicket due to his height. His brother, Paul, was an enthusiastic follower of local league cricket and was a regular at Greenside games both home and away.

The batsman quickly got on top, Fearon bowling 5 overs for 31, he was replaced by Tony Wallace who fared no better, his 4 overs costing 21.

I played a lot of second team cricket at Seaton Burn with Tony Wallace and I can honestly say I never saw him bowl and had no idea he could. It was only years later talking to John Dixon, who played with Tony at Greenside and Seaton Burn, that I found out that he used to be a left arm spinner in his youth!

John also recalls that Tony showed so much potential as a spinner he had a trial with Nottinghamshire CCC.

Paul Carrick remembers Tony's bowling at Greenside, saying as a youngster he was an outstanding spinner but he got a case of the "yips" and his confidence never recovered.

Ernie Bewick came and went for 23 from his 6 overs. Bewick was a larger than life character, well known throughout the league. He was born in a house on the edge of Greenside Cricket Field. He played there as a junior and progressed through the third and second teams into the first team, becoming part of the great Greenside team which dominated the league for ten years.

He did have a brief flirtation with Swalwell at the start of the 1969 season but returned to Greenside before the season was out. He joined Burnopfield in 1975 and later became pro at both Leadgate and Clara Vale. He also played for Sacriston.

Unfortunately his statistics are missing a lot of information, so whatever I publish here, simply wouldn't do the man justice.

Paul Carrick says that Bewick had "a brilliant, dry, sense of humour, not always appreciated or understood by people who didn't know him well."

He recalls playing a game at Greenside against Gateshead Fell. A batsman called Doug Hudson came down the stairs to bat, swinging his arms, playing imaginary cover drives and pull shots, an array of shots as he walked to the crease, past Bewick at mid off. Unfortunately Hudson was out first ball....as he walked back to the pavilion he had to walk past Bewick again, quick as a flash Bewick says to him "Never mind Doug, you were 24 not out on the way in!"

Carrick states that Bewick was an underrated bowler, a great competitor, he uses the words "Greenside Legend" to describe him. He was part of the Greeenside team that was so succesful in the 60's and 70's, winning the league ten years in a row. He goes on to say that as well as being right up there in speed with the very best fast bowlers of the day, Bewick was a very skilful bowler. As part of the quartet of Bill Jones, Ian Wishart and Alan Smith, Bewick and his fellow fast bowlers dominated the TSL for an unprecedented period of time.

The first wicket added 132 and it was the 31st over before Gibson was caught by John Mcgrady off the bowling of Shaun Stokoe for 21. His innings had included a single boundary.

Smartie describes Stokoe as "a right arm, medium pace inswing bowler, he was very accurate." There are no league records of Shaun Stokoe as a bowler.

Bill Graham came in at number three and scored 8 in a partnership of 33 before he was bowled by Shaun Stokoe. Carrick remembers bowling to Bill Graham as being tough. He says "the bloke never gave his wicket away, he was never caught in the ring playing an extravagent shot, his wicket had to be earned. It was invariably taken by a "bowlers dismissal" rather than batsman error." By that he means bowled, LBW or caught behind the wicket.

165 for 2.

David Bilclough was now bowling with Stokoe. He was a talented all rounder, a right arm medium pace bowler, on his day he could move the ball round and be unplayable. Described by

Paul Carrick as "a better batter than bowler and a very good fielder, also a really nice bloke!"

It was Bilclough who took the next wicket, Sean Smith batting at four, who was bowled for a score of 4.

Davie Watson came in at number five and he scored a quick 10, which included two boundaries, out of a partnership of 11 before he was LBW, a second wicket for Bilclough.

181 for 4 quickly became 183 for 5 when Shaun Stokoe bowled Smartie for 122 in the 44th over of the innings.

The 122 had included 19 fours & 2 sixes.

Graeme Sinton with 6 not out and Phil Myers with 0 not out finished the innings up as Seaton Burn made 188 for 5 from their 45 overs.

Shaun Stokoe had 13-1-44-3 and Bilclough 9-1-30-2 as the only bowlers to take wickets.

The scorebook I have for this game has no details of the second half of the game, only the batsman scores and the bowlers statistics.

That said, there were some very well known local cricketers in the Greenside team and it's worth taking a look and finding out a little about them.

Shaun Stokoe and John Mcgrady opened the batting for Greenside.

Shaun Stokoe came from Shotley Bridge and was part of a well known cricket family. His father Bill, was a talented cricketer and both Shaun and his brother Robert were both good enough to be professional cricketers for local sides. Indeed Shaun had been appointed Greenside professional in 1981 and would have been playing in that capacity on this day.

Smartie recalls a "left handed bat, very correct in his technique, he could play shots all round the wicket with a good defence. He was a complete batsman and a tough competitor, he neither asked for nor gave any quarter."

John Mcgrady's father, Albert, had played for Greenside and also in Minor Counties Cricket. John was a right handed batsman and good wicketkeeper. Technically he was a very good batsman, especially off the front foot. In 1990, whilst studying chemistry there, he went on to play six matches for Oxford University as a wicketkeeper, taking fifteen catches and two stumpings. He batted twice, scoring a total of 15 runs and a highest score of 14. Amongst the players he took the field against were Mathew Maynard, Peter Roebuck, Chris Tavare, Alec Stewart, Graham Thorpe, Peter Willey, Michael Atherton, Neil Fairbrother, Phil Defreitas, Robin Smith, Mark Nicholas and David Gower. It was Gower who took the catch which dismissed him for his top score of 14.

From Oxford he obtained his doctorate at the Australian National University in Canberra. He returned to Oxford in 2009 when he became a "fellow" at New College.

Stokoe made 34 before he was bowled by Rob Parkin and Mcgrady 28 before he was bowled by Bill Graham.

Bill Stokoe batted at three and he made 31 before he was caught by Phil Myers also off the bowling of Bill Graham. He was the father of Shaun and Robert Stokoe.

A right handed bat, he started his career at Consett, moving to Shotley Bridge in 1961 and remaining there until 1976, apart from two seasons, 67 and 68 at Beamish & East Tanfield.

He scored one century for Shotley, in 1965, an unbeaten 101. He played one season, 1977 at South Moor. When Shaun was appointed Greenside professional in 1982, Bill joined him until he effectively retired in 1986. Although he did turn out once for them in 1987. This game would have been at the end of his career. Another player who was technically very good. He was also a talented country and western singer!

Jim Watson came in at four and he scored 26 before he too was caught by Phil Myers off the bowling of Bill Graham. Watson was the captain throughout the period when Greenside dominated the league. He was a right handed batsman and a quick bowler who bowled big "inswingers" off the wrong foot. Described as a better person than he was a cricketer, and he was a great cricketer!

He made a lasting impression on a 14 year old Paul Carrick. During one match the batsman was given out, caught behind, as he came to walk off he became distraught, wicketkeeper Gordon Faulkner approached Watson and told him he wasn't sure the batsman had hit it. Watson immediately called the batsman back. The only time Carrick saw such a gesture during many, many years of cricket.

In 1951, whilst still a scholar at The Royal Grammar School in Newcastle, Watson made his first team debut for Greenside. In this season his best return was 9-31!

In 1952, playing for Durham Schoolboys, he took 9-29 against Northumberland Schoolboys.

In 1953 he would also play for Durham Juniors.

In 1954, whilst still a scholar, he took 50 League wickets in a season, despite playing only 13 games!

In 1957 he made his debut for Durham Seconds.

In 1958 he played his first match as a Greenside opener, scoring 109 against Leslies and following it up the next game with 101 against Seghill.

As a young man Watson had attended Cambridge University where he successfully studied for a Bachelor of Science degree. Whilst there he was good enough to play for the University Second Team. It's worth noting that in the late fifties a certain E.R.Dexter was playing for the Cambridge First Eleven, he would become better known as Ted Dexter, England Player, Captain and Selector. Another well known name from the period was opening batsman, H.C.Blofeld, Henry Blofeld, he would make a name for himself as part of The Test Match Special Team on the radio!

After leaving Cambridge he took up a post as a teacher in Surrey, playing only for Greenside if he returned to the area on holiday. He moved back to the area in 1965 but a back injury hampered his bowling from then on and he became an occasional bowler only.

He was a school headmaster, he died in very sad circumstances, during his retirement presentation. The four pall bearers at the funeral were his four fast bowlers, Bill Jones, Ian Wishart, Ernie Bewick and Alan Smith

The last wicket to fall was John Stokoe, batting at five, he was caught by Davie Gibson off the bowling of Rob Parkin. Part of the Stokoe dynasty, brother of Bill and Uncle to Shaun and Rob, he also played for Consett and Shotley Bridge. Carrick states every dressing room should have a John Stokoe! A tough player on the field and the life and soul of the dressing room off it! He was a good all rounder, batting right handed and bowling right handed medium pace. He was also a brilliant fielder. He had played for Shotley Bridge in the game in 1979 when Smartie got his first hundred.

Batsman six was Paul Kerry. He was a right handed bat, he was one of those cricketers who had the knack of scoring important runs, if the team was winning comfortably he would often fail with the bat, in a close match, a contest, he would more often than not, make a valuable and match winning contribution. He died relatively young of a heart attack. He was 25 not out at the end of the innings, batting with David Bilclough who was 1 not out.

The two wicket takers, Rob Parkin and Bill Graham had figures of 14-2-46-2 and 14-2-45-3. Ray Cardwell, who had opened the bowling with Parkin, 7.1-1-33-0, and Davie Watson 8-0-44-0 completed the bowling figures.

It had taken Greenside 43.1 of their allotted 45 overs to score the runs. Given that their top six all made at least 23 and without the full scorebook, it looks like a very professional performance by a very good, very experienced batting line up.

As for Smartie and his hundred, that was the second time he would score a hundred and end up on the losing side.

Seaton Burn

D. Smart		B S. Stokoe	122
D. Gibson	C J. Mcgrady	B S. Stokoe	21
W. Graham		B S. Stokoe	8
S. Smith		B D. Bilclough	4
D. Watson		LBW B D. Bilclough	10
G. Sinton	Not	Out	6
P. Myers	Not	Out	0
Extras			17
Total			188-5 Wkts

P. Carrick 0-22 M. Fearon 0-31 T. Wallace 0-21 E. Bewick 0-23
S. Stokoe 3-44 D. Bilclough 2-30

Greenside

S. Stokoe		B R. Parkin	34
J. Mcgrady		B W. Graham	28
W. Stokoe	C P. Myers	B W. Graham	31
J. Watson	C P. Myers	B W. Graham	26
J. Stokoe	C D. Gibson	B R. Parkin	23
P. Kerry	Not	Out	25
D. Bilclough	Not	Out	1
Extras			21
Total			189-5 Wkts

R. Parkin 2-46 R. Cardwell 0-33 W. Graham 3-45 D. Watson 0-44

On Saturday 8th September 1984 Seaton Burn played an away league fixture against Wallsend. This was the return fixture from earlier in the season. Once again I am grateful to Craig Johnson for his memories of the Wallsend players.

Seaton Burn found themselves batting again, although by slightly unorthadox means. Smartie and the Wallsend captain, Micky Jackson, worked together at Parson's.

The custom was both captains would walk to the middle of the wicket and the home captain, in this case, Jackson, would toss the coin and the visiting skipper call "heads or tails". Winning captain decides if he wants to bat or bowl.

As Smartie left the dressing room to go to the middle he said to Jackson "Howay then, are we going to spin up?"

Jackson replied "We don't need to do we?"

Smartie "Why?"

Jackson "What are you going to do if you win?"

Smartie "Bat!"

Jackson "Well this lot want you to see you bat, we will try our best to get you out mind, but they want to see you smash the league record, make sure it stays with a local lad!"

A third opening partner in three games as Gary Stephenson returned to the side.

Wallsend fielded a very different side from the fixture earlier in the season, with only four players returning from that game.

The bowling was opened by Maurice Johnston and Gary Walton.

Johnston was a right arm opening swing bowler and a handy middle order batsman. He was a Police Inspector who was based at Wallsend for part of his service. After Wallsend left the TSL he played a few games for Seaton Burn. Walton was one of the players from the earlier game.

After an uneventful first three overs, Walton stirred things up by removing Gary Stephenson and Bill Graham with the first two balls of the fourth over, bowling both of them.

Seaton Burn and Smartie in familiar territory at 10 for 2!

Davie Gibson came in at four and steadied the ship, scoring 12 as they added 43 for the third wicket. It was Walton who was again the wicket taker, this time a caught and bowled.

Two more wickets quickly followed as Walton's fellow opening bowler, Johnston, struck twice in four balls. Sean Smith for 4 and Billy Wilkinson for a duck were the unlucky batsman.

Seaton Burn now 63 for 5 and once again the innings hangs in the balance.

Graeme Sinton was next to try his luck and a cameo of 14, with three boundaries, as he and Smartie put on 55 for the sixth wicket before Sinton was LBW to Johnston.

Davie Watson came in at eight and struck six four's in an innings of 35. A partnership of 110, one run shy of tying a league 7th wicket record, with Smartie, ensured Seaton Burn passed 200 and a challenging score would be delivered. Watson was caught by Jackson off the bowling of Ian Cawthorne.

Cawthorne was a right arm swing bowler. He was an all rounder who was usually in either the runs or wickets. He worked in the brewery trade.

When Watson was out in the 44th over Phil Myers wasn't left with much of a chance and he was bowled for a duck off the last ball of the innings by Walton.

Seaton Burn had made 234 for 8 from their 45 overs. All credit to bowler Johnston who bowled 20 overs unchanged at the start of the innings to finish with 20-4-67-3. Fellow opening bowler Walton had 15-3-65-4 with Cawthrone being the other wicket taker 5-0-33-1.

Smartie was 147 Not Out when the innings closed.

The innings lasted 2 hours 40 minutes and included 21 fours & 4 sixes.

Wallsend sent out Ian Cawthorne and Bob Pyke to open the innings.

Cawthorne would normally bat in the middle to lower order.

Seaton Burn were to rely on the youthful pace of Rob Parkin and the wily experience of Billy Wilkinson to open the bowling.

Parkin opened with a maiden over. With his second ball, Wilkinson bowled Pyke for two. 2 for 1, became 3 for 2 when with the third ball of his second over Parkin bowled new batsman George Dunn for a single.

With the first and third balls of his third over Billy Wilkinson bowled number four batsman Mark Robson for a single and opening bat Cawthorne, for 2.

Robson was in his teen's at this time, and as was the way of many teams, would have been picked to inject some youth into the fielding and bat in the lower order. That said, he would go on to mature into a decent, attacking, middle order batsman.

Wallsend 7 for 4 and "Pep" had the astonishing figures of 3.3-0-5-3!

Batsmen five, Micky Jackson and six, Maurice Johnston, put on 7 for the fifth wicket. Jackson was caught by Sean Smith off the bowling of Parkin for 2. Wallsend 14 for 5.

Two more wickets fell at 17. Johnston was out for 2, caught by Phil Myers off Rob Parkin. Next to go was Terry Pears, caught by Bill Graham off Billy Wilkinson for a duck. Wallsend 17 for 7.

G.Lockwood, batting at 9, was next to go, bowled by Wilkinson for 4 and batsman 10, Billy Tubman, who top scored with 8, was next as Billy Wilkinson had him LBW.

Despite Parkin's last four overs all being maidens and reaping two wickets he was removed from the attack. He finished with excellent figures of 8-6-4-3!

Bill Graham's left arm spin replaced Parkin and with the last ball of his first over he bowled number 11, Gary Walton for a duck. Number 8 batsman Graham Turnbull was 1 not out, with 10 extras top scoring in the innings. Wallsend 33 all out in 17 overs.

Seaton Burn had won by 201 runs.

Billy Wilkinson finished with 8-3-18-6. Anyone who faced "Pep" will tell you how hard he was to face when he was on song. As stated earlier he finished this season with 49 wickets. Over the years his round arm action caused many batsmen problems, including some of the best in the league.

Bill Graham's one over cost him one run for the one wicket he collected.

Seaton Burn

D. Smart	Not	Out	147
G. Stephenson		B G. Walton	0
W. Graham		B G. Walton	0
D. Gibson	C & B	G. Walton	12
S. Smith		B M. Johnston	4
W. Wilkinson		B M. Johnston	0
G. Sinton		LBW B M. Johnston	14
D. Watson	C M. Jackson	B M. Johnston	35
P. Myers		B G. Walton	0
Extras			22
Total			234-8 Wkts
M. Johnston 3-67	G. Walton 4-65	G. Lockwood 1-33	I. Cawthorne 0-47

Wallsend

I. Cawthorne		B W. Wilkinson	2
R. Pyke		B W. Wilkinson	2
G. Dunn		B R. Parkin	1
M. Robson		B W. Wilkinson	1
M. Jackson	C S. Smith	B R. Parkin	2
M. Johnston	C P. Myers	B R. Parkin	2
T. Pears	C W. Graham	B W. Wilkinson	0
G. Turnbull	Not	Out	1
G. Lockwood		B W. Wilkinson	4
W. Tubman		LBW B W. Wilkinson	8
G. Walton		B W. Graham	0
Extras			10
Total			33 All Out
R. Parkin 3-4	W. Wilkinson 6-18	W. Graham 1-1	

It's worth looking at the league table, as well as Smartie's run total and centuries, Seaton Burn also had Billy Wilkinson with 49 wickets and Davie Gibson with 42. Smartie and Bill Graham were also selected by the Tyneside Senior League representative eleven.

Smartie's run total was a new league record, beating the previous one held by Pakistani test batsman, Qasim Omar, who had played for Sacriston.

Before he departed for Karachi to prepare for series against India and New Zealand, Omar wrote Smartie a letter, congratulating him on breaking the record. He was reported at the time as saying "I think it's a marvellous achievement for an amateur, I always thought David Smart was a very good cricketer who should have got more runs in the past. I said to him once, you have got all the shots and you are a very hard hitter, you should score many more."

Tyneside Senior League Table 1984
All teams played 26 games and there were no ties.

	WON 5PTS	WON 4PTS	LOST 1PT	LOST 0PTS	Drawn	Tied	PTS
Shotley Bridge	8	11	2	1	4	0	90
Annfield Plain	7	10	3	3	3	0	81
Swalwell	9	6	8	2	1	0	78
Reyrolle	10	5	4	5	2	0	76
South Moor	9	5	7	4	1	0	73
Burnopfield	9	4	7	2	4	0	72
Lintz	10	4	4	8	1	0	71
Blaydon	5	9	2	9	1	0	64
Greenside	6	6	8	5	1	0	63
Consett	4	9	5	7	1	0	62
Ryton	5	6	7	8	0	0	56
Seaton Burn	5	4	12	4	1	0	54
Sacriston	4	1	7	13	1	0	32
Wallsend	0	0	4	21	1	0	5

The number of batsmen who scored 500 runs in 1984 is a testimony to the quality of the League batting at this time. If you have a look at the bowling averages of the season, you can see the quality of the bowlers those batsmen faced!!!

League Batting Averages 1984
Qualification 500 Runs

	Runs	High Score	Comp Inns	Average
D. Smart (Seaton Burn)	1474	201no	21	70.19
W. Raja (Shotley Bridge)	912	155	13	70.15
C. Butts (Blaydon)	1089	103	19	57.32
S. Stokoe (Greenside)	948	150	18	52.67
C. Albone (South Moor)	805	121no	18	44.72
D. Jackson (Annfield Plain)	640	105no	16	40.00
I. Stokoe (Swalwell)	519	76	13	39.92
G. Hunter (Consett)	575	75	17	33.82
S. Clennell (Lintz)	595	96	18	33.06
N. Turner (Reyrolle)	657	109	20	32.85
M. Bell (Reyrolle)	586	86	20	29.30
B. Mccardle (Annfield Plain)	504	113no	18	28.00
C. Stephenson (Shotley Bridge)	591	89	22	26.86
I. Stoneman (Sacriston)	613	108	23	26.65
G. Clennell (Lintz)	516	59	21	24.57
P. Veitch (Blaydon)	587	69	25	23.48
S. Stanton (Ryton)	510	85no	22	23.18
N. Burdon (Swalwell)	526	63	25	21.04

League Bowling Averages 1984
Quaification 50 Wickets

	Overs	Runs	Wkts	Ave
R. Stokoe (Swalwell)	338	906	74	12.24
W. Raja (Shotley Bridge)	290	752	61	12.33
A. Halliday (Annfield Plain)	210	702	56	12.54
R. Cook (Lintz)	282	788	62	12.71
N. Hewison (Burnopfield)	192	677	52	13.02
I. Wishart (Ryton)	359	979	68	14.40
A. Smare (Reyrolle)	369	1106	76	14.55
F. Hilton (Sacriston)	229	831	56	14.84
C. Butts (Blaydon)	470	1285	84	15.30
R. Bainbridge (Lintz)	277	867	50	17.34
J. Carlyon (South Moor)	285	988	54	18.30
I. Stoneman (Sacriston)	288	1007	54	18.65

CHAPTER 9

SOUTH MOOR, ESSEX AND GREENSIDE

On Saturday April 27th 1985 Seaton Burn opened their league season with a home fixture against South Moor.

South Moor had finished fifth in the league last season. Opening bat Colin Albone had been fifth in the league averages with 805 runs at 44.72.

I am indebted to Ossie Barrass and Phil Shield for most of the information in respect of South Moor. Barrass was Mr "South Moor," player, official and author of the remarkable book "A History of South Moor Cricket Club."

Phil Shield played junior and senior cricket for the club. A gifted right handed batsman who hit the ball hard. He gained both league and county honours at under 13/16/18 and 19 level. He was also an excellent wicketkeeper, keeping wicket for the first team whilst still a junior.

A quiet and modest man he took the huge step in 1991 of going to play grade cricket in Tasmania, Australia. This was arranged through the club's connection with it's then professional, Clay Young.

In both 1989 and 1991 he featured in the league batting averages, in 1989, aged 17 or 18 he scored 500 runs at an average of 23.81 and in 1991 scoring 655 runs at 31.20. He also scored his first hundred in 1991 with 113 not out against Ryton.

In 1993 he left South Moor to play for Sacriston. He also had two seasons at Ryton in 2003-04 before returning to Sacriston. In 93 and 94 he scored over 500 runs in each season, and repeated the feat again in 2002. He would go on to score seven centuries in his career, with a best of 115 not out in 2002.

I recall Phil being a very good opening batsman, I distinctly remember a game at Sacriston when he square cut a short ball from Alan Francis in my direction at gully. It was hit very hard and to this day it is one of the very few catches I remember, if I hadn't caught it, it would have decapitated me! As Phil walked off the field, shaking his head, Smartie said to him "Unlucky mate, but he does that about twice a season!"

In 2010 he moved to Annfield Plain, scoring a 100 not out in one game that year to mark his debut season.

Their bowling attack was led by Jeff Carlyon. He had featured in last seasons league bowling average with 54 wickets at 18.30 each.

Smartie opened the batting with a familiar partner, Gary Stephenson.

Jeff Carlyon and David Shield opened the bowling. Both men were very good all rounders. Carlyon was a right arm fast bowler. He featured regularly in both the league representative sides and the league averages. His best season as a bowler was in 1982 when he took 70 wickets at 15.23 each. From 1981 to 1986 inclusive he took at least 54 wickets in each season. He also played two seasons at Shotley Bridge and two seasons at Beamish and East Stanley.

Shield began at South Moor as a junior and progressed through the ranks, becoming club captain. As a bowler he was a capable swing bowler. He went on to be a committee member and club chairman.

With the last ball of his first, the second over of the innings, Shield bowled Stephenson for 2. Seaton Burn 6 for 1.

Left hander Bill Graham batted at three and a partnership of 110 followed with Smartie for the second wicket. Graham making 32 before he was caught Wright off the bowling of change bowler, Ivor Burridge.

Burridge came from a cricketing family, both his grandfather, Tommy, and father, Jonty, being well known on the local cricket scene. He played for South Moor juniors and was another who progressed through the ranks. In 1969 he was a member of the second team which won the "Division B" League title. By the time he made the first team he was another considered as a genuine all rounder, opening the bowling, often bowling long spells, and a useful lower middle order batsman. He also had three seasons at Beamish and East Tanfield. In 1991 he returned to South Moor, going on to captain the seconds and become Club Chairman.

Another left hander, Davie Gibson came in at four, and another steady partnership, this time of 41, took the score to 157 before Gibson was bowled by second change bowler, Stephen Wells for 14.

Phil Shield recalls Wells being "pretty quick" and has a vivid recollection of him bowling at him in the nets while wearing "Doc Martin" boots! Unfortunately work commitments prevented him playing a lot more cricket within the next couple of seasons.

Another left hander, Richie Allan, came in at five but he was bowled by Wells second ball with no addition to the team score.

A brief partnership of just three with Phil Myers for the fifth wicket before Myers was caught by Carlyon off the bowling of Burridge for a duck.

Steve Armstrong, batted at seven. He was a compact, very reliable batsman and more than useful wicketkeeper.

Smartie was run out off the last ball of the 44th over for 118. The innings had included 13 fours and 2 sixes.

Billy Wilkinson was batting at eight and he and Armstrong took nine off the last over as Seaton Burn finished 184 for 6 off their allotted 45 overs.

Armstrong was 7 not out and Wilkinson 2 not out.

Wells was the pick of the bowlers with 10-0-49-2, with a wicket each for Shield and Burridge.

Colin Albone and David Shield opened the batting for South Moor. Albone first played for South Moor juniors and seconds in 1969. By the following season he was a first team regular. He scored runs throughout the 1970's before two seasons at Shotley Bridge, in 1982 and 83. He scored 3 centuries for Shotley, with a highest score of 119 against Wallsend. He returned to South Moor in 1984. He continued his good form in 1985, scoring 101 against Annfield Plain and 121 against Blaydon.

He was a regular in both the league batting averages and the league representative side. He was a very correct batsman, he had shots all round the wicket. Albone was good enough to play three seasons as a professional at Beamish and East Stanley, from 87-89 inclusive, before once again returning to South Moor. The club won several cups in the years that followed.

In 1991 Albone and West Indian Professional Dennison Thomas scored a then league record of 291 against Seaton Burn. Thomas scored 184, Albone contributed 122, this would be his sixth century.

Smartie also recalls Colin Albone, he remembers "a very gifted batsman, he could, and would, play shots all round the wicket. He was technically very correct. Even now, around fifty years later I still say a hundred I saw him score at Seaton Burn was one of the best centuries I ever saw. We had batted first and Bill Graham had scored a great ton for us, but South Moor, led by Colin's hundred rubbed them off and they won comfortably. As well as being an awesome batsman he was a really nice bloke off the pitch too."

Shield was also a very good player at this level, he had a good enough game where he could bat steadily or attack depending on the situation he found himself in. He had a highest score of 102 not out against Lintz this season.

Billy Stephenson and Davie Gibson opened the bowling for Seaton Burn.

Stephenson was a right arm fast bowler. He worked at Barclays Bank with Billy Wilkinson.

An excellent opening partnership of 61 for the first wicket saw off both of the opening bowlers. Although both economical in their spells, neither could take a wicket. Stephenson 7 overs for 18, replaced by the left arm spin of Bill Graham, and Gibson 10 overs for 21, replaced by the swing and seam of Billy Wilkinson.

It was Graham who struck first, having Shield caught by Smart for 23.

Matty Gowland came in at three and a steady partnership of 46 took the score to 107 when Billy Wilkinson bowled Albone for 57. Albone's innings had included 5 four's and a six.

The wicket had fallen with the second ball of the 32nd over, South Moor now needed 78 to win from 13.4 overs.

Michael Wright came in at four. His innings of 14 included a six and a four, as South Moor went for the runs. He was caught Smart off the bowling of Bill Graham with the score now at 130.

South Moor now require 55 runs off 8 overs.

Jeff Carlyon batted at five. A left handed batsman with a long reach, he could strike the ball powerfully off his front foot. His brief innings of 11 included a six off Bill Graham.

This was enough for Gibson to replace Graham in the bowling attack.

With the second ball of his new spell Gibson bowled Carlyon with the total now 153 for 5.

South Moor now need 32 runs to win from 32 balls.

New batsman was captain Colin Watson. Watson had been a young captain when appointed in 1984. Despite his age the club won The Divison A Knockout Cup that year. He was highly regarded as a leg spinner and a capable bat. Considered as being under bowled he left the club in around 1986, going to Kimblesworth. He returned to South Moor in 1990.

A partnership of 21 between Watson and number three batsman Gowland, took the score to 174 when Gowland was caught by Richie Allan off the bowling of Billy Wilkinson for 41.

South Moor now require 11 runs to win off 9 balls.

New batsman was Ivor Burridge. Burridge was regarded as someone who hit the ball hard, the pinnacle of his batting career coming with a match winning 50 in the 1984 Division A Cup Final at Swalwell.

The batsman had crossed before the catch was taken and with the next ball of the over, Watson was bowled by Wilkinson for 12.

South Moor now 174 for 6, 11 required with 8 balls left and two new batsman at the crease, Burridge and Ray Gray batting at 8.

Gray was a left handed batsman, another who came through the club junior system into senior cricket. Capable of clever defence and unorthadox aggression, regarded as a loyal club servant who never let the club down.

Gray managed a single off the fifth ball of the over, with a leg bye off last ball of the over.

The crucial second last over had cost Billy Wilkinson 3 runs but he had also taken the wickets of two batsman who were both set at the crease.

South Moor 176 for 6, require 9 runs from the last over, to be bowled by Davie Gibson.

Burridge scored a two off the second and third balls of the over. South Moor 180 for 6 require 5 runs off 3 balls to win.

Gibson bowled Burridge for four off the fourth ball of the over. New batsman Stephen Wells had two balls to score the five runs to win the game.

The fifth ball was a dot ball, no run scored. Wells, who was known as someone who could "give it a whack" now required a six off the last ball to win the game, a four will tie the match!

Gibson bowled him, Seaton Burn win by 4 runs!

Gray was 1 not out.

South Moor 180 for 8 from their 45 overs.

Davie Gibson's last three overs had gone for 17 runs but he had picked up three wickets, the crucial last over, with nine runs needed to win the match, had cost him four runs and he had picked up two wickets.

Gibson finished with 13-0-38-3, Billy Wilkinson 12-0-48-3 and Bill Graham 13-1-60-2.

Although South Moor were to finish bottom of the League this season, both Albone, 646 runs at 32.30 and Carlyon, 54 wickets at 20.07 would again feature in the league averages.

A great game of cricket to start the 1985 season!

Seaton Burn

D. Smart	Run	Out	118
G. Stephenson		B D. Shield	2
W. Graham	C M. Wright	B I. Burridge	32
D. Gibson		B S. Wells	14
R. Allan		B S. Wells	0
P. Myers	C J. Carlyon	B I. Burridge	0
S. Armstrong	Not	Out	7
W. Wilkinson	Not	Out	1
Extras			6
Total			184-6 Wkts

J. Carlyon 0-32   D. Shield 1-32   I. Burridge 1-65   S. Wells 2-49

South Moor

C. Albone		B W. Wilkinson	57
D. Shield	C D. Smart	B W. Graham	23
M. Gowland	C R. Allan	B W. Wilkinson	41
M. Wright	C D. Smart	B W. Graham	14
J. Carlyon		B D. Gibson	11
C. Watson		B W. Wilkinson	12
I. Burridge		B D. Gibson	4
R. Gray	Not	Out	1
S. Wells		B D. Gibson	0
Extras			14
Total			180-8 Wkts

W. Stephenson	D. Gibson	W. Graham	W. Wilkinson
0-20	3-38	2-60	3-48

On 21st May 1985 Smartie played at Gateshead Fell for a Combined Northumberland and Durham side in a game against Essex. The match was 50 overs a side, Essex had been both the County Champions and The John Player League Champions in 1984, and were a formidable side.

Former Seaton Burn wicketkeeper Kevin Corby was also in the combined eleven side.

Skipper Neil Riddell won the toss for the home side and asked Essex to bat. First wicket to fall was Graham Gooch, caught by Smartie off the bowling of Clyde Butts. England Test Player Derek Pringle top scored the innings with 50 as Essex scored 188 for 8 from their 50 overs. Shotley Bridge fast bowler Stuart Wilkinson taking one of the wickets to fall.

When the Combined Eleven batted, Essex opened the bowling with Neil Foster and Norbert Phillip. Foster played twenty nine tests for England and Phillip played nine tests for the West Indies.

Smartie came in at three. He and Richie Richardson added 77 for the second wicket. Richardson making 47 and Smartie 44 before he was bowled by Graham Gooch. Michael Roseberry and Andrew Lyght both scored 42 not out as the home side won by seven wickets.

On Saturday July 6th 1985 Seaton Burn played an away league fixture at Greenside Cricket Club. In 1984 Greenside had finished mid table, they undoubtedly had some quality players. Shaun Stokoe for example, had scored three centuries that season as he scored 948 runs.

Paul Carrick has again kindly provided some memories of the time.

The Seaton Burn innings opened promptly at 2.30pm. Bill Graham was Smartie's opening partner on this occasion.

Carrick describes the young version of himself finding it a tough task to bowl to Smartie and Bill Graham. He remembers that they had a very different approach to batting but that they were a very effective opening pair. The left handed Graham looking to rotate the strike, finding gaps for singles and occasional two's, Smartie, right handed, more aggressive, always looking to get on the front foot, leaving little margin for error.

Shaun Stokoe and Paul Carrick opened the bowling for Greenside.

It was Carrick who took the first wicket, Bill Graham caught by John Mcgrady for 7. Seaton Burn 15 for 1 after 5.4 overs.

Richie Allan batted at three, a partnership of 64 for the third wicket took the score to 79 when Allan was caught by Shaun Stokoe off the bowling of change bowler Michael Fearon for 19.

Allan had struck four boundaries in his innings.

Steve Armstrong came in at four, now playing as just a batsman. It was not to be his day, after a partnership of 3, Armstrong was out caught by Bill Stokoe off the bowling of second change bowler, David Bilclough, for a duck.

The score was now 82 for 3 after 19.5 overs.

New batsman Tim Garfield, was new to the club, he was also the new wicketkeeper. He was originally from Market Harborough in Leicestershire. He worked for the sports council and when he moved to Kenton Bank Foot he asked a colleague, Doug Ferguson, who played for Wallsend, if he could recommend a club. Ferguson told him Seaton Burn. He had previously played for Bishop Auckland. He had played a handful of games for the club before this one. Smartie recalls that he was a good wicketkeeper and batsman, he could play shots all round the wicket.

Bilclough's fifth over cost him 9 runs, his sixth over 11 runs as he was hit out of the attack, replaced by Shaun Stokoe, his 6 overs costing 31 for the wicket of Armstrong.

Fearon bowled ten consecutive overs before his eleventh went for 12 runs and he too, was replaced. His 11 overs had cost 44 runs for the wicket of Allan.

Paul Carrick was the replacement bowler.

The last nine overs saw ten fours and a six scored as Smartie and Garfield added 172 for the 4th wicket. This was a league record partnership at the time.

Garfield finished on 92 not out. His half century had come off 102 balls and the innings contained 11 fours and 2 sixes.

Smartie was 120 not out. His innings had lasted 2 hours and 35 minutes. His half century was scored off 117 balls and his century from 211 balls.

His innings had contained 12 four and 2 sixes.

Seaton Burn had scored 254 for 3 off their allotted 45 overs.

John Mcgrady and Shaun Stokoe opened the batting for Greenside.

Shaun Stokoe was a left handed batsman. He had started his career at Shotley Bridge in 1973. In 1977 he was appointed professional at Philadelphia in the Durham Senior League. He stayed there for four years before moving to Greenside.

He had great success as a batsman, scoring over a 1,000 runs in the 1989 season. He also scored 15 centuries, with three in 1984 and 1989. His highest score was 150, which came in 1984 and his three centuries in 1989 were all undefeated. In total he scored 10,269 runs in The Tyneside Senior League and would have been looked upon as one of the best local batsman of this, or any era of the league.

No Davie Gibson today, so the bowling was opened by Billy Stephenson and Billy Wilkinson.

Carrick, as many do, remembers Billy Wilkinson well, describing him as a bowler who didn't give much away, landing the ball "on the spot" with great regularity.

A brisk opening partnership of 50 off just 10 overs saw Greenside make an excellent start. With the first ball of the eleventh over, Stephenson had Mcgrady caught by Bill Graham for 17.

Brian Clark came in at three. A left handed bat who was always cheerful around the dressing room, a mild man who enjoyed his cricket. He sadly passed away recently.

Sixteen runs added for the third wicket before Clark was also caught by Bill Graham off the bowling of Stephenson, for 9.

The next few overs saw a steady fall of wickets.

Alan Wheeler batted at four. He played most of his career at Blaydon, moving to Greenside in his latter years. A right handed batsman, usually in the middle order who was very good at putting the bad ball away. He was one of those players who you could rely on to score runs when you needed them most. Paul Carrick remembers as a 16 year old watching Wheeler bat against Stuart Wilkinson of Shotley Bridge in his prime. He recalls how nervous he was watching "Wilkie" tear in down the bank at Greenside and Wheeler taking everything that was thrown at him and scoring runs too. He says he learnt a lot about batting just from watching this encounter.

Ten runs were added for the third wicket when, with the first ball of his ninth over, Billy Wilkinson bowled Shaun Stokoe for 45. His innings had contained eight boundaries.

Greenside 76 for 3 after 17.1 overs.

New batsman Bill Stokoe failed to shine and with one run added, he was stumped by Tim Garfield off the bowling of Stephenson for a duck.

Greenside 77 for 4.

John Stokoe came in batting at number 5.

A partnership of 22 for the fifth wicket steadied things for Greenside but with the score at 99, John Stokoe was caught by Bill Graham off the bowling of Stephenson for 11.

99 for 5 quickly became 99 for 6.

Next in was Tony Wallace who I caught off the bowling of Billy Wilkinson for a duck.

Ironically I played a lot of second team cricket with Tony Wallace when he came to play at Seaton Burn. He worked as a hospital porter at the R.V.I in Newcastle and was a lad who always had a smile on his face. He was a right handed batsman who liked to hit the ball hard and straight, a useful second team performer.

Tommy Dobson batted at number eight. He was a right handed batsman, small in stature, but a good player through the offside, especially square of the wicket. He has been described as a "fantastic fielder." He would later go on to play for Seaton Burn.

A brisk partnership of 47 between Wheeler and Dobson followed. Two balls of Billy Wilkinson's 15th over going for six from Dobson's bat.

This heralded a double bowling change. Stephenson replaced by the left arm spin of Bill Graham, Wilkinson by the fast bowling of Rob Parkin.

It was Parkin who made the breakthrough, bowling Dobson with the fourth ball of his second over for 25. The innings had included two fours and two sixes.

Greenside were now 146 for 7 from 33.4 overs.

109 still needed from 11.2 overs, a tall order.

New batsman David Bilclough seemed to be up for the challenge. While Wheeler batted steadily at the other end, Bilclough had a "go." He scored 38 in good time, four four's and a six, as he took the fight to the bowlers. His innings ended with the score on 209 after a partnership of 63 when he was caught by Billy Stephenson off the bowling of Bill Graham.

With the score now 209 for 8 and just 15 balls left the odds were now in Seaton Burn's favour, especially with the departure of Bilclough.

Wheeler added three off the next ball and new batsman Paul Carrick was then caught by Billy Stephenson off the first ball he faced from Bill Graham.

Carrick was only 16 at this time, he later developed into an excellent batsman, he liked to put bat to ball and was good enough to score two centuries in one season in the TSL and a third in the then newly formed NTSL. His highest score was 124 not out. He scored 7715 runs over his league career.

With Greenside now 212 for 9 and just thirteen balls remaining, the score was clearly now beyond them.

So, given the scoring system,your team gets a point if you are not all out, Wheeler and number 11, Michael Fearon played out the last two overs from Parkin and Bill Graham for maiden's to bag the point for their team.

Alan Wheeler was 56 not out. His half century containing five boundaries. Fearon was a resilient 0 not out.

Seaton Burn had won by 42 runs.

Billy Stephenson was the pick of the bowlers, 15-1-59-4, but all four used had contributed, Billy Wilkinson 15-5-70-2, Bill Graham 8-1-40-2 and Rob Parkin 7-2- 33-1.

The week after this game, Saturday 13th July 1985, Live Aid rocked the world. It was a major event at the time, undoubtedly missed by club cricketers all over the country as they followed their own passion.

Seaton Burn

D. Smart	Not	Out	120
W. Graham	C J. Mcgrady	B P. Carrick	7
R. Allan	C S. Stokoe	B M. Fearon	19
S. Armstrong	C W. Stokoe	B D. Bilclough	0
T. Garfield	Not	Out	92
Extras			16
Total			254-3 Wkts

S. Stokoe	P. Carrick	M. Fearon	D. Bilclough
0-85	1-82	1-44	1-31

Greenside

J. Mcgrady	C W. Graham	B W. Stephenson	17
S. Stokoe		B W. Wilkinson	45
B. Clark	C W. Graham	B W. Stephenson	9
A. Wheeler	Not	Out	56
W. Stokoe	St T. Garfield	B W. Stephenson	0
J. Stokoe	C W. Graham	B W. Stephenson	11
T. Wallace	C S. Graham	B W. Wilkinson	0
T. Dobson		B R. Parkin	25
D. Bilclough	C W. Stephenson	B W. Graham	38
P. Carrick	C W. Stephenson	B W. Graham	0
M. Fearon	Not	Out	0
Extras			11
Total			212-9 Wkts

W. Stephenson	W. Wilkinson	W. Graham	R. Parkin
4-59	2-70	2-40	1-33

Although only early July, the fortunes of the three teams mentioned didn't really pick up. South Moor finishing bottom of the league, Seaton Burn second bottom and Greenside third bottom.

I think this reflects how strong the Tyneside Senior League was at this time. If you look at the league averages, you will see Smartie was second in the batting, Shaun Stokoe from Greenside was third and Colin Albone from South Moor eigth. South Moor also had Jeff Carlyon ninth in the bowling averages as one of only nine bowlers to take 50 wickets this season.

You will also see that Felling have now replaced Wallsend from the 1984 season. All teams played 26 games.

1985 League Table

	WON 5PTS	WON 4PTS	LOST 1PT	LOST 0PTS	Drawn	Tied	PTS
Swalwell	13	6	4	0	3	0	96
Shotley Bridge	11	7	2	2	3	1	90 1/2
Lintz	6	12	2	3	3	0	83
Annfield Plain	7	7	8	3	3	2	78
Burnopfield	5	10	6	3	2	0	73
Blaydon	2	12	2	7	2	1	64 1/2
Consett	4	6	11	1	4	0	59
Sacriston	8	1	6	7	3	1	55 1/2
Reyrolle	7	1	6	7	3	2	53
Felling	3	7	4	9	3	0	50
Ryton	4	3	6	11	2	0	40
Greenside	4	2	9	9	2	0	39
Seaton Burn	2	3	10	7	3	1	37 1/2
South Moor	4	1	8	11	2	0	34

League Batting Averages 1985
Qualification 500 Runs

	Runs	High Score	Comp Inns	Average
D. Jackson (Annfield Plain)	1100	140no	17	64.71
D. Smart (Seaton Burn)	1027	120no	21	48.90
S. Stokoe (Greenside)	804	104no	19	42.32
R. Stokoe (Swalwell)	692	103no	17	40.71
C. Butts (Blaydon)	552	96no	15	36.80
M. Brown (Burnopfield)	736	91	21	35.05
G. Hunter (Consett)	696	89	20	34.80
C. Albone (South Moor)	646	93	20	32.30
D. Parnaby (Felling)	545	81	17	32.06
G. Clennell (Lintz)	534	89no	17	31.41
D. Collingwood (Shotley Bridge)	597	101no	20	29.85
D. Metcalfe (Sacriston)	650	103	22	29.55
A. Khan (Burnopfield)	585	88	20	29.25
N. Burdon (Swalwell)	611	114	21	29.10
R. Coulson (Felling)	574	124no	20	28.70
G. Wilkinson (Lintz)	552	93no	20	27.60
M. Bell (Reyrolle)	507	62	19	26.68
C. Stephenson (Shotley Bridge)	548	104	21	26.10
I. Robson (Lintz)	517	74	21	24.62
P. Veitch (Blaydon)	546	69no	24	22.75

League Bowling Averages 1985
Qualification 50 Wickets

	Overs	Runs	Wkts	Ave
N. Pickering (Swalwell)	241	602	58	10.38
R. Stokoe (Swalwell)	308	737	67	11.00
W. Raja (Shotley Bridge)	447	1136	98	11.59
C. Butts (Blaydon)	394	963	78	12.35
R. Cook (Lintz)	329	755	61	12.38
D. Parnaby (Felling)	354	988	59	16.75
I. Stoneman (Reyrolle)	323	1112	65	17.11
A. Khan (Burnopfield)	417	1061	54	17.39
J. Carlyon (South Moor)	325	1084	54	20.07

CHAPTER 10

SACRISTON AND BURNOPFIELD

On Saturday 31st May 1986 Seaton Burn played a league match at Sacriston. Sacriston had finished 8th last season and would finish 4th bottom this season. Seaton Burn would finish 3rd bottom. Paul Henshall, 788 runs at 35.82 and David Hickmott, 532 runs at 24.18 both made the league batting averages this season. Hickmott also made the league bowling averages with 48 wickets at 21.71.

David Hickmott has kindly provided some memories of this day and his Sacriston team mates.

Hickmott was from Western Australia and club professional.

He had arrived at Sacriston as a 23 year old from Freemantle District Cricket Club in Australia with north east legend Mike Hirsch. Hirsch had teed up the introduction to Sacriston and also arranged a cricket coaching job at Bow School in Durham.

He represented the league under 25 side this season. In the Wilkinson Cup Final he bowled eight overs and finished with 3 for 23 in a narrow win over the Northumberland County League.

He describes the north east as having it a bit tough in 1986. The cricket club was the hub of the community, a place where everyone gathered for a few drinks and a bit of fun.

Following the miners strike he says the cricket club played an important part in keeping the community together.

He made many friends in that time, including the aquisition of three brothers in law, Richy, David and Barry Strong, and a wife, Marj!

Hickmott enjoyed the attitude of the north east people to life, emotional, passionate and very real, and thats without discussing the Newcastle-Sunderland football rivalry!

He recalls going for his first pint in England with "Hirschy." When he ordered a pint of scotch, Hickmott, who at that time had never heard of scotch ale, thought he was getting a pint of whiskey! He would go on to develop a taste for Mckewans Scotch!

He is pretty sure that whatever Aussie cricketers were paid, a fair portion made its way back to the clubs over the club bar.

Seaton Burn batted first, wicketkeeper Tim Garfield now promoted to open the batting with Smartie.

The bowling was opened by the two Aussies, professional David Hickmott and Paul Henshall.

As a bowler Hickmott says that he was medium pace, his stock ball being a leg cutter but that he also got a lot more movement off the pitch rather than through the air. He liked to use variations in pace, in his younger days he recalls being described on the radio as "faster than he looked!"

Smartie recalls that he was a "medium quick who was accurate."

Hickmott remembers using the Gunn & Moore cricket ball rather than his preferred Dukes ball. The problem was they wouldn't stay round and one side could go flat quite quickly, making them difficult to bowl with. That said, he understood the financial reasoning behind the decision so made the best of it.

Hickmott describes his Aussie team mate Henshall as a fellow Western Australian who he played regularly against in Perth. He was a very talented batsman and effective bowler. He was a medium pace bowler who could bowl both in swing and off cutters to the right hander. Off the field he enjoyed a good sing song, "Roll a Silver Dollar" being a particular favourite.

Hickmott made an early breakthrough when he bowled Garfield for three with the total just 17.

This brought Edgar Ridley to the crease at three. Ridley was predominantly a second team opener at this stage of his cricket career, rarely playing in the first team but proving a reliable right handed opening batsman and effective spin bowler in the second eleven.

Ray Cardwell recalls that Edgar was affectionately compared to Geoffrey Boycott in the second team, mainly for his slow scoring......or should that be for his defensive style and qualities?

It may also have referred to the high number of run outs that Edgar was involved in, seldom his fault!

He rarely missed a game, despite playing to a good age, and he always maintained an infectious enthusiasm for the game.

Despite the "Boycott" jokes, at second team level, Edgar was a man who opposing teams often found difficult to get out, often as a number of his batting partners came and went, he would see us through a "sticky" patch and he kept us competetive in many second team games.

He was also Club Chairman for many years.

Ridley was bowled by Henshall for a single with the third ball of the tenth over as Seaton Burn reached 36 for 2.

The normally reliable left hander Bill Graham came in at number four. Today wasn't to be his day as he was caught behind by Askew off the bowling of Henshall, also for a single, as Seaton Burn struggled to 53 for 3 off 17.5 overs.

Steve Armstrong came in at number five.

Hickmott and Henshall bowled 11 overs and 12 overs each in their opening spells, Jeff Wilkinson replacing Hickmott, Martin Armitage, an occasional bowler replaced Henshall.

A fourth wicket partnership of 63 between Smart and Armstrong pulled Seaton Burn back into the game before Armstrong was run out with the score on 116.

Davie Gibson batted at six and he and Smart added 62 for the fifth wicket, Gibson being stumped by wicket keeper Micky Askew off the bowling of Wilkinson for 15.

Seaton Burn now 178 for 5 with 3 overs and 4 balls remaining of the innings.

Peter Ford came in at seven and finished 4 not out.

Smartie was 143 not out. His innings had lasted 2 hours 52 minutes and contained 11 four's and 9 sixes. There were 9 extras in the innings and the other batsman scored a total of 44 runs in the 45 overs!

Seaton Burn were 196 for 5 wickets after their 45 overs.

Henshall was the best of the bowlers, 18-4-58-2, with a wicket each for Hickmott and Wilkinson.

Martin Armitage and Barry Edwards opened the batting for Sacriston. Armitage had previously played for Middlesbrough. Edwards used to bat in glasses. They generally batted well together, often getting the side off to good starts. Unfortunately both left the club two thirds of the way through the season.

Davie Gibson and Graeme Nixon opened the bowling for Seaton Burn. Nixon was a right arm medium fast bowler, he would have been around 16 at this time and good enough to play for the county under 16's. He was a first team regular from around this young age and developed into a very useful opening bowler. As a batsman he was a good player of spin and slow bowling, liking to hit the ball straight and in the "v."

Kevin Corby, who kept wicket to Graeme later in his career, describes him as "a seamer who swung the ball, with a fast arm action his pace was hard to judge. He gave a lot of thought on how to get the batsman out."

His father, Stewart, played a lot of cricket for Seaton Burn over the years and it was great to see his grandson, Graeme's son, Callum, make his debut for the second team during 2020.

Stewart Nixon was another I would play a lot of second team cricket with. I was chatting with him over the pandemic summer at the cricket field, reminiscing as old cricketers do and he told me that he had scored a first team hundred back in the day. I had no idea, despite many shared hours at cricket!

When pressed on the matter he modestly informed me that it was back in the early 70's against Greenside. For the record, that would have been the Greenside which dominated the league for ten years or so and most of the time had four outstanding fast bowlers for those years!

Kevin Corby later loaned me a "weekly newsletter" from 1976. It mentioned a Seaton Burn win at Annfield Plain, with a "whirlwind" 50 by Stewart Nixon from only 23 balls and featuring 4 sixes and 5 fours! He was a useful medium pacer in the years I played with him too.

With the score at 33 Armitage was caught by Steve Armstrong off the bowling of Nixon for 14 in the 12th over. A steady start for Sacriston.

Paul Henshall came in at number three. He finished eleventh in the league batting averages this season with a high score of 91.

Henshall was selected for the full League Representative side this season and scored a creditable 31 not out against The Durham Senior League.

Dave Hickmott recalls that Henshall was a strong batsman all round the wicket. He favoured the drive, he was always looking for runs and liked to keep the scoring rate high.

A short lived stand of 7 before Edwards was stumped by Tim Garfield, also for 14, and also off the bowling of Nixon.

Sacriston 40 for 2 in the 14th over.

David Hickmott batted at four, he had a good enough season to appear in the league batting averages this season and had a top score of 98 not out.

Smartie recalls a "right handed batsman who hit the ball very hard."

Hickmott himself says that he "scored more runs of his back foot than the front, with plenty of pulls and hooks and that I didn't mind using "cow" corner!"

After bowling ten overs and taking 2 for 42 Nixon was replaced in the bowling attack by Bill Graham.

Graham made an impact almost immediately. With the fifth ball of his first over he had Henshall caught by Graeme Nixon for 17.

Sacriston 68 for 3 off 21.5 overs.

The new batsman was Alan Gray. I can't remember anything about his batting but I joined Northumbria Police with Alan in 1987 and do recall him saying he had played a season at Sacriston after also playing at Langley Park. David Hickmott recalls that Alan drove a red sports car and was always immaculately turned out, sounds about right!

With only 5 runs added for the fourth wicket Gray was bowled by Davie Gibson for 2.

At this point Gibson was clearly bowling well, after 12 overs he had 1-25, I did notice though, that very unusually for Gibson, he had bowled seven no-balls and a couple of wides at this point.

David Hickmott would point out that later, as the match got very close, how the ten extras the Seaton Burn bowlers conceded may have just turned what at the end, was a very tight match.

Sacriston 78 for 4 off 22.2overs.

This brought Colin Turnbull to the crease batting at six. He was club captain and he had a very useful season with the bat this year. Hickmott was looking threatening at the other end.

The next ten overs saw a single boundary ....but also included four sixes!

Gibson was replaced after bowling an opening stint of 17-1-54-1, this had included 9 no-balls and 2 wides, very rare for Davie!!!

He was replaced in the bowling attack by Rob Parkin. His first over went for 13 as Sacriston went for the runs. The partnership would be worth 63.

With the last ball of the 36th over Bill Graham broke the partnership when he had Turnbull caught by Peter Ford for 20. The innings had contained 2 fours and a six.

Sacriston now 136 for 5 off 36 overs and require 60 off 9 overs to win.

Mick Lavelle was next in. Hickmott recalls a "good fellow, who I enjoyed many good nights with." A stand of 25 for the sixth wicket before Lavelle was run out for 7.

Sacriston 161 for 6.

Micky Askew batted at 8. The wicketkeeper, he was "a farmer by trade, he regularly enjoyed a little whiskey tipple, always entertaining, he used to get a dangerous glint in his eye after a few drinks!" He scored 4 before Parkin had him caught by wicketkeeper Garfield.

Sacriston 171 for 7 off 40.4 overs. 26 runs needed from 3.2 overs.

The new batsman was Jeff Wilkinson. Hickmott recalls "a club stalwart who always tried his heart out for the club, he always kept us entertained with his many stories, none of which should ever find their way into print!"

Hickmott hit the last ball of the 43rd over from Bill Graham for six.

Sacriston 185 for 7 off 43 overs, now require 11 from two overs. Hickmott was 86 not out.

Wilkinson got a single from the second ball of the 44th over, which was being bowled by Rob Parkin.

Hickmott hit the next ball, the third ball of the over for six, took two off the fourth ball, played the fifth ball for a dot ball....... then hit a boundary off the last ball.

Sacriston, 198 for 7 off 44 overs, had won by three wickets with an over to spare.

Hickmott was 98 not out. His innings had included just three boundaries....but he had also hit seven sixes, including at least one off each of the four bowlers used.

Around 35 years later Dave Hickmott can still recall this game, he, modestly in my opinion, says that "the game was decided in very gloomy conditions, with me swinging like a rusty gate and missing more than I hit. Fortunately the cricket gods were smiling on us as we scraped home, despite the Herculean effort of David Smart."

Wilkinson finished 5 not out.

Each bowler used had picked up at least one wicket, Gibson 1-54, Nixon 2-42, Graham 2-58 and Parkin 1-40.

As for Smartie, this was the third time he would score a century and finish on the losing side!

Hickmott was invited back to Sacriston the following season. He has fond memories of the place and people, especially of time spent coaching the juniors. Harry Hubber, Alan Clarke, Andy Lavelle, Melly Betts, Ian and Paul Jones, all went on to play some good cricket at various levels.

Hickmott on his final return to Australia would see out his cricket career where he started, with Freemantle District Cricket Club. They went on to win the 1992/93 50 Over Title against a near Test strength Midland Guilford side at The W.A.C.A. This would be his last Grade A game.

His describes his other career highlight as winning the A Grade Bowling Averages at Freemantle in 1984-85.

Seaton Burn

D. Smart	Not	Out	143
T. Garfield		B D. Hickmott	3
E. Ridley		B P. Henshall	1
W. Graham	C M. Askew	B P. Henshall	1
S. Armstrong	Run	Out	20
D. Gibson	St M. Askew	B J. Wilkinson	15
P. Ford	Not	Out	4
Extras			9
Total			196-5 Wkts
D. Hickmott	P. Henshall	J. Wilkinson	M. Armitage
1-40	2-58	1-46	0-46

Sacriston

M. Armitage	C S. Armstrong	B G. Nixon	14
B. Edwards	St T. Garfield	B G. Nixon	14
P. Henshall	C G. Nixon	B W. Graham	17
D. Hickmott	Not	Out	98
A. Gray		B D. Gibson	2
C. Turnbull	C P. Ford	B W. Graham	20
M. Lavelle	Run	Out	7
M. Askew	C T. Garfield	B R. Parkin	4
J. Wilkinson	Not	Out	5
Extras			17
Total			198-7 Wkts
D. Gibson 1-54	G. Nixon 2-42	W. Graham 2-58	R. Parkin 1-40

In between the Sacriston fixture and Smartie's next League hundred he did score another one!

On Sunday 22nd June 1986 Smartie hit 104 not out in a cup match against Bedlington. This innings contained fourteen four's and three sixes.

The purpose of this book is to focus on The Tyneside Senior League, so after a quick "well done Smartie" we shall move on!

On Saturday 5th July 1986 Seaton Burn played a home League fixture against Burnopfield. Burnopfield would finish sixth in the League this season, with Neil Hewison, 8th in the batting averages, 677 runs at 37.61, Malcolm Brown 10th in the batting averages with 502 runs at 35.86 and Kevin Petrie finishing 4th in the bowling averages, 62 wickets at 15.61 each.

Once again I'm indebted to Dave Sweeney for the information he has provided about the Burnopfield players. As this is Smartie's second ton against Burnopfield, this chapter will concentrate on those who didn't play in the first game.

Smartie opened the batting with the left handed Bill Graham. The bowling was opened by Neil Hewison and Tim Collins.

A steady opening partnership ensued. Collins was hit out of the attack early after he had bowled just three overs, 0-21, including three boundaries.

He was replaced by Kevin Petrie. Petrie was a good medium quick bowler who could nip and swing the ball both ways. With the second ball of his third over he had Bill Graham caught by his brother, Stephen Petrie, for 17.

Seaton Burn 55 for 1.

This brought Richie Allan, another left hander, to the crease. After taking a single off the first ball he faced, Allan added a couple of boundaries before he was bowled by Kevin Petrie for 9.

Seaton Burn 78 for 2.

The new batsman was Davie Gibson, the third left hander in a row.

Bowling wise, Hewison was now replaced by Alan Beck, his opening spell had been 8-1-33-0.

After dismissing Allan in his 6th over, Kevin Petrie bowled Gibson in his 7th over, for 7.

Petrie had bowled 7-1-22-3.

Seaton Burn 93 for 3 in the nineteenth over.

This brought wicketkeeper Tim Garfield to the wicket. Last season Smartie and Garfield had set a new league record partnership for the fourth wicket with a stand of 172.

The pair of them set about the Burnopfield bowlers.

Beck was taken out of the attack after 5-0-35-0.

Petrie's next five overs went for 32.

Mickey Small was brought on to replace Beck and opening bowler Hewison, to replace Petrie.

Small fared no better than Beck, 6-0-49-0 so he was replaced by opening bowler Collins.

Smartie and Garfield had taken the score to 276, a stand of 183, and also a new league record for the highest league 4th wicket partnership, beating their own record by 11!

It was Hewison who got the breakthrough, having Garfield caught behind by Stephen Petrie for 79.

Garfields innings had lasted 83 minutes and included 11 fours and a six. His fifty had come from 70 balls.

The wicket had fallen with the fourth ball of the 43rd over.

Gary Stephenson came in at six and with the last ball of the innings he was stumped by Stephen Petrie off the bowling of Collins for 3. The last wicket added 16 off just 8 balls.

Seaton Burn were 292 for 5 wickets off their allocated 45 overs.

Smartie was 155 not out. His innings had lasted 2 hours and 41 minutes, it contained 11 fours and 8 sixes. His 50 had come from 64 deliveries and the 100 from 107 balls faced.

Kevin Petrie with 12-1-54-3 was the pick of the bowlers, with a wicket each for Hewison, 15-1-82-1, and Collins, 7-0-52-1.

Burnopfield opened the batting with David Mitchinson and Ian Cottingham. Mitchinson was a stylish batsman and an excellent fielder. He played cricket for a number of clubs in the North East, including Seaton Burn and whilst at Annfield Plain he suffered another Smartie ton. He was however, better known as a footballer, a central defender playing for Whitley Bay, Blyth Spartans and Gateshead amongst others. Sadly he died in November 1991 after a battle with cancer.

Cottingham was a steady bat who also played for Whickham, as did his father David before him. He was not a regular first team cricketer.

Davie Gibson and Rob Parkin opened the bowling for Seaton Burn.

Both bowlers opened with tight spells, the first 7 overs going for just 11 runs. With the first ball of the eighth over, Parkin bowled Mitchison for 6.

This brought Neil Hewison to the crease.

Parkin and Gibson continued to bowl well, giving few runs away, although Hewison hit the first boundary of the innings in the twelfth over.

With the third ball of the fourteenth over, Parkin had opener Cottingham caught behind by Garfield for 11.

Burnopfield 25 for 2 after 13.3 overs.

New batsman Tommy Nichols immediately gave the innings some momentum, after getting off the mark with a single, he hit the first and third balls of Gibson's next over for four.

Two more boundaries for Nichols from balls one and four from Parkin's next over with a two and a single added for good measure.

Parkin was removed from the attack and spinner Bill Graham came on to bowl.

With the third ball of Graham's first over, Nichols was caught by Davie Gibson for 21. The innings had included four boundaries and the partnership added a quickfire 24 in 24 balls!

Burnopfield 49 for 3 off 17.3 overs.

This brought Micky Small to the crease batting at four.

Gibson was replaced in the bowling attack by Graeme Nixon, presumably through injury, as Gibson had bowling figures of 10.4-0-25-0.

Small had got off the mark with a boundary off Bill Graham and he took another one off Nixon's first ball as he too showed positive intent.

Bill Graham took his second wicket in just three overs with the third ball of the 22nd over when he caught and bowled Small for 9.

Burnopfield 66 for 4 off 22.3 overs.

Alan Beck came in at number six. There then followed a partnership of 101 as both Hewison and Beck set about the Seaton Burn bowlers. Hewison being particularly harsh on Nixon.

It was Bill Graham who once again broke the partnership, having Beck caught by Davie Watson for 49. His innings had contained 3 fours and a six. The pair had scored 101 in just over 14 overs!

Burnopfield 167 for 5 after 37.2 overs.

They still needed 125 run to win off just over 7 overs.

New batsman Fred Charlton was not a regular first team player but he was a decent second team player. He was one of a number of members of the Charlton Family, including Keith and Gary, who played their cricket at Burnopfield. He hit a six and a four in an innings of 19 as he and Hewison continued to play their shots.

Graeme Nixon was hit out off the attack when his tenth over went for 19. He was replaced by Richie Allan's medium pace swing.

However it was Hewison who was was next to go, caught by Gary Stephenson off the bowling of Bill Graham for 97.

His innings had included 8 fours and 5 sixes.

Burnopfield now 213 for 6 and the game effectively over.

When Charlton was run out with the score at 227, this brought Stephen Petrie in at nine to join his brother Kevin who was batting at eight.

Stephen had a lot of success as a batsman at second team level but he was never quite able to transfer that to first team level. He was a very good fielder and a useful wicketkeeper.

Kevin was a capable lower order batsman who liked to hit the ball hard. Unfortunately his playing career was cut short by work and family commitments.

These two ensured Burnopfield got a precious point for not being dismissed, with Kevin 5 not out and Stephen 2 not out.

Bill Graham, 14-1-89-4 and Rob Parkin 8-1-24-2, were the only wicket takers for Seaton Burn.

Seaton Burn won by 60 runs.

Seaton Burn

D. Smart	Not	Out	155
W. Graham	C S. Petrie	B K. Petrie	17
R. Allan		B K. Petrie	9
D. Gibson		B K. Petrie	7
T. Garfield	C S. Petrie	B N. Hewison	79
G. Stephenson	C S. Petrie	B T. Collins	3
Extras			22
Total			292-5 Wkts

N. Hewison 1-82 T. Collins 1-52 K. Petrie 3-54 A. Beck 0-35
M. Small 0-49

Burnopfield

D. Mitchinson		B R. Parkin	6
I. Cottingham	C T. Garfield	B R. Parkin	11
N. Hewison	C G. Stephenson	B W. Graham	97
T. Nichols	C D. Gibson	B W. Graham	21
M. Small	C & B	W. Graham	9
A. Beck	C D. Watson	B W. Graham	49
F. Charlton	Run	Out	19
K. Petrie	Not	Out	5
S. Petrie	Not	Out	2
Extras			13
Total			232-7 Wkts

D. Gibson 0-25 R. Parkin 2-24 W. Graham 4-89 G. Nixon 0-73
R. Allan 0-13

Swalwell were the new League Champions in 1986, with relatively new boys Felling finishing as runners up in just their second season in the League.

All teams played a maximum of 26 games and this season saw just one tie, between Felling and Annfield Plain.

Tyneside Senior League Table 1986

	WON 5PTS	WON 4PTS	LOST 1PT	LOST 0PTS	Drawn	Tied	PTS
Swalwell	11	11	1	1	2	0	102
Felling	7	12	2	3	1	1	88 1/2
Shotley Bridge	6	13	2	3	2	0	86
Annfield Plain	9	5	5	5	1	1	73 1/2
Blaydon	5	10	4	5	2	0	71
Burnopfield	8	5	7	5	1	0	68
Greenside	8	3	9	4	2	0	63
Lintz	5	6	7	7	1	0	57
Consett	4	7	6	7	2	0	56
Reyrolles	5	5	5	10	1	0	51
Sacriston	5	3	10	7	1	0	48
Seaton Burn	1	6	10	8	1	0	40
South Moor	4	2	11	8	1	0	40
Ryton	4	1	10	9	2	0	36

On the batting front, Mark Harper, the West Indian Pro at Blaydon set a new league aggregate for runs scored, an incredible 1863, and Wasim Raja, Shotley Bridge's Pakistan Test Player set a new highest Individual Score, 202, both passing previous records set by Smartie in 1984.

Small consolation for Smartie, he did, once again, score over 1000 runs in a season, 1056 to be precise!

The number of batsman who made 500 runs this season, 22, would suggest that this was a season for the batsmen. The league bowling qualification was reduced to 45 wickets, still a great achievement, but again would support the theory it was a batting year!

League Batting Averages 1986
Qualification 500 Runs

	Runs	High Score	Comp Inns	Average
M. Harper (Blaydon)	1863	180no	17	109.53
I. Stokoe (Swalwell)	707	85no	11	64.27
D. Smart (Seaton Burn)	1056	155no	21	50.29
W. Raja (Shotley Bridge)	902	202	19	47.47
S. Stokoe (Greenside)	851	125	18	47.27
R. Stokoe (Swalwell)	783	116	17	46.06
D. Jackson (Annfield Plain)	990	119	25	39.60
N. Hewison (Burnopfield)	677	97	18	37.61
G. Hunter (Consett)	684	96no	19	36.00
M. Brown (Burnopfield)	502	107no	14	35.86
P. Henshall (Sacriston)	788	91	22	35.82
I. Robson (Swalwell)	603	105no	17	35.47
W. Gibson (Shotley Bridge)	609	77	18	33.83
C. Albone (South Moor)	531	69	16	33.19
R. Coulson (Felling)	566	81	18	31.44
C. Stephenson (Shotley Bridge)	708	104	24	29.50
D. Leonard (Felling)	698	92	25	27.92
W. Armstrong (Consett)	634	84	23	27.57
P. Veitch (Blaydon)	628	85	23	27.30
D. Collingwood (Shotley Bridge)	570	58	21	27.14
D. Hickmott (Sacriston)	532	98no	22	24.18
N. Burdon (Swalwell)	507	88no	21	24.14

League Bowling Averages 1986
Qualification 50 Wickets

	Overs	Runs	Wkts	Ave
R. Stokoe (Swalwell)	378	897	89	10.08
W. Raja (Shotley Bridge)	488	1316	108	12.19
J. Riley (Annfield Plain)	360	1130	91	12.42
K. Petrie (Burnopfield)	277	968	62	15.61
D. Parnby (Felling)	345	969	59	16.42
M. Fearon (Greenside)	273	985	59	16.69
R. Cook (Lintz)	284	926	52	17.81
N. Robinson (Blaydon)	382	1376	77	17.87
M. Nolan (Felling)	236	827	45	18.37
P. Carrick (Greenside)	312	1087	59	18.42
D. Nevin (Lintz)	222	889	45	19.75
J. Carlyon (South Moor)	334	1068	54	19.77
G. Clennell (Lintz)	291	941	45	20.91
S. Smith (Ryton)	357	1244	59	21.08
D. Hickmott (Sacriston)	319	1042	48	21.71

CHAPTER 11

LINTZ AND SOUTH MOOR

On Saturday 4th May 1987 Seaton Burn played an away league fixture at Lintz Cricket Club. Lintz had finished 8th in the league last season. They would finish second bottom this season, but in fairness, they had a league high nine matches washed out with the weather. They had three bowlers in the league averages last season, Bob Cook, 52 wickets at 17.81, David Nevin, 45 wickets at 19.75 and Graeme Clennell, 45 wickets at 20.91.

Graeme Clennell has provided some information on his teammates of the day.

Seaton Burn batted first and Smartie and Bill Graham opened the innings. Bill had an excellent season with the bat this year, making 456 runs at 25.33, he finished 12th in the league batting averages.

Bob Cook and Graeme Clennell opened the bowling for Lintz.

Graeme Clennell has some high praise for Bob Cook. He was known as Tommy to his team mates after starting as a 13 year old junior at Lintz. He was a right arm fast bowler, "the best bowler ever to play for Lintz. He was a really skilful fast bowler with a smooth, rythmical action, he opened the bowling for over 20 years for us, moving the ball in the air and darting it off the pitch."

He was the first Lintz player to play for Durham CCC in the Minor Counties Championship. He also represented the Tyneside Senior League for many years as well, also playing for the League Cricket Conference, essentially an All England Side.

He was offered professional terms by Derbyshire CCC but decided it wasn't for him and he continued to play for Lintz.

He played his entire careeer with Lintz. He twice took 9 wickets in an innings in Tyneside Senior League matches, 9-32 and 9-27, he also had an 8-7 against Seaton Burn in 1974.

He took 1,268 wickets in the league plus many, many more in cup competitions. He represented the league on many occasions and Durham CCC when they were in the Minor Counties. He had a fearful partnership with his fellow fast bowler, Bob Bainbridge.

Smartie describes Bob Cook as "quality, just quality, sheer class, for a local league cricketer, there was him and Wilkie (Stuart Wilkinson, Shotley Bridge) who were at least as quick as any professional I played against. The thing with Cookie was, he would swing the ball as well as being very accurate. Of all the bowlers I played against, if anyone had the better of me, it was Bob Cook, I had my days against him, a few successes, but believe me, he was well out in front! He was a lovely lad off the field as well."

In his next league innings after scoring 201 not out Smartie was bowled for nine.......... by Bob Cook

Graeme Clennell was regarded by many as one of the best all rounders to play in the league. He was another one who played his entire career at Lintz.

He twice returned bowling figures of 7-36, against Greenside and Sacriston. Jack Chapman has Clennell taking 1,089 league wickets and he took 5 wickets in an innings at least 40 times.

Smartie recalls Graeme Clennell as "a very, very, good cricketer. As an all rounder you couldn't say he was a better batter or bowler because he was so good at both. As a bowler, he didn't have a stock ball as such, but he would bowl you four or five different deliveries an over, plugging away on line and length at a decent pace with his variations."

After ten overs Seaton Burn were going well, 48 for 0 wicket and Clennell was replaced by spinner Michael Edmunds.

Graeme Clennell remembers Edmunds as another who started as a 13 year old at Lintz. A "very good off spin bowler who was very successful for over 30 years at Lintz at either keeping the runs down or taking wickets. This was no mean feat as a spinner on a field as small as ours at Lintz. He was also a very loyal one club man."

Smartie laughs out loud when you mention Edmunds, "If anyone had the wood over me it was Micky Edmunds, well him and Cookie, he always seemed to get me out! Sometimes I had scored a few, sometimes not!"

He describes Edmunds as "a very good off break bowler, he bowled it flat and could push it through, but it was the variations he had that were the problem, and the clever cricket brain he had to use those variations."

With Cook bowling tightly at one end, the runs were flowing at the other, Edmunds 4 overs going for 35 before he was replaced by Stuart Clennell.

Graeme Clennell describes brother Stuart as another who came through from the under 13 side. He was "under used as a bowler, especially in his early years, but with Bob Cook, Bob Bainbridge, the other Clennell and Dave Nevin ahead of him opportunities were limited. A good seam bowler he would suddenly produce an unplayable delivery, just ask Richie Richardson who found himself bowled middle stump after being on the wrong end of one such delivery. He still plays the occasional game now, 47 years after the first."

After bowling 9 overs for 23, Cook's tenth over was hit for 11, and he was replaced by his opening partner, Graeme Clennell, as Lintz fought for a wicket.

It was Stuart Clennell who got the breakthrough, bowling Smartie for 103. His innings had taken 1 hour and 35 minutes and contained 12 fours and 6 sixes.

Seaton Burn 146 for 1 after 27.3 overs.

Richie Allan came in at three but was caught by Bob Cook also off the bowling of Stuart Clennell, for a duck.

Seaton Burn 154 for 2 off 29.5 overs.

Wicket keeper Tim Garfield was next in, Tim had shown his capabilities with the bat since joining the club a couple of seasons earlier, he and Smartie had twice broken league partnership records.

Graeme Clennell's second spell didn't fare much better than the first and after another five overs he was replaced by Bob Cook.

A partnership of 31 took the score to 185 when Bill Graham was caught by Hood off the bowling of Stuart Clennell for 64. His innings had taken 2 hours and 5 minutes and had contained

9 fours and a six. His last four scoring shots were all boundaries as Seaton Burn looked to up the pace.

Seaton Burn 185 for 3 off 36 overs.

Billy Wilkinson was batting at 5 but before Billy could get going, with just one more run added, Garfield was bowled by Cook for 13, an innings which had included a six and a four.

Gary Stephenson batted at 6, he and Billy Wilkinson continued with the aggressive stance and added 39 in just over six overs before Wilkinson was caught by Cook off the bowling of Stuart Clennell for 23. Typically his innings had included a couple of fours and a six.

Seaton Burn 225 for 5 after 43 overs.

Phil Myers was the new batsman and he and Stephenson took Seaton Burn to the close of innings, Stephenson 18 not out and Myers 3 not out.

Seaton Burn had finished 233 for 5 wickets off their 45 overs.

Stuart Clennell was the pick of the bowlers, 13-3-66-4, with Bob Cook, the only other bowler to take a wicket, 18-2-70-1.

Lintz opened the batting with Stuart Clennell and Paul Cameron.

Graeme Clennell describes his brother, Stuart, or "Stuers," as being one who it "was obvious from an early age that he was going to be a good batsman. Whether playing on the beach, in the garden or in the street, nobody could get him out, he didn't hit it far but he watched the ball onto the bat.

We joined Lintz at nine years old. Stuart would go on to become a very attacking opening batsman, just as likely to hit the first ball for six as play it down. If you pitched it up he generally hit it back where it came from, usually over your head for six. He played for Durham at Under 15 and Under 19 level.

He scored two hundreds in 20 over matches, one at Under 18 level and one at first team level, at Hylton. He was certainly my equal as a batsman but perhaps just not as lucky. He is still taking wickets and scoring runs 47 years after his debut and enjoys playing with his son, Josh."

Paul Cameron was a right handed wicketkeeper/batsman who had started his career at Burnopfield. Graeme Clennell recalls that he was "a very talented, quick scoring batsman who loved to play the cut, a shot he used to great effect. He was a very accomplished wicketkeeper, representing Durham at Under 19 level. His son Oliver, also a wicketkeeper/batsman would also go on to play for the club.

A new opening bowling attack for Seaton Burn, the youthful Graeme Nixon would bowl the first over with Ian Tinlin bowling the second.

Tinlin was a steady, reliable right arm fast/medium bowler. As a batsman though, his quirky personality came through, at some point Ian had found he could bat both left and right handed! When he went to the crease, his team mates didn't know which way he was going to bat! He was an intelligent, soft spoken, quiet man off the pitch and a pleasure to play cricket with.

Although he played mainly second team cricket, he had his moments in the first team and certainly wasn't out of his depth at that level when he did play.

I can recall a second team game at Seaton Burn when Ian had the first nine wickets to fall. I was brought on first change at the other end. Early in my second or third over I had the batsman plumb LBW, I deliberately didn't appeal to give Ian his chance at taking all ten wickets. Two or three balls later the same batsman edged one to first slip, the fielder there took an amazing one handed diving catch to close the innings. Ian finished with nine wickets and that amazing catch!

The first wicket fell in Graeme Nixon's fifth over when he had Stuart Clennell caught by Richie Allan for 28. The innings had contained 5 fours and a six.

Lintz 38 for 1 off 8.3 overs.

This brought Freddie Hood to the crease, Hood who had previously played for Burnopfield, had been wicketkeeper on the day Smartie had scored his double hundred, was known as a hard hitting batsman, today would be no exception!

Graeme Clennell says he could write a whole book about the eccentricity of Fred! He describes him as a "talented wicketkeeper/ batsman, he was just as capable of batting all day for nothing or cutting loose and hitting 80 off 50 balls! I have fond memories of batting with Hood one day after Gordon Baker had set us batting targets. He wanted us to be 100 off 30 overs, we got to 90 off 25 overs, well ahead of pace, Fred came up to me inbetween overs and says to me "we better slow down, Gordon wants us to be 100 off 30 overs! A complete one off, once met, never forgotten!"

The fall of the first wicket didn't spare Tinlin from being replaced in the bowling attack after just 4 overs, 0-15.

His replacement was Richie Allan. Richie was a right arm medium pace swing bowler, he was an occasional bowler rather than a regular. His three overs went for twenty as Hood and Cameron set about their task.

As the score ticked steadily up, a double bowling change was made after 15 overs. Nixon had bowled a steady first spell, 8-2-29-1 and he was replaced by the left arm spin of Bill Graham.

Billy Wilkinson with his right arm swing replaced Allan.

With the second ball of his third over, Wilkinson had Cameron caught behind by Tim Garfield for 28. The innings had contained four boundaries.

Lintz 83 for 2 off 18.2 overs.

The new batsman was Graeme Clennell. Smartie says that Clennell was "a very correct batsman. He was a clever enough cricketer, and had the batting game to support him being a situational batsman. If the situation called for resolute defence or putting bat to ball, Clennell had the technique and ability to adapt."

Clennell and Hood then really took the attack to the Seaton Burn bowlers.

They added 114 off 22 overs.

Bill Graham's last four overs went for thirty four, as first he and then Billy Wilkinson were hit out of the attack. Wilkinson's last two overs going for twenty five!

Graham finished with 9-0-42-0 and Wilkinson 11-1-69-1.

Wilkinson was replaced by Smartie. He was a right arm medium pacer in these days, he only bowled occasionally rather than regularly but he had taken enough wickets at this level to have bowled more.

Graeme Nixon was brought back to replace Graham.

It was the 40th over before Seaton Burn took a wicket. Graeme Clennell was caught by Richie Allan off the fourth ball of the over for 55. The innings had included four boundaries and three sixes.

Lintz 197 for 3 off 39.4 overs. They required 37 to win off 5.2 overs.

Bob Cook came in at five. As well as being a stand out fast bowler, Cook could also bat a bit too! His top score was 116 in 1978 against Ryton. On that occasion he and John Lott, who scored 68, had added a league record of 157 for the 9th wicket partnership. This was at least the second occasion when Cook had been a good enough bat to feature in league batting records.

On 19 June 1975 he and fellow fast bowler Bob Bainbridge had added an unbeaten 76 for the eight wicket against Blaydon. Cook was 49 not out and Bainbridge 29 not out.

Graeme Clennell recalls Cook as "a batsman who usually dealt in boundaries!"

The score had reached 213 when Seaton Burn got the wicket they desperately needed, Freddie Hood, caught by Ian Tinlin off the bowling of Graeme Nixon for 84. The innings had included 9 fours and 4 sixes.

Lintz were now 213 for 4 off 41.2 overs, they now require 21 off 3.4 overs.

The new batsman was Gordon Baker, probably the last batsman Seaton Burn would wish to see at this point. Baker played his entire career at Lintz, following his father, also Gordon, who was well known first of all as a player, then as an umpire in the league.

He would score over 9,000 runs in the Tyneside Senior League plus a further 3,000 in the Northumberland and Tyneside Senior League following amalgamation in the year 2000. He was captain of Lintz for many years.

As a batsman Graeme Clennell says that Baker was "a really talented cricketer, a right handed batsman who I got to know when I first played with the juniors in 1974. He is a good friend to this day. As a junior he was a top all rounder, representing Durham at Under 19 level. I still don't know why he stopped bowling as he was very good, with an action like Basil D'Oliveira.

For the record D'Oliveira was a fast/medium paced right armer.

He was just as good opening as he was at number four, he would choose to bat at four when he was captain. He was an attacking batsman who was a large part of the formidable line up we had in the 80's and 90's.

He was a selfless player and captain who took the responsibility of being captain to new heights.

As a captain, Gordon T Baker, known as GTB. was so competitive it was unbelievable, it was like Lintz winning was like life or death to him. I remember one game, after we had lost, he went and sat in the bottom corner of the field by himself for ages, certainly until after we had all been showered and gone to the bar, but I loved that, because I was the same on the pitch, although I was a more relaxed off it. I think that's why we were good friends. I think some of that "never say die" attitude rubbed off on the lads as well, remember we didn't have a pro to rely on like a lot of teams.

There is one incident which is still fresh in my mind. I love my music, always have, in 1996 I had a ticket for Oasis at Maine Road, Manchester, this was a massive gig as it's their home turf, it was the start of the season and I missed the first match. We won but failed to bowl the opposition out, gaining only four points instead of the five we could have had. We missed out on the league title to Felling by one point, to this day, that's my fault!

I could handle Gordon, maybe others couldn't understand his passion to win, I could. Nothing would stand in the way of trying to make Lintz the best side around.

He was the League Player of the Year in 1999 at the age of 40 and would still be playing today if illness hadn't cut short his career."

Smartie recalls Baker as being "a really good bat, as a captain he gave you nothing on the field, he played the game very hard, very, very competitive, to the point of being hard work to deal with on the field. A nice bloke off the cricket field but the ultimate opponent on it!"

Cook hit a two and a six off the remainder of the over plus a leg bye, Lintz now 222 for 4 off 42 overs.

With the first ball of the 43rd over Smartie bowled Cook for 17. The innings had contained a four and a six. The shoe was on the other foot in a manner of speaking, as Smartie freely admits Cookie got him enough times!

Lintz were now 222 for 5 off 42.1 overs.

The new batsman was the left handed Alan Bell. Graeme Clennell recalls that Bell had started his career at Lintz as a junior but would play most of his cricket as Tantobie. He did return to Lintz for a couple of seasons of senior cricket, including this one.

He was run out without scoring in the same over.

Lintz now 222 for 6.

Edward Largue came in at number 8. He was widely known as "Ted". He played all his career at Lintz, making his debut in 1964 and playing his final game in 1989. He scored at least 6832 runs, with one league century, 101 not out in 1974.

Graeme Clennell remembers Largue as "a quality top order batsman, he was a major player in our league title win in 1982. He suffered a lot with injuries, resulting in two new hips but even then, remarkably, he continued to play and scored an incredible century against Chester Le Street at Ropery Lane. Both his sons, Mark and Iain played for the club."

Largue hit the fifth ball of the over for four.

Lintz 226 for 6 off 43 overs, require 8 to win.

Graeme Nixon was to bowl the 44th over, three dot balls then with the fourth ball of the over he had Gordon Baker caught by Ian Tinlin for no score.

Lintz 226 for 7 off 43.4 overs, still require 8 to win.

The new batsman was David Payne. He was also known as "Window." Graeme Clennell recalls that he was "a right handed bat, he was another who came through from Lintz Juniors, a real club player, he was happy to bat late on the first team rather than bat three or four for the seconds every week. He was a good batsman and a really good fielder, he always gave everything he had. He was one of those lads of the type that every club needs."

Payne was now the non striker as Largue and Baker had crossed before the catch was taken.

The next ball of the over, the fifth, saw Largue bowled by Nixon for 4.

Lintz were now 226 for 8 off 43.5 overs. Still 8 required to win.

Michael Edmunds batted at number ten. Smartie was to bowl the last over.

Payne took a single off the first ball, 7 to win.

Edmunds faced the second ball, a dot ball, no run.

The third ball was a no-ball......6 to win off 4 balls.

Edmunds got off the mark with a single from the fourth ball, 5 runs to win off 3 balls.

Payne got the third ball away for two, 3 runs to win off 2 balls.

Payne then took a single off the second last ball of the over, Lintz require 2 runs to win off 1 ball.

The last ball, of course, being the no-ball earlier in the over.

Edmunds got bat on ball, the batsmen ran a single, Lintz 233 for 8 off their 45 overs, match tied!

Payne was 4 not out, Edmunds 2 not out.

Graeme Nixon's last 4 overs had cost him 19 runs but he had picked up four wickets in the spell, including the key wickets of Hood and Graeme Clennell. He had also bowled a double wicket maiden in the crucial 44th over. He finished with 12-3-48-5.

Smartie finished with 6-0-30-1.

Honours even, an excellent day of hard, competitive, village cricket.

Seaton Burn

D. Smart		B S. Clennell	103
W. Graham	C F. Hood	B S. Clennell	64
R. Allan	C R. Cook	B S. Clennell	0
T. Garfield		B R. Cook	13
W. Wilkinson	C R. Cook	B S. Clennell	23
G. Stephenson	Not	Out	18
P. Myers	Not	Out	3
Extras			9
Total			233-5 Wkts
R. Cook	G. Clennell	M. Edmunds	S. Clennell
1-70	0-60	0-35	4-66

Lintz

S. Clennell	C R. Allan	B G. Nixon	28
P. Cameron	C T. Garfield	B W. Wilkinson	28
F. Hood	C I. Tinlin	B G. Nixon	84
G. Clennell	C R. Allan	B G. Nixon	55
R. Cook		B D. Smart	17
G. Baker	C I. Tinlin	B G. Nixon	0
A. Bell	Run	Out	0
E. Largue		B G. Nixon	4
D. Payne	Not	Out	4
M. Edmunds	Not	Out	2
Extras			11
Total			233-8 Wkts
G. Nixon	I. Tinlin	R. Allan	W. Wilkinson
5-48	0-15	0-20	1-69

W. Graham 0-42 D. Smart 1-30

126

On Saturday 16th May 1987 Seaton Burn played an away League fixture at South Moor Cricket Club.

South Moor had finished second bottom of the league in 1986, but Colin Albone had featured in the league batting averages, 531 runs at 33.19 and Jeff Carlyon had finished 12th in the league bowling averages, 54 wickets at 19.77 each, this season they would finish bottom of the league.

As this was Smartie's second hundred against South Moor, only those players who didn't feature in the earlier game will be featured. I am once again indebted to Phil Shield for information on the South Moor lads.

Seaton Burn batted first, Bill Graham again being Smartie's opening partner. Graham was having good season with the bat, he would make the league batting averages this season with 456 runs at an average of 25.33.

The bowling would be opened by the useful and reliable Jeff Carlyon and David Shield.

An opening stand of 112 put Seaton Burn in the driving seat.

Shield had been taken out of the attack after five overs for twenty five, he was replaced by George Sanders Jnr.

George Sanders Snr was associated with South Moor Cricket Club most of his life. Over the years he held almost every role there was to hold at the club and was made a life member.

George Sanders Jnr came through the club junior system, playing for the second team which won the "B" Division in 1969. He was a good left handed batsman and an excellent slow to slow medium right hand bowler who could cut or spin the ball from off to leg.

With Smartie dominating the strike, it was the 27th over before Graham was bowled by Carlyon for 24. Carlyon was to bowl unchanged throughout the innings, 23 straight overs, no easy task!

Davie Gibson, another left hander,came in at three.

A partnership of 60 followed, Gibson, like a lot of left handers was a graceful batsman to watch.

It was Smartie who was out next, bowled by Jeff Carlyon. He had scored 113 and batted for 123 minutes. His 50 had come after

47 minutes and included 6 fours and a six. The 100 had come in 107 minutes and included 9 fours and 3 sixes. The final total was 10 fours and 3 sixes.

This brought wicketkeeper Tim Garfield to the crease. He and Gibson added a further 26 before Gibson was caught by Carlyon off the bowling of Shield with the last ball of the 44th over.

Another left hander, Richie Allan came in at five, he and Garfield took 7 off Carlyon's 23rd and last over. Garfield was 11 not out, Allan 4 not out.

Thanks to Carlyon's amazing effort, South Moor had only used three bowlers, Carlyon 23-1-73-2, Shield 15-0-90-1 and Sanders 7-0-36-0.

Seaton Burn 206 for 3 wickets from their allotted 45 overs.

David Shield and Ernie Wilson opened the batting for South Moor.

Shield had played in the previous game listed ealier.

Ernie Wilson has been described by Ossie Barrass as "a wit, a talker and an opening batsman of considerable skill." He previously played for Vickers Armstrong in the Tyneside Senior League. He would play for South Moor for over 20 years, at different times, depending on the needs of the team, sometimes as a wicketkeeper, sometimes as an off break bowler. In his day he was good enough to score a century for South Moor, at a time when centuries were not that common.

The bowling was to be opened by Davie Gibson and Graeme Nixon. South Moor were soon in trouble, Gibson bowling Wilson with the last ball of the first over for a duck.

The new batsman was Jeff Carlyon. A big ask, bowling 23 overs straight then bat at number three. With the score on 8, Carlyon was caught and bowled by Gibson for 1.

Tony Wordsworth came in at number four, he was in the same class at school as Phil Shield. They played junior cricket at under 13, under 16 and under 18 level, where they had a strong side. Wordsworth was a useful batsman and excellent fielder. He was Colin Albone's nephew but he only played one or two seasons of senior cricket. He was bowled by Gibson for 9, with the score now at 20.

South Moor were 20 for 3 after 12.1 overs.

Kevin Carr batted at number five.

Both Nixon and Gibson were giving nothing away. After bowling 4 maidens in a row, including a wicket maiden, Gibson was rested after ten overs, his figures were 10-5-11-3.

He was replaced by the left arm spin of Bill Graham.

Nixon had to wait a little longer for his first wicket, in his eleventh over he had Carr caught by Gibson for a duck.

South Moor 42 for 4 off 21.4 overs.

Bill Boyd batted at six. He had began his cricket career as a junior at Beamish and East Tanfield. He joined South Moor in 1967 and was part of the side that won the "B" Division in 1969. He was a useful bat and occasional bowler at both senior levels of the game. He was another who served the club as an administrator for many years.

After scoring 7 of an 8 run partnership, Boyd was caught behind by Tim Garfield off Nixon as South Moor struggled against some tight bowling.

South Moor 50 for 5 off 24.1 overs, Shield still batting well, mixing patience with balanced aggression.

George Sanders came in at number seven. After his 15th over, the 30th of the innings, Nixon was replaced by yours truly.

I was ostensibly a second team fast bowler, I had a very slingy action, leading me to bowl too many four balls in the first team. I had opened the bowling for the first team in the second game of the season and managed to get Davie Collingwood LBW with a slower ball. Because of my slingy action I rarely got LBW decisions so as well as my first ever first team wicket it was a rarity all round, Davie had no idea how unlucky he was!

I had also opened the bowling a few weeks later against Greenside, I had 10-2-25-2, taking the wickets of Shaun Stokoe and Ronnie Platford. As stated elsewhere I will take Collingwood, Stokoe and Platford as my first three "A" division league wickets!

Smartie describes me as a bowler who "could swing it a bit but one who didn't make use of his height, the slingy action meant that the bowling arm didn't come over straight, but that didn't stop him developing into a good second team bowler who took some big wickets in the first team too."

As Bill Graham, bowled at one end, I was fortunate enough to bowl Sanders for 21. The score was now 118 for six.

Stephen Gray batted at number eight. He was the brother of Ray Gray and an all rounder. He was a decent bowler and as a batsman he could "give it a whack down the order." The brothers lived in a street facing the cricket ground.

With the score now on 131, he was caught by Graeme Nixon off my bowling for 3.

South Moor now 131 for 7.

New batsman was Michael Smith. He had started out as an under 13 player at South Moor with his brother, David. Dad, John, was scorer for South Moor and used to run the juniors. Michael played at all levels with South Moor. He was an attacking left handed batsman and could bowl left arm spin or medium pace. He also played at Kimblesworth and Burnhope. He sadly died in his late forties following a heart attack.

Davie Gibson replaced Bill Graham for the last couple of overs as Seaton Burn pushed to try and bowl South Moor out.

Shield carried his bat for 81 not out, his innings had lasted 45 overs and contained 11 fours and a six.

Smith was 4 not out.

South Moor 146 for 7 off 45 overs.

Three of the four bowlers used had wickets, Davie Gibson being the stand out with 12-5-17-3, Graeme Nixon had 15-5-39-2 and I had 7-0-33-2.

Seaton Burn had won by 60 runs.

Seaton Burn

D. Smart		B J. Carlyon	113
W. Graham		B J. Carlyon	23
D. Gibson	C J. Carlyon	B D. Shield	46
T. Garfield	Not	Out	11
R. Allan	Not	Out	4
Extras			9
Total			206-3 Wkts

J. Carlyon 2-73   D. Shield 1-90   G. Sanders 0-36

South Moor

D. Shield	Not	Out	81
E. Wilson		B D. Gibson	0
J. Carlyon	C & B	D. Gibson	1
T. Wordsworth		B D. Gibson	9
K. Carr	C D. Gibson	B G. Nixon	0
W. Boyd	C T. Garfield	B G. Nixon	7
G. Sanders		B S. Graham	21
S. Gray	C G. Nixon	B S. Graham	3
M. Smith	Not	Out	4
Extras			20
Total			146-7 Wkts

D. Gibson 3-17   G. Nixon 2-39   W. Graham 0-39   S. Graham 2-33

The 1987 Tyneside Senior League Table

All teams played 26 games, there was only one tie all season, the one described earlier between Lintz and Seaton Burn.

	WON 5PTS	WON 4PTS	LOST 1PT	LOST 0PTS	Drawn	Tied	PTS
Felling	10	8	0	0	8	0	90
Swalwell	10	5	3	1	7	0	80
Reyrolle	7	6	1	5	7	0	67
Consett	5	8	1	4	8	0	66
Shotley Bridge	7	5	3	3	8	0	66
Blaydon	3	8	1	7	7	0	55
Greenside	5	5	2	7	7	0	54
Burnopfield	6	3	6	5	6	0	54
Seaton Burn	5	1	10	3	6	1	47 1/2
Sacriston	2	4	7	5	8	0	41
Annfield Plain	2	3	7	6	8	0	37
Ryton	4	1	7	8	6	0	37
Lintz	3	1	5	7	9	1	35 1/2
South Moor	1	2	7	9	7	0	27

One noticeable thing about this year's table is the amount of games that were washed out, Lintz for example lost more than a third of their games to the weather, no-one lost less than six games to the "British Summer."

Consequently the qualifying runs for the League Batting Averages was cut from 500 to 450, the bowling qualifying was dropped from 50 wickets to 45.

Make no mistake, either is still a great achievement given the quality of cricketers listed below!

League Batting Averages 1987
Qualification 450 Runs

	Runs	High Score	Comp Inns	Average
M. Lal (Felling)	831	103no	6	138.50
S. Nayak (Reyrolle)	585	101no	10	58.50
W. Thomas (Blaydon)	930	103	16	58.13
R. Coulson (Felling)	611	95	12	50.92
D. Hickmott (Sacriston)	667	104no	14	47.64
D. Jackson (Annfield Plain)	786	84	19	41.37
D. Smart (Seaton Burn)	779	113	19	41.00
C. Stephenson (Shotley Bridge)	584	135	16	36.50
S. Stokoe (Greenside)	550	97no	17	32.35
G. Hunter (Consett)	496	68	16	31.00
A. Peart (Burnopfield)	494	60	18	27.44
W. Graham (Seaton Burn)	456	69	18	25.33

League Bowling Averages 1987
Qualification 45 Wickets

	Overs	Runs	Wkts	Ave
S. Gillespie (Swalwell)	269	582	71	8.20
S. Nayak (Reyrolle)	265	606	53	11.43
M. Lal (Felling)	302	746	55	13.56
G. Halliday (Ryton)	273	714	51	14.00
C. Pleasants (Felling)	274	747	52	14.37
D. Brown (Shotley Bridge)	257	672	44	15.27
D. Jackson (Annfield Plain)	320	1020	52	19.62
K. Petrie (Burnopfield)	302	1067	49	21.78

CHAPTER 12

GREENSIDE AND FELLING

On Saturday April 30th 1988 Seaton Burn played a home league fixture against Greenside. This season saw the number of overs per innings increased to 50.

I don't have the scorebook for this fixture so this piece will be scorecard based and will lack the detail of other matches.

Once again, Paul Carrick has filled in the gaps in my knowledge of the Greenside players.

Greenside had finished 7th in the league last season and would finish 12th this season. Ronnie Platford would make this seasons batting averages with 508 runs at 26.74. Shaun Stokoe had been engaged as Club Professional but persistent knee trouble meant he missed a lot of cricket and had to resign his position, although he did play a few games as an amatuer.

Seaton Burn batted first, another new opening partner for Smartie, Duncan Affleck. Affleck was a left handed batsman, he rarely gave his wicket away.

The bowling was opened by Paul Carrick and Andrew Hawley.

Hawley was a right arm, medium pacer. He had played junior cricket at Greenside where he was thought of as a good young cricketer. He progressed through the ranks to the first team. Carrick says that he was one of those bowlers who always seemed to put the ball on a nagging length where he was hard to get away. Hawley later became a competitive body builder!

Smartie made 107, his innings had included 12 fours and 4 sixes.

He was bowled by Dave Bilclough.

Affleck was caught by Shaun Stokoe off the bowling of Carrick for 14.

Richie Allan batted at three, he was bowled by Michael Fearon for 8.

Davie Gibson batted at four, he was caught by Tommy Dobson off the bowling of Clive Rogerson for 41. Rogerson had come to the club from Stocksfield with a good reputation, he was a right arm slow/medium pacer, he was another who always put the ball on the spot on a nagging length. Not necessarily a wicket taker but certainly could tie one end up.

Wicketkeeper and now captain, Tim Garfield came in at five, he was caught and bowled by Bilclough for 5.

Bill Graham batted at six, he was to finish 6 not out.

According to the scorebook, G.Thompson came in at seven. Neither Ray Cardwell or I have any idea who this is. There was however an E.Thomson, Eddie, who played for the club at the time. We both believe that this was Eddie Thomson. A right handed batsman, normally in the top four for the second team. He was a decent second team batsman. He was bowled by Rogerson for 1.

Billy Wilkinson next in at eight, he was bowled by Bilclough for 2.

Davie Watson batted at nine, he was 2 not out.

Ray Cardwell and I were the unused batsmen!

There were 3 extras.

Seaton Burn scored 191 for 7 off their 50 overs.

The bowling figures were as follows

Carrick 1-34, Hawley 0-18, Fearon 1-33, Golightley 0-23

Willoughby 0-36, Rogerson 1-25, Bilclough 2-19

David Golightley was the son of Greenside and Seaton Burn batsman, Eddie Golightley. I played a lot of second team cricket with Eddie and I enjoyed both the cricket and his company, a lovely man. It was no surprise when Paul Carrick described David in the same way. As a bowler Carrick says he was a medium pacer who had the knack of taking vital wickets.

Although wicketless today, Robert Willoughby was a left arm spinner. On his day, like many spinners, he could be very difficult to play. He had started as a junior at Greenside and they were his only club.

Greenside opened the batting with Shaun Stokoe and Angus Mclanders. Mclanders was a right handed batsman who had been a junior at Greenside. He didn't play much in his early senior years, came back to the club and then only played for two or three years more.

The bowling was opened by Davie Gibson and Ray Cardwell.

This was to be Davie Gibson's best season as a bowler for Seaton Burn, taking a career high 67 wickets. He was a very talented all rounder, an excellent right arm fast bowler and very watchable left handed batsman, he was also a brilliant fielder, especially in the covers.

Ray Cardwell was now in his third spell with the club, having left the area twice for work, a right arm medium paced bowler and great club man, as well as second team captain for a few years. He also held the post of Treasurer for many years, from the mid-80s until 2007, that's one job I wouldn't envy him!

Stokoe was caught behind by Garfield for a single off the bowling of Gibson.

Mclanders was bowled by Gibson for 5.

David Golightley batted at three. A right handed batsman, described by Paul Carrick as "a good batter."

He was bowled by Billy Wilkinson for 6.

Paul Carrick came in at four. He was caught by Bill Graham off the bowling of Billy Wilkinson for 32.

Clive Rogerson batted at five, he was to top score the innings with 62. He was stumped by wicketkeeper Garfield off the bowling of Bill Graham.

Dave Bilclough batted at six. He was caught by Smart off the bowling of Gibson for 48.

Tommy Dobson came in at seven. I caught him off the bowling of Gibson for 3.

Ronnie Platford was next in at eight. He was bowled by Bill Graham for a duck.

Michael Fearon batted at nine, he was to finish 20 not out.

Andrew Hawley came in at number ten. A right handed batsman, very good defensivley, he could be obstinate in defence, although he could be limited in his shots. He was run out for 3.

Robert Willoughby was last man, a right handed batsman. He finished nought not out.

There were 7 extras in the innings.

Greenside 188 for 9 wickets from their 50 overs.

Seaton Burn won by three runs.

Davie Gibson was the key bowler, taking 4 for 55. Only Cardwell finished wicketless, 0 -13, with Billy Wilkinson 2-79 and Bill Graham 2-36.

The century against Greenside was Smartie's 15th in the Tyneside Senior League Division "A".

Seaton Burn

D. Smart		B D. Bilclough	107
D. Affleck	C S. Stokoe	B P. Carrick	14
R. Allan		B M. Fearon	8
D. Gibson	C T. Dobson	B C. Rogerson	41
T. Garfield	C & B	D. Bilclough	5
W. Graham	Not	Out	6
E. Thomson		B C. Rogerson	1
W. Wilkinson		B D. Bilclough	2
D. Watson	Not	Out	2
Extras			3
Total			191-7 Wkts

P. Carrick 1-34   A. Hawley 0-18   M. Fearon 1-33   D. Golightley 1-23

A. Willoughby 0-35   C. Rogerson 1-26   D. Bilclough 2-19

Greenside

S. Stokoe	C T. Garfield	B D. Gibson	1
A. Mclanders		B D. Gibson	5
D. Golightley		B W. Wilkinson	6
P. Carrick	C W. Graham	B W. Wilkinson	32
C. Rogerson	St T. Garfield	B W. Graham	62
D. Bilclough	C D. Smart	B D. Gibson	48
T. Dobson	C S. Graham	B D. Gibson	3
R. Platford		B W. Graham	0
M. Fearon	Not	Out	20
A. Hawley	Run	Out	3
A. Willoughby	Not	Out	0
Extras			7
Total			188-9 Wkts

D. Gibson 4-55   R. Cardwell 0-13   W. Wilkinson 2-79   W. Graham 2-35

On Saturday June 4th 1988 Seaton Burn played a home league fixture against Felling. Felling won the league in 87, 89, 90 and 91 before moving to the Durham Senior League.

They had an opening bowling attack of Madan Lal and Chris Pleasants, one, a proven test match player and the other a proven Minor Counties player, with excellent support bowlers in Nolan and Feetham.

As a batting unit Madan Lal was clearly the lynchpin of their batting, but the abilities of Leonard, Selkirk and both Coulson's should not be underestimated.

This game is another without a scorebook and therefore any information comes from a newspaper scorecard and is very limited.

I have been very fortunate in that Joe Tyson, who was heavily involved with Felling and indeed local cricket for many years has provided pen pictures of the Felling team that day.

Tyson was actually from Percy Main, it was there, aged eight, that he first got involved with the game. Initially as a scorer, then progressing through the juniors into the senior teams. He stayed with Percy Main until his marriage when he moved South of the Tyne.

He played for Swalwell, Reyrolle and Wark in the West Tyne League before moving to Felling. He was a top four batsman, opening many times at Felling with Dave Leonard and giving the innings a good start on many occasions.

Unfortunately Tyson was forced to retire as a player at around 34, this was when he took up umpiring.

Whilst at Felling he became heavily involved with the club. He secured many sponsorships, including one with his own employers, The Newcastle Building Society, who would also go on to sponsor the league.

As Durham rose to first class status Tyson also became involved. This resulted in Felling staging Durham Second Team games, including visits from Derbyshire, Hampshire, Sussex, Worcestshire and Yorkshire.

He also organised benefit games for John Wright, Derbyshire and New Zealand, David Bairstow, Yorkshire and England, Arnie

Sidebottom, Yorkshire and England and John Birch of Nottinghamshire. The last game resulted in Notts playing for three days in the build up to a new season.

The Building Society Chief Executive, Bill Midgley, was also Durham County Cricket Clubs Chief Executive, and Joe Tyson was the perfect choice to be appointed as Chairman of Durham Groundsman Tom Flintoft's Testimonial Committee. It was very rare for a cricket county to award a testimonial year to a non player. The highlight event among the many was a game against Yorkshire. Flintoft died in June 2020 aged 86.

Tyson moved into umpiring around 30 years ago, first of all in the Tyneside Senior League, he also became Chair of the Umpires Association of The League. He now stands as an umpire in The North East Premier League.

He recalls many highlights from his umpiring career, but the one that sticks out most was the day an air ambulance stopped play at Hetton Lyons!

Today he has no involvement with any club, I'm grateful his memory of the Felling players was so good.

Returning to this fixture, Seaton Burn batted first. Smartie opened the batting with Peter Ford. Ford was a right handed batsman, largely a second team cricketer, with a solid defense.

Madan Lal and Chris Pleasants opened the bowling for Felling. They were widely regarded as being one of the best opening bowling attacks in the league at this time.

Madan Lal was a genuine Test All-Rounder. A medium paced right arm bowler and good lower order batsman. He was a member of the Indian Squad that won the 1983 World Cup. He played 39 tests for India, scoring 1042 runs at 22.65 each, with a top score of 74. He also took 71 test wickets at an average of 40.08 each. His test debut was in 1974 and his last test match in 1986, both against England.

He also played 67 one day internationals for India, scoring 401 runs at 19.10 and taking 73 wickets at 29.27. His one day international debut was in 1974 and his last game in 1987. He signed for Felling in 1988. He played eight seasons for Felling and as well as being an outstanding all-rounder he is also remembered as "bucket hands" for his catching. He was very popular with all at the club and is credited with turning the club around "on and off the field."

Chris Pleasants was from Felling and known as "Mr Felling." A left arm fast bowler, who had a reputation for moving the ball, and a right handed batsman. In 1977 he had trials with Northamptonshire. He was good enough to be a professional at both Benwell and Bill Quay. He played minor counties cricket for Northumberland between 1987 and 1991, with a best of 5-46.

Peter Ford was out early for a duck, caught by Leonard off the bowling of Madan Lal.

The left hander Richie Allan batted at three, he scored only 2 before he was bowled by Pleasants.

All rounder and another left hander, Davie Gibson batted at four. A reliable performer with the bat, he once again steadied the ship as he made 26 before he was caught by Madan Lal off the bowling of Pleasants. This was to be the second top score of the innings.

Phil Myers came in at five, making 12 before he was caught by Phil Robinson off the bowling of Brian Feetham. Feetham was another Felling lad, he was Mr Reliable with his patience, as he wouldn't often get a bowl because of the strength of the opening attack. When he had the opportunity he often came up with creditable performances.

Wicketkeeper Tim Garfield was next in at six. He was bowled by Micky Nolan for a single. Nolan was also from Felling. He was usually first change bowler who could move the ball considerably. He was a quiet member of the team but very competitive.

Graeme Sinton batted at seven. He played most of his cricket in the second team due to the continental shift pattern he worked. He was LBW to Nolan without scoring.

Billy Wilkinson came in at eight, another left hander, he also failed to score as he was caught by Madan Lal off the bowling of Feetham.

Steve Graham came in at nine, I can't remember a thing about this game, I scored 2 before I was caught by Leonard off the bowling of Nolan.

Smartie describes me as a "very, very determined batsman, he was never going to give his wicket away, a grafter. A good puller of the short ball and a reasonably sound defence. I recall a fifty against South Moor when he smacked Dennison Thomas around the park."

A bit like this game, I can't remember scoring fifty against South Moor, never mind hitting Dennison Thomas around!

A youthful Graeme Nixon, he would have been around 19 at this time, batted at ten, he was also left handed. He scored 4 before he was bowled by Nolan.

Last man was Ian Tinlin. A reliable right arm fast/medium bowler, Tinlin had the strange capability of batting left or right handed, there is no record of which way he batted on this day.

Ray Cardwell recalls one particular season where Ian batted left handed for half the season and right handed for the other half! He scored 1 not out today, most importantly this allowed Seaton Burn to achieve a batting point and also Smartie to reach 100 not out.

His innings had included sixteen fours and a six.

With 12 extras from their 50 overs Seaton Burn had scored 160 for 9.

Each of the four bowlers used took at least one wicket, Micky Nolan with 4-20 being the best of them. Madan Lal had 1-41, Chris Pleasants 2-55 and Brian Feetham 2-35.

Dave Leonard and Alan Selkirk opened the batting for Felling.

Leonard was a one club man and a reliable opening bat. He was also an excellent wicketkeeper, known for taking many spectacular catches. His son, Paul, is now making the headlines at Felling, being the first bowler to take all ten wickets in a North East Premier League fixture.

Selkirk joined Felling with his brother, Malcolm, from Wardley who played in the North East Durham League. He was a steady batsman, either opening or lower down the order. He was a very capable wicketkeeper whose opportunities were limited by the quality of his opening batting partner!

Davie Gibson and Steve Graham opened the bowling. Davie Gibson was a good performer at this level, right arm fast bowler, accurate, a regular wicket taker, capable of bowling sides out on his own.

You would struggle to find two more different fast bowlers than us two. Gibson had a lovely smooth run up and action, he made fast bowling look effortless. I was all arms and legs and effort with my slingy action.

In truth I have no recollection of this game, no-one was more surprised than me when I saw that the scorecard I had showed that I had opened the bowling and took two wickets in the game.

Given the other bowlers in the team, Ian Tinlin, Grame Nixon and Billy Wilkinson, I can only think the scorer must have misheard the bowlers name, still, I shall go with the scorecard until someone can prove otherwise.

I was a right arm fast/medium bowler, fast in the second team, medium in the first team because of the difference in class of the players. I had a slingy action and was renowned amongst my team mates for bowling short and could, on occasion, be erratic.

I asked Ray Cardwell, who captained me a lot in the second team, including the season I took 67 league wickets, for his honest opinion of me as a cricketer. Be careful what you ask for!

Ray says as a bowler, I was very competitive, erratic and single minded! He does go into detail....very competitive, he states I wasn't a swing bowler or a bowler who moved the ball off the wicket consistently, but that I always bowled as fast as I could and gave 100% and was a match winner on several occasions!

Ray feels describing me as erratic might be harsh, but that as a captain it was hard to set a field for me, as no-one, me included, knew where the ball was going to pitch! He is sure this baffled some batsman and got me a few wickets!

He does recall a second team game against Swalwell where I took the last wicket to win the game for us and the ball pitched on the bails! I remember that game too, I had opened the bowling unchanged, had four wickets and then a couple dropped in the slips or behind the wicket, I remember being knackered and just bowling as fast as I could ....scorebook says bowled Graham and five for!

Ray goes on to describe how single minded I was. That he thought my view was that it was me against the batsman and that I would never duck the challenge. He says my attitude was that I wanted that wicket at all cost and nothing else mattered, it didn't matter how the game was panning out, I wanted that wicket at any cost, to the point where I could be confrontational if required!

As a captain Ray says I was a good weapon to have in his armoury and that I proved to be a match winner on quite a few occasions. As a batsman he says I played straight, scoring valuable runs and as a fielder had a safe pair of hands in the gully, taking some great catches and making the position my own.

An honest and I think fair assessment of Steve Graham the cricketer, cheers Ray!

Back to the Felling match and I'm still sticking with the scorecard!

Dave Leonard,who had a good enough season to score 571 runs at an average of 27.19, was bowled by Davie Gibson for 11.

The scorecard shows Alan Selkirk was caught by Smartie off my bowling for 2.

Bobby Coulson batted at three. He joined Felling from Craghead. He was a stylish left hander, usually batting at three. In 1985 Coulson and John Littleton scored a league record 222 for the third wicket against Ryton. He was bowled by Davie Gibson for 3.

Undoubtedly the big wicket was that of Madan Lal who came in at four. He finished fourth in the league batting averages this season, 686 runs at an average of 49.00.

Madan Lal was bowled by Billy Wilkinson for 67. This would have been the wicket which opened the door for Seaton Burn.

Billy Coulson, brother of Bobby and also signed from Craghead. A very capable batsman who played many important innings for the club over the years. He could hit the ball a long way and could be relied upon to take wickets when called upon. He batted at five, records show I bowled him for 9.

Nigel Young came in at six, another one club man, a very good right handed batsman, these days he is a leading light in the running of the club and coaching the juniors. He had the second highest score of the Innings, 29, before he was LBW to Billy Wilkinson.

Colin Boddy batted at seven. He had joined the club from Bill Quay having previously played at Reyrolle. He was a stylish opening bat who was capable of good scores on his day. He was LBW to Davie Gibson for 2.

Phil Robinson was yet another Felling lad. He was very popular with his team mates, although often on the wrong end of practical jokes! He occasionally opened the batting and was a reliable cricketer. He was at batting eight today and was bowled by Davie Gibson for 5.

Micky Nolan came in at nine and was unbeaten on 6 at the end of the innings. When the team required quick runs he could be relied upon to put bat to ball.

Fast bowler Chris Pleasants batted at ten, he was caught by Phil Myers off the bowling of Billy Wilkinson for 4.

Last man was Brian Feetham, he liked to tell a good story about how competitive he was with the bat, even though he was normally ten or eleven on the card! He was 3 not out at the end of the allotted 50 overs.

There had been 16 extras in the innings.

Davie Gibson had bowled unchanged from one end, his 25 overs going for 69 runs but he had picked up four wickets. Billy Wilkinson had 3-45, including the very important wicket of Madan Lal, and I ended up with 2-34.

When the dust had settled, Felling were 159 for 9 from their overs, Seaton Burn had won by one run!

Over 30 years later, I can still remember the fact that we beat Felling by one run, I can't however remember a single other thing about it!

Seaton Burn

D. Smart	Not	Out	100
P. Ford	C D. Leonard	B Madan Lal	0
R. Allan		B C. Pleasants	2
D. Gibson	C Madan Lal	B C. Pleasants	26
P. Myers	C P. Robinson	B B. Feetham	12
T. Garfield		B M. Nolan	1
G. Sinton		LBW B M. Nolan	0
W. Wilkinson	C Madan Lal	B B. Feetham	0
S. Graham	C D. Leonard	B M. Nolan	2
G. Nixon		B M. Nolan	4
I. Tinlin	Not	Out	0
Extras			12
Total			160-9 Wkts
Madan Lal	C. Pleasants	M. Nolan	B. Feetham
1-41	2-55	4-20	2-35

Felling

D. Leonard		B D. Gibson	11
A. Selkirk	C D. Smart	B S. Graham	2
R. Coulson		B D. Gibson	3
M. Lal		B W. Wilkinson	67
W. Coulson		B S. Graham	9
N. Young		LBW B W. Wilkinson	29
C. Boddy		LBW B D. Gibson	2
P. Robinson		B D. Gibson	5
M. Nolan	Not	Out	6
C. Pleasants	C P. Myers	B W.Wilkinson	4
B. Feetham	Not	Out	3
Extras			18
Total			159-9 Wkts

D. Gibson 4-69   S. Graham 2-34   W. Wilkinson 3-45

The 1988 Tyneside Senior League Table
All teams played 26 games, there was only one tie all season.

	WON 5PTS	WON 4PTS	LOST 1PT	LOST 0PTS	Drawn	Tied	PTS
Swalwell	13	7	1	1	4	0	90
Felling	11	7	4	1	3	0	90
Burnopfied	10	7	3	3	3	0	84
Blaydon	9	7	2	6	2	0	77
Shotley Bridge	8	5	5	4	4	0	69
Consett	4	10	2	6	3	1	67 1/2
Sacriston	6	6	3	6	5	0	62
Seaton Burn	6	5	6	6	4	0	60
Annfield Plain	9	1	6	6	4	0	59
Lintz	3	6	6	6	5	0	50
Ryton	3	7	7	5	0	1	41 1/2
Greenside	0	3	11	8	4	0	27
South Moor	1	1	7	11	6	0	22
Reyrolle	2	0	5	15	4	0	19

League Batting Averages 1988
Qualification 500 Runs

	Runs	High Score	Comp Inns	Average
P. Burn (Sacriston)	947	123	13	72.85
W. Thomas (Blaydon)	1003	110	16	62.69
D. Smart (Seaton Burn)	1005	107	17	59.12
M. Lal (Felling)	686	89 no	14	49.00
N. Courtney (Swalwell)	918	101	20	45.90
G. Halliday (Ryton)	848	104 no	19	44.63
I. Robson (Swalwell)	640	86 no	17	37.65
A. Peart (Burnopfield)	595	210 no	16	37.19
G. Hunter (Consett)	587	94	16	36.96
R. Stokoe (Burnopfield)	588	93 no	17	34.59
N. Burdon (Shotley Bridge)	680	104 no	20	34.00
P. Veitch (Blaydon)	741	96	22	33.68
M. Brown (Burnopfield)	542	79	18	30.11
D. Leonard (Felling)	571	89	21	27.19
R. Platford (Greenside)	508	99	19	26.74
I. Somerville (Blaydon)	579	76	23	25.17
C. Stephenson (Shotley Bridge)	530	98	23	23.04

League Bowling Averages 1988
Qualification 50 Wickets

	Overs	Runs	Wickets	Average
M. Lal (Felling)	313	864	70	12.34
R. Stokoe (Burnopfield)	304	714	57	12.53
N. Courtney (Swalwell)	357	1036	80	12.95
W. Thomas (Blaydon)	380	1194	91	13.12
C. Pleasants (Felling)	325	826	58	14.24
M. Urwin (Burnopfield)	301	929	65	14.29
F. Hilton (Sacriston)	251	846	58	14.59
T. Cooley (Annfield Plain)	295	904	61	14.82
D. Gibson (Seaton Burn)	437	1061	67	15.84
R. Cook (Lintz)	294	964	50	19.28
G. Clennell (Lintz)	349	1211	56	21.63
G. Halliday (Ryton)	360	1181	51	23.16

CHAPTER 13

CONSETT AND ANNFIELD PLAIN

On Saturday June 10th 1989 Seaton Burn played a home league fixture against Consett. Consett had finished sixth last season. Gordon Hunter, who was their standout cricketer at this time, had finished in the league averages, scoring 587 runs at an average of 36.96 and a high score of 94.

Seaton Burn had finished a respectable eigth last season.

Once again no full scorebook for this one, scorecard details only taken from the local media of the time.

Dave Wilkinson, who was first team wicketkeeper at Consett for many years, has provided some information on his team mates of the day.

He also recalls enjoying some great "banter" with Smartie over the years, both on the field and off the field, having a pint in "the Drift" after the game. He enjoyed watching Smartie bat over the years but not so much when he was keeping wicket against him!

SBCC 1989

TYNESIDE SENIOR LEAGUE outfit Seaton Burn pictured in a happy mood are:

Back row (left to right) Steve Graham, Peter Ford, David Gibson, Bill Wilkinson, David Smart and Duncan Affleck.

Front row (left to right) Ray Cardwell, Paul Myers, Steve Hope, Richard Allen, Graham Nixon.

Seaton Burn batted first, Smartie opening the batting with one of his regular opening partners, the left handed Billy Graham.

The Consett bowling attack was opened by Ian "Rocky" Stoneman and the left arm Neil Remmer.

Stoneman was well known throughout the league as a larger than life cricketer, he was an excellent all rounder, very destructive with bat or ball.

The phrase "hard hitting" has been used to describe quite a few players in this book, the one player it definately applied to was "Rocky." I remember a game at Reyrolle when he was smashing our bowlers all round the park. Billy Wilkinson decided to try and "buy" his wicket by tossing a few up......after a couple of floaters were deposited on the nearby A185 a new plan was called for!

Dave Wilkinson recalls that Stoneman had "more clubs than a golf bag" but that he was an accurate right arm medium/pace bowler and as a batsman he could turn the game very quickly with his big hitting.

His father Jack, who had played club cricket for Whickham, was a very well liked and respected umpire in the league for many years. He would always stand with Derek Murray and the pair were popular among younger players in particular as they would often slip you bits of advice as the day progressed!

Ian's son Mark would make a bit of a name for himself as a cricketer too, first of all with Durham, then Surrey, eventually opening the batting for England.

Wilkinson describes Remmer, known affectionately amongst the Consett lads as "Ginge," as being a very quick left arm bowler. He had come through the juniors at Consett. He had his moments batting too!"

Remmer played most of his career at Consett but he did also have four seasons at Burnopfield from 2002 to 2005 inclusive. He is credited with taking over 350 wickets in the Tyneside Senior League and a further 250 in the Northumberland and Tyneside Senior League. He achieved his best bowling figures of 8 for 40 in 1998. He was good enough to play representative cricket for the Tyneside Senior League on a number of occasions.

Bill Graham was out for 14 when Stoneman bowled him.

Steve Hope batted at three, he was probably keeping wicket in this game as well. A useful right handed batsman. He was also bowled by Stoneman, this time for a single.

All rounder Davie Gibson came in at four, and not for the first time over the years, he found an innings in trouble and he once again he set about putting it right, scoring 28 before he was bowled by change bowler Gary Steadman. Wilkinson says that Steadman was "very quick, although he was sometimes erratic."

League records show that Steadman first played for Consett in 1988. During the 1993 season he moved to Annfield Plain. He would spend the 2002 season at Burnopfield before returning to Annfield Plain. He took at least 350 wickets in the Tyneside Senior League and a further 119 in the Northumberland and Tyneside League. His best return was 7 for 14 in 1992. This season he also took a career high 51 wickets in a season.

Michael Dancer was batting five, in his late teen's at this time, he was an excellent all round sportsman, good enough as a young footballer to be given trials and rumours of a contract offer from Nottingham Forest. He didn't play much cricket before heading off to University, to train as a teacher if memory serves me well, but he was undoubtedly talented. He scored 8 before he was caught by Wilkinson off the bowling of Remmer.

This brought Ray Cardwell to the crease, Club Treasurer and ultimate club man, he made 12 not out as the overs ran out.

Smartie was 101 not out. His innings had included nine fours and two sixes.

There were 17 extras in the innings as Seaton Burn reached 182 for 4 wickets off their 50 overs.

Consett had used five bowlers during the innings, Stoneman 2-50, Remmer 1-33, Steadman 1-30, Gordon Hunter 0-40 and Wally Armstrong 0-15 had also bowled.

Consett opened the batting with Gordon Hunter and Gary Steadman.

Gordon Hunter was a true Consett stalwart, he started his career in the 60's, after playing in the juniors he made his senior debut with one game in 1965. He developed into a brilliant left hand bat, who would very regularly feature in both the league averages and the league representative side, and a right arm slow bowler who was capable of turning a game. He is now one of the groundstaff at Consett.

He had 5 years from 1973 to 1977 inclusive as professional at Langley Park. He then returned Consett and became captain. His last game was in 2004 and he is credited with 14,276 runs at 29.93 in The Tyneside Senior League with five centuries and a best of 108 not out. In 1989 he hit a career best 725 runs in a League season.

His bowling record is a little more incomplete but he has at least 394 wickets with a best of 8 for 34.

Smartie remembers him as "a lovely bloke, a proper gentleman, as a batsman he was left handed, he was very graceful, an elegant batsman who was strong through the covers. He was also a good off break bowler, especially when he was younger."

Gary Steadman was a true all rounder, as well as being a fast bowler he was a good enough batsman to open the batting or bat in the middle order.

Davie Gibson and Graeme Nixon opened the bowling for Seaton Burn.

Hunter had made 22 when he was caught by Smartie off the bowling of Davie Gibson.

Steadman was out for 5, bowled by Graeme Nixon.

John Handy batted at three, he had joined Consett from South Moor in the 80's. Dave Wilkinson recalls "a strong right handed batsman, he batted "up the order," a good slip fielder. Sadly he passed away a couple of years ago."

He scored 27 before Billy Wilkinson caught him off the left arm spin bowling of Bill Graham.

Robert Stokoe, batting at four, is the same one mentioned earlier at Greenside. Dave Wikinson describes him as "one of a number of Stokoe's who have all been excellent at cricket. A class left arm bowler and right hand batsman. He always had a theory of some kind!"

He scored 42 before Bill Graham trapped him LBW.

Walter (Wally) Armstrong batted at five. He played from the mid 60's onwards, he was a very quick bowler in his day, renowned for his action, which included bowling with his tongue sticking out! He was captain today and despite the hundred from Smartie, Armstrong was to play the decisive innings in the match. He was to finish 61 not out.

Armstrong also had a few years playing at Marston, and although he now lives in Lancashire he is still in regular contact with Consett CC.

Number six batsman was Robert (Chappa) Chapman, he was a right handed, middle order bat. He could adapt his game to graft for quick singles or was equally adept at launching the ball over the boundary. He had played junior cricket for Consett and his son is now first team wicketkeeper.

He was 13 not out as Consett, with 15 extras in the innings, scored 185 for 4 and won comfortably by six wickets.

Seaton Burn had used six different bowlers to try and win the game.

Davie Gibson 1-47 Graeme Nixon 1-35 Billy Wilkinson 0-29

Bill Graham 2-38 Ray Cardwell 0-15 Raymond Wilkinson 0-10.

Raymond Wilkinson was Billy Wilkinsons son, he didn't play a lot of cricket, very little first team cricket, but he did manage to win the club single wicket before he went off to join the Navy.

Seaton Burn

D. Smart	Not	Out	101
W. Graham		B I. Stoneman	14
S. Hope		B I. Stoneman	1
D. Gibson		B G. Steadman	28
M. Dancer	C D. Wilkinson	B N. Remmer	8
R. Cardwell	Not	Out	12
Extras			17
Total			182-4 Wkts
I. Stoneman	N. Remmer	G. Steadman	G. Hunter
2-50	1-33	1-30	0-40
W. Armstrong			
0-15			

Consett

G. Hunter	C D. Smart	B D. Gibson	22
G. Steadman		B G. Nixon	0
J. Handy	C R. Wilkinson	B W. Graham	27
R. Stokoe		LBW B W. Graham	42
W. Armstrong	Not	Out	61
R. Chapman	Not	Out	13
Extras			16
Total			185-4 Wkts
D. Gibson	G. Nixon	W. Wilkinson	W. Graham
1-47	1-35	0-29	2-38
R. Cardwell	R. Wilkinson		
0-15	0-10		

On Saturday June 17th 1989 Seaton Burn played an away league fixture at Annfield Plain. Last season Annfield Plain had finished just below Seaton Burn in the league at ninth. None of their batsman had made the league averages although Australian Professional Troy Cooley had featured in the league bowling averages with 61 wickets at 14.82. Cooley would later make a name for himself as a bowling coach, including as coach to the England team during the 2005 Ashes Series.

He was replaced by all rounder Livingston Lawrence for this season. Lawrence was from The Leeward Islands in the West Indies. A right handed batsman and off spin bowler, he did represent the West Indies B Team on a tour to Zimbabwe in the 1986-87 season.

It should be noted that Cooley did return to Annfield Plain for the 1990 season and with some success.

Graham Robinson has given me an insight into some of the Annfield Plain players. Robinson was well known among Tyneside Senior League Cricketers, much admired for playing his cricket to the standard he did with only one arm. He never let his disability bother him, first playing at Beamish and East Tanfield before moving to South Moor for a number of years. Whilst there he would open the bowling under the captaincy of the late Bert Steward. Robinson regards Steward as the best captain he played under during a lengthy career.

He then moved to Annfield Plain. I recall playing against him in the second team, a nagging medium pacer who got a bit of swing if my memory serves me well.

After ten years opening the bowling there he moved South with work. He was a sports journalist, covering Newcastle United, before joining the Sunday People and Sunday Mirror and then retiring.

Upon returning to the area he joined Reyrolle before injury forced him to retire aged 40.

Once retired he looks back fondly on his cricket memories, always saying that as a bowler he enjoyed his biggest challenge, bowling to Smartie, recalling that Smartie "always came out on top."

As both Robinson and Smartie travel round the North East watching their son's play, they would occasionally cross paths, reminiscing about days gone by as only old cricketers do!

Seaton Burn won the toss and elected to bat first.

Smartie opened the batting with Bill Graham.

Annfield Plain opened the bowling with Ken Walters and Dave Mitchinson. Mitchinson had played for Burnopfield in 1985 when Smartie had scored an earlier ton, he would also play at Seaton Burn in his career.

A steady start was made, Walters was replaced by Lawrence after bowling 5-0-20-0.

Mitchinson was replaced by Kevin Mccardle after 9-0-37-0.

With the last ball of the 22nd over Lawrence had Graham caught by Geoff Mcconnell for 24.

Seaton Burn 91 for 1 from 22 overs.

Steve Hope was batting at three today, he had scored 7 out of a partnership of 28 when he was caught by Alan Greener, also off the bowling of Lawrence.

Seaton Burn 119 for 2 from 27.3 overs.

This brought Davie Gibson to the crease. The remainder of the innings became a battle between Smart and Gibson against Lawrence and Mccardle as both batsmen remained unbeaten and both bowlers bowled unchanged.

The unbroken partnership was 125. Seaton Burn posted 244 for 2 wickets from their 45 overs. The innings included 15 byes and 25 extras in total.

Lawrence had figures of 18-1-94-2 and Mccardle 13-0-68-0.

Annfield Plain opened the batting with Ron Walters and Livingston Lawrence.

Davie Gibson, fresh from his unbeaten 60, and Graeme Nixon opened the bowling for Seaton Burn.

An opening stand of 26 got Annfield Plain off to a steady start until Nixon caught and bowled Walters for 8 with the third ball of the eighth over.

A bit of deja vou for Nixon as this brought the identical twin brother of the departing Ron, Ken Walters, to the crease at three!

Graham Robinson recalls that "only their parents could tell Ron and Ken apart. Both men would go on to become teachers. When Ron..... or was it Ken.....dislocated his shoulder fielding in the slips for Annfield Plain, the other was violently sick on the field and unable to continue. Both were excellent all rounders who had started their cricket careers at Burnhope."

An excellent partnership of 65 followed. Nixon was taken out of the attack after bowling ten overs and replaced by the left arm spin of Bill Graham.

With the first ball of his spell, Graham bowled Lawrence for 52. The innings had contained five boundaries.

Annfield Plain 91 for 2 from 21.1 overs.

Dave Mitchinson came to the wicket at four.

Gibson's last over, his eleventh, was the last over of his opening spell, 11-0-40-0. He was replaced by fellow opening bowler, Nixon, who now switched ends.

In the second over of his new spell, Nixon bowled Ken Walters for 24.

Annfield Plain now 107 for 3 from 24.4 overs.

Geoff Mcconnell batted five today. He was a Police Officer by profession and had been heavily involved with Lanchester before joining Annfield Plain. His son, Andrew, would also go on to play first team cricket for Annfield Plain and also follow his father into the police.

Only a single was added for the fourth wicket when Mitchinson was bowled by Nixon for 9 from the last ball of the 27th over.

Annfield Plain 108 for 4 from 27 overs.

All rounder Kevin Mccardle batted at six. A right arm, medium pace bowler, often opening bowler or first change and a powerful middle order batsman. Kevin was one of the son's of long term Annfield Plain servant, Arthur, and brother of Brian. Brian who would go on to captain the side, was another all rounder.

Athur's grandson, Kevin's son, Adam, still plays for the club. Arthur was his greatest supporter until he passed away. Adam is a medium paced bowler who is aggressive and gives his all. He doesn't hang around when he is batting and likes "a hit." In the same mould as his dad, he wears his heart on his sleeve.

With only four more runs added to the total, with the last ball of the 28th over, Bill Graham removed Mcconnell, LBW for 5.

Annfield Plain now 112 for 5 from 28 overs.

This brought the very experienced wicketkeeper/batsman Paul Gilfellon to the crease. Robinson describes him as "one of the best wicketkeepers to grace the Tyneside Senior League." He played numerous times for the League representative side. Originally from Craghead, he originally joined Chester Le Street before moving to Annfield Plain.

A stand of 49 followed as Gilfellon and Mccardle set about rebuilding their innings and trying to get a platform to chase the runs down.

It was Bill Graham who broke the partnership, with the score on 161, he had Mccardle caught by Ray Cardwell for 38. Mccardle had struck five fours and a six.

Annfield Plain 161 for 6 from 33.5 overs, now require 84 runs to win from 11.1 overs.

Stephen Donnelly batted at number at eight today. Robinson recalls that "he was one of the Donnelly dynasty, brought up within a stone's throw of Enterprise Park. Dad Terry, was an excellent servant to the club behind the stumps and married to Liz, brother of long term skipper, Alec Patterson. All three brothers, Stephen, Andrew and Phil went on to represent Annfield Plain."

A stand of 47 between Gilfellon and Donnelly then put Annfield Plain right back in the game. A Gilfellon six from Bill Graham's ninth over saw him replaced by opening bowler Davie Gibson.

Graham had 9-2-45-3.

With the score on 208, Gibson caught and bowled Gilfellon for 27. He had hit a four and a six in his knock.

Annfield Plain 208 for 7 from 41 overs.

They now required 37 from 24 balls to win.

New batsman, number nine, was Alan Johnston. Robinson remembers "a more than nippy opening bowler who also had many years with Lintz."

With the score at 217 Donnelly was run out.

Annfield Plain 217 for 8.

Batsman number ten was Charlie Brinton. Brinton was another "local lad, who could give the ball a bit of a tweak, he could chip in with useful runs."

With the fifth ball of the 44th over Graeme Nixon bowled Johnson for 8.

Annfield Plain now 225 for 9 wickets off 43.5 overs.

They required 20 to win from 7 balls as last batsman Alan Greener walked to the crease.

Greener is remembered as a "loyal club man who always gave 100%. He went on to have a great career as a Tyneside Senior League Umpire."

Davie Gibson who had already scored an unbeaten 60, then opened the bowling with an eleven over spell, plus a further three overs in his second spell, was asked to bowl the last over.

He conceded three singles off the bat and a couple of extras as Annfield Plain scored 230 for 9 wickets from their 45 overs.

Brinton was 5 not out, Greener 3 not out.

There had been 15 extras in the innings.

Davie Gibson finished with 15-0-60-1 and Graeme Nixon 21-3-98-4 as Seaton Burn won by 14 runs.

A great day of hard fought village cricket.

Seaton Burn

D. Smart	Not	Out	124
W. Graham	C D. Mcconnell	B L. Lawrence	24
S. Hope	C A. Greener	B L. Lawrence	7
D. Gibson	Not	Out	60
Extras			25
Total			244-2 Wkts
K. Walters	D. Mitchinson	L. Lawrence	K. Mccardle
0-20	0-37	2-94	0-68

Annfield Plain

R. Walters	C & B	B G. Nixon	8
L. Lawrence		B W. Graham	52
K. Walters		B G. Nixon	24
D. Mitchinson		B G. Nixon	9
D. Mcconnell		LBW B W. Graham	5
K. Mccardle	C R. Cardwell	B W. Graham	38
P. Gilfellon	C & B	D. Gibson	27
S. Donnelly	Run	Out	22
A. Johnson		B G. Nixon	8
C. Brinton	Not	Out	5
A. Greener	Not	Out	3
Extras			29
Total			230-9 Wkts

D. Gibson 1-60   G. Nixon 4-98   W. Graham 3-45

The 1989 Tyneside Senior League Table
All teams played 26 games, there was only one tie all season.

	WON 5PTS	WON 4PTS	LOST 1PT	LOST 0PTS	Drawn	Tied	PTS
Felling	8	12	3	1	2	0	93
Lintz	8	9	4	3	2	0	82
Swalwell	8	7	6	2	2	1	78 1/2
Sacriston	7	9	3	5	2	0	76
Consett	4	12	5	3	2	0	75
Blaydon	5	9	7	4	1	0	69
Shotley Bridge	6	6	6	3	3	2	68
Annfield Plain	5	6	9	3	3	0	61
Greenside	3	8	8	5	2	0	57
Burnopfield	5	5	5	9	2	0	52
Ryton	6	1	10	6	2	1	48 1/2
Seaton Burn	4	4	6	10	2	0	44
Reyrolle	4	3	5	12	2	0	39
South Moor	1	1	15	8	1	0	25

League Batting Averages 1989
Qualification 500 Runs

	Runs	High Score	Comp Inns	Average
M. Lal (Felling)	992	91no	11	90.18
L. Lawrence (Annfield Plain)	1099	163no	16	68.69
S. Stokoe (Greenside)	1056	130no	17	62.12
W. Thomas (Blaydon)	858	121no	17	50.47
W .Raja (Sacriston)	795	120no	17	46.76
G. Clennell (Lintz)	791	99	18	43.94
N. Hewison (Burnopfield)	683	113	16	42.86
I. Somerville (Blaydon)	808	101	20	40.40
G. Hunter (Consett)	725	103	19	38.15
J. Dumighan (Swalwell)	839	120no	22	38.14
D. Leonard (Felling)	703	120	19	37.00
W. Ackerman (Swalwell)	594	85	17	34.94
R. Coulson (Felling)	591	147no	17	34.76
T. Nichols (Burnopfield)	694	137no	20	34.70
D. Smart (Seaton Burn)	726	124no	21	34.57
C. Stephenson (Shotley Bridge)	671	77	20	33.55
P. Veitch (Blaydon)	725	79no	22	32.95
N. Burdon (Shotley Bridge)	605	82no	19	31.84
G. Kerry (Greenside)	725	88no	17	30.88
S. Lishman (Greenside)	573	105no	19	30.16
D. Golightley (Greenside)	596	96	20	29.80
J. Dunn (Reyrolle)	651	106	22	29.59
R. Stokoe (Consett)	529	65	18	29.39
D. Gibson (Seaton Burn)	534	60no	20	26.70
B. Scott (Ryton)	500	69	21	23.81
P. Shield (South Moor)	500	63no	21	23.81

League Bowling Averages 1989
Qualification 50 Wickets

	Overs	Runs	Wickets	Average
R. Cook (Lintz)	215	604	51	11.84
M. Lal (Felling)	311	825	55	15.00
W. Raja (Sacriston)	454	1254	81	15.48
W. Thomas (Blaydon)	452	1258	80	15.72
C. Pleasants (Felling)	343	978	62	15.77
S. Lishman (Greenside)	340	1092	65	16.80
W. Ackerman (Swalwell)	249	863	50	17.26
I. Stoneman (Consett)	371	1093	62	17.62
G. Clennell (Lintz)	358	1114	60	18.57
M. Urwin (Burnopfield)	337	1180	56	21.07
D. Sweeney (Burnopfield)	360	1254	51	24.59

CHAPTER 14

BLAYDON AND GREENSIDE

On Saturday April 28th 1990 Seaton Burn played an away league fixture at Blaydon. This should have been the second week of the season but the entire programme for the previous weekend had been washed out!

Blaydon were an excellent side at this time. They would finish third in the league this season. They had three batsmen in the league batting averages this year, Wes Thomas was third in the batting averages 1014 runs at 56.33, Ian Somerville had 763 runs at 34.68, and Paul Veitch had 603 runs at 25.12. Thomas was also third in the bowling averages with 75 wickets at 13.77.

I only have a scorecard rather than scorebook for this fixture, so details of the game are basic. However Peter Carroll has furnished a lot of information about the Blaydon players.

Carroll was a Blaydon stalwart who featured for the club for many years. He was also entrusted by Jack Chapman with all of his Tyneside Senior League records and documentation, without the help of Peter Carroll, there would be a lot more holes in this work.

Carroll was a Magistrate and for many years Club Secretary. He arrived at the club in 1969. He was renowned for his late swing. On his debut he took 7-41 and he finished that season with 102 wickets.

He was a regular problem for Seaton Burn.

On 28th May 1977 Blaydon visited Seaton Burn. Carroll was to bowl Smartie for 81. Stewart Nixon chanced his arm with the next ball, hoisting it to square leg where Joe Mcabe took the catch. The batsman crossed as the ball was in the air so Bill Graham had the dubious honour of facing the hat trick ball. He was bowled for 48 to complete the hat trick. This was the pivotal point in a close match which Blaydon won by only 8 runs.

Throughout his career he was to take 1,353 wickets for Blaydon First Team. His victims included Test Match Players, Desmond Haynes, John Bracewell, Clayton Lambert, Ali Zia, Dilip Doshi, Claremont Depeiza, Derek Parry and Qasim Omar.

He took 100 first team wickets in a season four times.

He took 9-35 in the Aynsley Johnson Cup Final against Burnopfield

He also "chipped in" with 498 second team wickets! He tells the tale of sitting eating Sunday Lunch one day when he got the call that the second team were short, dashing off and taking 10 Felling wickets with the gravy from his lunch still on his chin!

Records show that was 14th July 1991 and he bowled 20 overs for his 10 for 28!

His highest score with the bat for the first team was 45 against Chopwell.

Smartie remembers him as "an inswing bowler, medium paced but very, very accurate, he would just nag away at you."

Seaton Burn won the toss and elected to bat.

Smartie opened the batting with the left handed Richie Allan. Allan was Smartie's settled opening partner for a number of years. He was well known throughout the league, and he refused to let his deafness stand in the way of his cricket or his popularity off the field. Everyone knew "Richie".

The bowling was opened by Wes Thomas and Ian Reid.

Thomas was quick, right arm fast, he took 857 wickets in six and a half seasons for Blaydon. Smartie remembers he was "quick, just quick, he was good and accurate with it, but the abiding memory is just "pace."

In 1988 Thomas scored a century and took ten wickets in a match against Lintz. His bowling figures that day were 9 -3-27-10. He bowled eight of the batsman and had two LBW!

Reid was a right arm fast/medium bowler. He made his debut for the club in 1984. In total he had 616 wickets for Blaydon. He passed 50 wickets in eight successive seasons for Blaydon and was regularly selected for the league under 25 side. 1989 was a standout season for Reid, an incredible 138 wickets for the second team. His best bowling figures were 7-45 against Sacriston in 1996.

Allan was out for 19. He was caught behind by Heasman off the bowling of Thomas.

Peter Heasman didn't bat in this game, he was however, an excellent wicketkeeper. He came to Blaydon late in his career. In his debut season with the club, 1988, he took 40 catches and had 7 stumpings. He would finish his Blaydon career with 214 catches and 72 stumpings. His highest score with the bat was 30 not out, achieved in 1999, his last season with the club.

This brought Steve Hope to the crease. He was a young man with not a lot of first team cricket behind him at this time. I do recall seeing him score a brilliant unbeaten 50 here for the second team a year or two earlier, so it was clearly a ground he liked. He was a right handed bat and did keep wicket for a while.

His brother, David, a wicketkeeper, also played for Seaton Burn for a while.

Dad Ian was a regular spectator at the cricket field and his butcher's shop was a favourite "coffee stop" of mine whenever I was put on foot patrol in Wideopen!

Hope scored 47, he was caught behind by Heasman bowled Plender.

Davie Gibson batted at four, he scored 25 before being caught by Thomas off the bowling of Plender.

Bill Graham was next in, he didn't have time to get off the mark and finished as he started, nought not out.

Smartie was 159 not out! His innings had contained 17 fours and 7 sixes.

Seaton Burn 263 for 3 wickets from their 50 overs.

Blaydon had used six bowlers, Thomas had 16-1-61-1 and Reid 8-0-51-0.

Plender had finished with 13-3-60-2. A right handed bowler, described as mainly a second team cricketer at this level. Known as a whole hearted performer who gave everything for the team. He left the club to play for Washington after six season in the early nineties.

Derek King had figures of 5-0-28-0. He was a left arm medium pacer. He would take 165 wickets for the club over his career. In 1990 he took 47 wickets in the season, including a match winning 4-6 against Annfield Plain. His best bowling was 5-26 against South Northumberland in 1991. After three seasons, 94-96 at Ryton, he returned to Blaydon where he became second team captain.

All rounder Micky Noon had figures of 4-0-34-0. He had joined Blaydon in 1980 from Wallsend Cricket Club. He would take 136 wickets for Blaydon. His best bowling figures were 4-10 against Sacriston in 1980. As he didn't bat today, now would be a good time to mention that Noon also scored 4159 runs for Blaydon, including seven half centuries and a highest score of 65. He was also a keen photographer, providing many action shots of his teammates!

Ian Somerville had 4-0-20-0. I didn't know he could bowl and was surprised to see "Somers" on the list of bowlers. He describes himself as a very, very, occasional leg spin bowler. He remembers being brought on to bowl in this game, it was his first bowl for "a season or two" and Smartie was on 90 odd at the time!"

For all the years cricket he played he bowled 60.2 overs, he had 7 maidens, at a cost of 303 runs for 11 wickets. The average cost was 27.55.

He does tell a story that he and John Hodgson, aged 17 or 18, went on a coaching course run by Doug Ferguson. Ferguson was a very well respected coach and would go on to coach the Italian National Team during the late nineties. He was, as probably all coaches were at the time, traditional in method, hit the ball in the "v." Ian describes him as a "brilliant" coach. He did however tells "Somers" that "he would never score a first team fifty but will take a hat full of wickets!"

Blaydon's innings was opened by the right handed Paul Veitch and the left handed Ian Somerville.

Veitch would be best described as an aggressive opening batsman, he could and would get after bowlers from the first ball. He is the son of former Blaydon Chairman, Bill Veitch.

He made his first team debut in 1980, with one innings of 0 not out.

He would go on to have a tremendous cricket career. He scored 1,000 runs eight times in a season. His 12,393 aggregate runs has him second in Blaydon's history. He scored his maiden century in the 494th innings of his career, he scored five more in his last thirty eight innings! Whilst at Blaydon he featured in 30 partnerships of 100 or more.

He would go on to play as a professional at both Ryton and Chopwell.

Smartie recalls one occasion during the tea interval when Veitch told Alan Francis he was "going to hit him for six first ball of the innings. Sure enough, first ball of the innings Veitch hit "Frankie" for six!

After his first two overs "Frankie" had gone for over 20, so I took him off and brought on Shaun Herriot and Phil Turnbull. One of them got Veitchy and another wicket fell, so I took Herriot off and brought "Frankie" back. He took the next eight wickets and we won the game!"

Ian Somerville was the perfect counter to Veitch's aggressive play. He had a calmness about his play, he was perfectly capable of scoring quickly but did it with typical left handers elegence. He possessed excellent technique and was a classical driver of a cricket ball.

He made his first team debut in 1981 and played until 2005.

He scored 1000 runs a club record 11 times, including 9 seasons in a row, from 1988-96 inclusive. In the 1993 season he scored 1662 runs.

In 1983, a championship winning year for the club, he was second in the league batting averages. He was also selected for the league under 25 team that year. In 1988 he captained The Durham Cricket Association Under 25 team against an Irish Union Team.

He finished with the most centuries by an amateur for Blaydon, 13, and scored 97 half centuries for good measure. He scored 23406 runs for Blaydon, with a highest score of 160 not out, at an average of 26.76.

"Somers" continued to score runs when Blaydon moved into the North East Premier League, including a century before lunch against Gateshead Fell in 2002.

Somerville himself says that "I consider myself very lucky to have played for Blaydon. More often than not we turned up to find the grass cut, the wickets pitched and site screens up. I fielded, batted and showered and went into the bar whilst someone else took the screens down, watered the wicket and put the flags away, the little things which make cricket really. When it rained we ran for the dressing room while a hoard of volunteers covered the wicket, this was not the case for many players at many clubs.

I clearly remember Freddie Hilton at Sacriston, he was in the middle of bowling us out, when he had to leave the field to put the boiler on for the tea and get the teas ready for the interval!

A huge thank you to all those volunteers at Blaydon and my hat goes off to those players who all those players who filled these sort of roles, also a word of admiration to those who turned up, batted at eight, didn't get a bowl and would field third man at both ends, those players who turned out to make the numbers up and make sure the rest of us got a game. They were just as much a part of the team as the rest of us, without these guys, nobody could play."

Smartie describes Somerville as being "very, very good in his Tyneside Senior League days, a solid batsman, difficult to dislodge and he would always put the bad ball away for four."

He goes on to say that, in his opinion, Somerville would go on to become an even better batsman when he moved up to the higher class cricket of The Premier League.

In my opinion probably Somerville's greatest achievement is that he did all of the above for one club, as an amateur. A truly remarkable cricketer.

Somerville recalls Smartie as someone "I was lucky enough to get to know as an opponent and as a team mate playing for the TSL. I remember one game in particular, we were opening up against The Durham Senior League at Swalwell.

Stephen Peel was bowling, he was the brother of the excellent keeper and top all round bloke, Tommy Peel. Smartie "clothed" one for six over the old scoreboard. It was a really short boundary there because of the odd shape of the old ground. Peel was a ferocious competitor and not best pleased, true to his nature he couldn't help himself, "that would never have been a six at The Fell."

At the end of the over Smartie and I had a little chuckle.

Stephen Peel rarely bowled badly, he may say differently, but knowing him, probably not!

However, what happened next was bound to happen, a few balls later Smartie got one out of the middle of the bat, this one would have been six at the MCG never mind the Fell, it disappeared over the fence and possibly landed at Blaydon Rugby Club!

Smartie piped up "I bet that would have been six at The Fell."

I loved the banter and always enjoyed Smartie's company, whether on the field or off it. We spent a few times putting the world to rights, around the field at Greenside and other cricket fields.

I remember seeing Smartie at a one day international at The Riverside. As we were walking round the ground we bumped into Gordon Halliday, the well respected Northumberland bat and ex Ryton Pro. Conversation was flowing well until Halliday mentioned that Smartie should turn out for the Northumberland Over 50 side. The response was short and "to the point," as Smartie so often was.

He reminded Halliday that Northumberland had repeatedly ignored him, for whatever reason, when he was in his pomp. It was obvious that this still bugged Smartie, and I know we can all agree, he was one of the best, if not the best, bat in Northumberland and should have played many, many times, it was perhaps "that to the point" that the County was afraid of.

That said, at least the suggestion of him playing Over 50's for the county was better than mine, I was only 42 when I was asked to play for Durham!"

Davie Gibson and Graeme Nixon opened the bowling for Seaton Burn.

Veitch and Somerville, as they did many times, got Blaydon off to a good start.

Veitch was the first wicket to fall, caught by Ray Cardwell off the bowling of Davie Gibson for 31.

Somerville would go on to make 69 before he was caught by Steve Hope off the bowling of Billy Wilkinson.

Paul Kennedy batted at three. He was a right handed batsman. He was thought of as being certainly good enough to play at this level but home and work commitments meant he never fulfilled his full potential. He left and returned a few times, always a classy looking batsman, he had two scores of over 50 in 1992 and three scores over 50 in 1993, including a highest score of 78.

Kennedy made 11 before Richie Allan caught him off the spin of Bill Graham.

Wes Thomas had batted four, he was to score a match winning 115 not out. I played in this game and I can remember as the game reached it's end, it was practically dark, Davie Gibson, who was certainly a fast bowler rather than a medium pacer, bowling flat out and Thomas just picking him apart. This innings contained 6 fours and 9 sixes, the innings lasted 61 minutes and he faced 64 balls for his 115!

Thomas was an incredible cricketer. Purely looking at his batting for Blaydon, he scored 11,621 runs from 11,755 balls! He hit 536 career sixes, 3 fives and 1081 fours!

He scored 14 centuries for Blaydon. His highest score, 215 not out was made against Lintz and included 17 fours and 13 sixes. For good measure his brother, Dennison, scored 134 for South Moor, on the same day!

His most remarkable days cricket came on 15th May 1988 against Lintz. When Blaydon batted he scored 110, the century coming off just 88 balls. When Lintz batted, he bowled eight of them and had two LBW!

Thomas had the bowling figures of 9-3-27-10!

It is the only recorded instance of a player scoring a century and taking ten wickets in a Senior Match in Durham.

To heap more grief on Lintz, in the return match he had the first nine wickets down, only a dropped catch with the last pair at the wicket then Ian Reid nipping in at the other end to take the last wicket prevented him taking 20 wickets in the two matches against Lintz.

Unfortunately the Wes Thomas story had no happy ending. He played his last match for the club against Shotley Bridge on 31st July 1993. Charlie Stephenson, among those noting that Wes wasn't himself. A short while later he was diagnosed as being terminally ill, he died on 1st February 1994.

Blaydon held a testimonial for Wes and his family, which he attended. Clyde Butts captained a side containing Jimmy Adams, Phil Simmons, Clayton Lambert, Eldine Baptistse and Roger Harper. Wes was well enough to make a speech standing on a seat in the bar.

A great cricketer and person, taken far too young.

Brian Scott had batted five, he was a useful right handed bat and bowler, a publican by trade. This limited his appearances for the club and he only played three years here before work took him away from the area. He did score 3 fifties for the club, with a high score of 98. As a bowler he took 21 wickets, with a best of 3 for 4, ironically, against Seaton Burn. Today, however, he was caught by Smartie off the bowling of Bill Graham for a duck.

David "Charlie" Minnikin came in at six. A right handed batsman, he joined the club in 1987 from Ryton. He was club captain in 1989, a year in which Minnikin scored his highest score of 125 not out. He scored 3170 runs for the club at an average of 17.42, including five fifties and one hundred. He was LBW to Billy Wilkinson for 1.

Derek King batted at seven. He was a right handed batsman and right handed medium pace bowler, a genuine all rounder. He made his first team debut for Blaydon in 1984, making five in his only innings.

His bowling was described earlier, as a batsman he scored 2026 runs for the club, at an average of 11.71. In 1988 he fell just short of a 500 run season, with 479. Incredibly for a player of his talent, he never made a 50, his highest score being 44.

Today, I caught him off the bowling of Davie Gibson for 7.

Just as a non cricket aside, a few years later, my first wife and son's had two season tickets at St James Park, I policed every

Newcastle home game for years, first of all on the Special Patrol Group and then as part of the dedicated football unit. During a quiet spell, I can't remember what year or even what game, pre match I called up to see the family, sitting almost directly behind them a couple of rows back, was Derek King! Small world!

Ian Reid came in at eight and he would finish with an unbeaten 11.

Reid was a right handed batsman, in the side for his bowling. Over his Blaydon career he scored 1555 runs, with a highest score of 43 not out.

There were 19 extras as Blaydon reached 264 for 6 and won the game by four wickets.

Davie Gibson finished with 17.1-3-80-2, Graeme Nixon 13-0-83-0, Billy Wilkinson 10-3-46-2 and Bill Graham 6-1-37-2.

A remarkable game in that it had two brilliant centuries by two of the stellar players of their time.

Ian Somerville recalls Blaydon being a "very sociable side at this time, especially when "Charlie" Minnikin was captain. They took their cricket seriously, but that they definately enjoyed each others company off the field, as well as trips to Shotley and Seaton Burn in particular. Good company, excellent teas and a few beers in The Drift afterwards.

The drill for Blaydon was to arrive at the ground, enjoy the game, hopefully win, the nights out were always better after we won, then out on the town.

I especially recall one night at Seaton Burn when Veitchy and I got kitted out with me as a vicar and him as a tart, we did have a party to go to! When we walked in The Drift all the Seaton Burn lads cheered and we even got a wolf whistle or two, well Veitchy has got amazing legs! I don't think anyone was surprised though, it was Blaydon after all!"

Funnily enough Smartie remembers this night as well, he remembers Richie Allan trying to put his hand up Veitchy's skirt, much to Veitchy's horror and everyone else's amusement!

Somerville adds that "In The TSL there were many great players, we all know about Steve Atkinson, Stu Wilkinson, Ian Wishart, Bobby Cook, David Jackson, Donald Brown, the list is endless. I learnt a lot from watching those guys. I went on to make friends with many of them, often through playing with them in The TSL representative sides, from the under 18s, under 25's, to the Wilkinson and Presidents Cup sides. Even more names spring to mind, Jeff Carlyon, Gordon Baker, Jim Smith and Freddie Hilton.

Often my chauffeur for these games was my much missed friend Alan Murray. Alan was also my cricket idol and mentor and he and his brother Derek would always insist on a massive pub lunch en route to these representative games.

I enjoyed my time with Blaydon in the North East Premier League but it was never the same as The TSL. Many Premier League players appear not to enjoy playing, it all seems a little too serious. After the game, a glass of orange, if they went to the bar at all. Don't get me wrong it's tough cricket, it is enjoyable at times but it's not the TSL.

Good games, some excellent cricketers, great mates, often from both teams, and some great nights. Possibly the best example I can give to show what I mean is one occasion when I was having a drink with my old mate Jack Chapman. A Blaydon player had scored a fantastic hundred at Gateshead Fell, by the time he got in the bar, Jack and I were the only supporters in the place. He had a soft drink and went home.

I recall scoring a hundred in The TSL and I never bought a drink all night, I was pretty much carried around by my team mates. We were singing, dancing and drinking into the small hours, as they celebrated my success with me. Then it was off to someone's house, waking up feeling rough and looking round and seeing pretty much all of my team mates were there with me. Priceless memories."

Seaton Burn

D. Smart	Not	Out	159
R. Allan	C P. Heasman	B W. Thomas	19
S. Hope	C P. Heasman	B W. Plender	47
D. Gibson	C W. Thomas	B W. Plender	25
S. Graham	Not	Out	0
Extras			13
Total			263-3 Wkts

W. Thomas 1-61 I. Reid 0-51 W. Plender 2-60 D. King 0-28
M. Noon I. Somerville
  0-34   0-20

Blaydon

P. Veitch	C R. Cardwell	B D. Gibson	31
I. Somerville	C S. Hope	B W. Wilkinson	69
P. Kennedy	C R. Allan	B W. Graham	11
W. Thomas	Not	Out	115
B. Scott	C D. Smart	B W. Graham	0
D. Minnikin		LBW B W. Wilkinson	1
D. King	C S. Graham	B D. Gibson	7
I. Reid	Not	Out	11
Extras			19
Total			264-6 Wkts

D. Gibson 2-80 G. Nixon 0-83 W. Wilkinson 2-46 W. Graham 2-37

On Monday 27th August 1990 Seaton Burn played a league fixture at home to Greenside. Greenside would finish 5th in the league this season. Paul Carrick with 671 runs at 51.62 and Steve Lishman 539 runs at 31.70 would both make the league batting averages.

Lishman would miss this game, just as well for Seaton Burn, on 13th May 1989 he had taken 10-44 against them, I played in that game, managing the third highest score of 15 before I was bowled.

This game would feature Smartie's fourth hundred against Greenside.

Paul Carrick has once again provided an insight to the Greenside players who haven't featured previously.

Greenside captain David Golightley won the toss and elected to bowl.

Carrick recalls that Golightley was "an attacking captain, a good thinker about the game, a nice lad who was a good skipper to play for."

Smartie and the left handed Richie Allan opened the batting for Seaton Burn.

Greenside opened the bowling with Paul Carrick and Ernie Bewick. With the score on 19 Allan was caught by Clark off the bowling of Carrick for 6.

This brought another left hander, Davie Gibson to the crease. Bewick was removed from the attack after he had bowled 5-1-11-0 and replaced by Michael Burdon.

Carrick describes Burdon as "a talented all rounder. A right arm off spin bowler. His brother Neil was well known throughout the league for his time at Shotley Bridge. Michael was one of the funniest fellas I came across in the dressing room."

Carrick after he had bowled 6-2-11-1 was replaced by Mark Whittaker. Carrick remembers "a young lad at this time, a left arm fast bowler but one who rarely played as he was also a good footballer." He would bowl only three overs, 0-21 before Carrick then came back for a second spell.

Burdon fared little better and after six overs 0-35, he was replaced by David Golightley.

Gibson and Smartie had added 104 for the second wicket, taking the score to 123 for 2 when Gibson was caught by Stokoe off the bowling of Golightley for 36. His innings had included four boundaries.

This brought Gary Stephenson out to bat at four. A former regular opening partner of Smartie, his cricket was now suffering from the horrendous shift pattern he worked, play a weekend, miss a weekend, very difficult to perform at this level with that kind of regime.

Carrick's second spell of 6-4-3-0 ended after the 30th over and he was replaced by Shaun Stokoe.

Golightley took himself off after bowling the 38th over of the innings and was replaced by Carrick for a third spell. Golightley had figures of 8-1-50-1.

With the score at 166 and the third ball of the 43rd over Stephenson was caught by Whittaker off the bowling of Carrick for 9.

Yet another left hander, Bill Graham came out batting at five. He would finish on 21 not out, with four boundaries.

Smartie was 126 not out. The innings had contained fourteen fours and five sixes from 141 balls.

Paul Carrick, despite going for a few in his last four overs, finished with 18-6-51-2 and Shaun Stokoe 10-2-33-0.

Seaton Burn had scored 219 for 3 from their allotted 50 overs. The innings had contained 18 extras.

Greenside opened the innings with Shaun Stokoe and Greg Kerry.

Greg Kerry was the son of former Greenside player Paul Kerry. He was an excellent all rounder. A right arm medium/ fast bowler, who extracted extra bounce because he was tall and had an upright action. As a batsman he was right handed, a good opening bat, he was equally adept at both driving and cutting.

Seaton Burn opened the bowling with Davie Gibson and David Felton.

Smartie also kept wicket in this game, it was something he did from time to time depending on the availability of others.

Stokoe took the first ball and scored a single off the second to get off the mark. A leg bye was taken from either the third or fourth ball of the over.

Smartie clearly recalls Davie Gibson bowling the fifth ball of the over to Shaun Stokoe, Smartie took it behind the stumps. The whole team went up appealing for a catch, all except Smartie, he didn't think Stokoe had hit it. Stokoe immediateley "walked."

Smartie spoke to him in the bar after the game and told him he didn't think he had hit it, Stokoe told him it had come off his gloves, that he had hit it and was out, he always "walked" and he knew if the circumstances were reversed that Smartie would have done the same.

When he relayed this story to me Smartie had said it was one of the things his father had told him to do, "if you hit it, you walk!"

I think it also tells of the respect there was among the top cricketers in the league at the time, they all wanted to play their cricket hard, they would begrudge you every run you scored and every wicket you took, but in the bar afterwards both teams would mingle and talk freely. Those that knew each other through representative cricket, especially so.

So Greenside were 2 for 1 of five balls!

David Golightley came in at three.

Both Kerry and Golightley made aggressive starts, after 8 overs the score was 39 for 1 with both bowlers having conceded 19 runs off their four overs.

Felton was replaced by Graeme Nixon. This coincided with Gibson finding his radar, his next four overs costing him just five runs.

Kerry and Golightley had taken the score to 63 when Kerry was run out for 30. His innings had contained five boundaries.

This brought Michael Burdon to the wicket batting at four. As a batsman Carrick describes Burdon as being "very good all round the wicket, as a youngster he had grown up playing on the hard decks of Shotley Bridge and consequently this made him very good off the front foot, driving in particular."

With the score on 70 Golightley was run out for 22, his innings had contained three boundaries.

Greenside 70 for 3 and the game evenly poised.

Paul Carrick batted at five today.

Smartie describes Carrick as a batsman who "had a good all round game, he could score all round the wicket, he was a powerful hitter when the occasion demanded it."

Nixon was replaced in the attack by Billy Wilkinson. His figures were 9-0-35-0. Gibson continued to keep it tight from one end, at this point he had figures of 14-2-42-1.

It was clear that Seaton Burn were going to have to bowl Greenside out to win the game.

They couldn't force another breakthrough. An unbroken stand of 150 between Burdon and Carrick saw Greenside home comfortably with ten balls to spare.

Burdon finished with 65 not out. His innings contained nine fours.

Carrick was 72 not out. His innings had contained seven fours and two sixes.

Gibson bowled unchanged throughout the innings, finishing with figures of 24.2-3-83-1. Billy Wilkinson had 11-0-65-0.

Greenside won by 7 wickets.

Seaton Burn

D. Smart	Not	Out	126
R. Allan	C Clark	B P. Carrick	6
D. Gibson	C S. Stokoe	B D. Golightley	34
G. Stephenson	C Whittaker	B P. Carrick	9
W. Graham	Not	Out	21
Extras			16
Total			219-3 Wkts

P. Carrick 2-51   E. Bewick 0-11   M. Burdon 0-35   M. Whittaker 0-21
D. Golightley   S. Stokoe 0-33
  1-50

Greenside

S. Stokoe	C D. Smart	B D. Gibson	1
G. Kerry	Run	Out	30
D. Golightley	Run	Out	22
M. Burdon	Not	Out	65
P. Carrick	Not	Out	72
Extras			30
Total			220-3 Wkts

D. Gibson 1-83   D. Felton 0-19   G. Nixon 0-35   W. Wilkinson 0-65

Tyneside Senior League Final Table 1990
All teams played 26 games, there were no tied matches this year!

	WON 5PTS	WON 4PTS	LOST 1PT	LOST 0PTS	Drawn	Tied	PTS
Felling	12	9	1	2	2	0	99
Lintz	12	7	2	2	3	0	93
Blaydon	9	9	2	3	3	0	86
Swalwell	9	7	4	4	2	0	79
Greenside	9	5	3	5	4	0	72
Shotley Bridge	9	2	6	6	3	0	62
Sacriston	8	3	4	8	3	0	59
Annfield Plain	6	4	3	7	6	0	55
Consett	5	4	2	10	5	0	48
Ryton	4	4	8	6	4	0	48
Burnopfield	5	3	3	13	2	0	42
South Moor	5	1	4	12	4	0	37
Seaton Burn	3	2	13	8	0	0	36
Reyrolles	4	0	5	14	3	0	28

League Batting Averages 1990
Qualification 500 Runs

	Runs	High Score	Comp Inns	Average
S. Bhave (Ryton)	1141	133no	15	76.06
M. Lal (Felling)	892	95	12	74.33
W. Thomas (Blaydon)	1014	115no	18	56.33
P. Carrick (Greenside)	671	88	13	51.62
T. Cooley (Annfield Plain)	743	111no	15	49.50
G. Taylor (Swalwell)	760	96	16	47.50
D. Smart (Seaton Burn)	982	159no	21	46.76
D. Metcalfe (Sacriston)	753	82	20	37.65
G. Hunter (Consett)	522	107	14	37.28
P. Cameron (Lintz)	729	121	20	36.45
N. Hewison (Burnopfield)	767	143	22	34.86
W. Raja (Sacriston)	557	111	16	34.81
I. Somerville (Blaydon)	763	83no	22	34.68
C. Stephenson (Shotley Bridge)	638	115	20	31.90
C. Young (South Moor)	606	93	19	31.89
S. Lishman (Greenside)	539	72	17	31.70
S. Clennell (Lintz)	592	101no	19	31.15
D. Brown (Shotley Bridge)	596	62	20	29.80
T. Nichols (Burnopfield)	688	92	25	27.52
G. Clennell (Lintz)	588	102	23	25.56
P. Veitch (Blaydon)	603	69no	24	25.12
T. Peel (Sacriston)	523	74no	21	24.90
J. Dunn (Reyrolle)	531	61	22	24.13

League Bowling Averages 1990
Qualification 50 Wickets

	Overs	Runs	Wkts	Ave
M. Lal (Felling)	401	905	77	11.75
R. Cook (Lintz)	314	892	69	12.92
W. Thomas (Blaydon)	363	1033	75	13.77
D. Brown (Shotley Bridge)	418	1055	76	13.88
C. Pleasants (Felling)	497	1211	86	14.08
W. Raja (Sacriston)	356	929	64	14.51
G. Clennell (Lintz)	351	859	58	14.80
F. Hilton (Sacriston)	205	757	51	14.87
R. Bainbridge (Annfield Plain)	302	760	50	15.20
M. Urwin (Swalwell)	258	875	56	15.62
A. Dumighan (Swalwell)	336	942	55	17.12
C. Young (South Moor)	284	997	53	18.81
D. Sweeney (Burnopfield)	355	1014	51	19.88

CHAPTER 15

BURNOPFIELD

On Sunday 5th May 1991 Seaton Burn played at Bill Quay in a Tyneside Charity Bowl match. Smartie added another century to his list scoring 101 out of a Seaton Burn total of 143-4. His innings contained eleven fours and six sixes. Bill Quay were 126 all out in reply. Opener Jeff Tudor made 45 and Graeme Nixon with 4-51 and David Felton 4-53 led the Seaton Burn bowlers.

On Saturday 10th August 1991 Seaton Burn played an away league match at Burnopfield.

No scorebook available for this game so the details are from Smartie's records and local media.

Once again Dave Sweeney has provided me with information about the Burnopfield players and again we shall look at the players who haven't been mentioned in previous games.

Last season Burnopfield had finished 11th in the league. Neil Hewison, 767 runs at an average of 34.86 and Tommy Nichols, 688 runs at an average of 27.52 had made the batting averages. Dave Sweeney had once again made the league bowling averages, 51 wickets at an average of 19.88 each.

Burnopfield were to finish the league in ninth position at the end of this season. Only Dave Sweeney would make the league averages this season, with 67 wickets at 22.10 each.

Burnopfield batted first. They must have soon been in trouble as their first four batsman were all out for single figures.

The bowling for Seaton Burn was opened by Graeme Nixon and Andrew White. This is the first time White features in the book and would have been very early in his cricket career. A slow/medium right arm bowler, relying on accuracy and movement to take his wickets, incredible to think, now in 2020, 30 years later, he is first team captain and still taking wickets.

Kevin Corby describes White as being "at the other end of the spectrum (from David Felton) regarding his pace, pitching the ball on the spot regularly, at a pace a lot of batsman felt uncomfortable with."

Cade Brown, who had played three seasons as "Whitey" had started out in the first team remembers him as "a man of the highest integrity, passion, spirit and tenacity. Whitey was, and last time I checked the internet, remains, one of the most respected cricketers in the north east and a genuine icon of the club. Andrew by his own admission, wasn't one that we reflect on as a player who could have been on the pro circuit but a better team man and a genuine guy you simply wouldn't find. He was hard to face, just enough swing complemented his enormous guile and patience as a medium pace bowler. The struggles of even the best players in the north east were validated annually if you had to face him in the single wicket.

Many great players thought they could get on top of "Whitey," not many of them did, and the cheeky grin on the face after removing a Somerville, a Veitch or an Armstrong, was a sight that gave our team a huge lift.

A punt, a pint, whatever the social occasion, he was there, always with outstanding banter. Andrew White would be in the all time great human eleven, probably as captain!"

Paul Allen was a hard hitting batsman and useful wicketkeeper, was top of the order. He was one of six Allen brothers who had started their cricket journey at North Durham C.C. Two of the brothers, Keith and Graeme also played at Burnopfield, alongside Dave Sweeney. He was bowled by Graeme Nixon for 3.

Fellow opener, Michael Fishwick was a Western Australian and club professional. He also played as a pro at North Durham, South Shields, Whickham and Kimblesworth. He was a stylish batsman, twice while at Whickham he scored 1,000 runs in a season. He still coaches cricket at Durham School. He was bowled by Nixon for a duck.

Micky Small batting three, had a rare failure as he was caught by Gary Stephenson, for a single off the bowling of White.

Captain Tommy Nichols batted at four. He had made the league averages the previous season. He also had an off day as he was caught by Gary Stephenson off the bowling of Nixon for nought.

Neil Hewison batted at five. He had another excellent season last season. He set about repairing the damage, scoring 27 before he was also bowled by Nixon.

David Baxter was another who could be described as hard hitting. He was also a useful swing bowler and an excellent gully fielder. A Burnopfield lad, who prior to the pandemic was still playing for Annfield Plain First Team. He had scored his maiden first team hundred against Annfield Plain using Dave Sweeney's borrowed SS Turbo bat!

Baxter batted at six and he scored 37 as the Burnopfield middle order rallied a bit. He was caught by Billy Wilkinson off the bowling of Graeme Nixon.

Gregg Peacock was at number seven. Another Burnopfield lad who followed his dad, Jack, as a player for the club. Jack is still Club President. Gregg was a stylish left handed bat and a more than useful slow left arm bowler. He was also another excellent fielder. His cricket career was curtailed as he became a successful businessman, travelling all over the world. So much so he met his wife, Cheryl, in Singapore! He now lives in Canary Wharf in London with Cheryl and their daughter, but he often returns to Burnopfield Cricket Club when in the area visiting his mum and dad.

He scored 2 before Nixon trapped him LBW to give him his fifth wicket.

Keith Allen batting eight with 26 pushed the Burnopfield score on, before he was caught by Peter Ahmed off the bowling of Nixon. Allen was the second of the cricketing family. He was a successful slow left arm bowler and a steady, if dour, batsman. As well as Burnopfield he also played at North Durham and Ryton. He is now a highly respected umpire.

Number nine, Dave Sweeney top scored the innings with 38, he was the last wicket to fall, bowled by Billy Wilkinson. Dave described himself much earlier in the piece, but it should not be forgotten that he did score a hundred in second team cricket so he was a more than useful number nine.

Numbers ten and eleven, Dominic Quinn 4 not out and Graham Heppell 13 not out, ensured Burnopfield got their batting point.

Quinn was a good, "skiddy" medium quick bowler, another who hit the ball hard when batting. He enjoyed success at both first and second team level. He played at both Burnopfield and Consett, with his brothers, Joe and John.

Heppell was a prodigous swing bowler. Early on in his career he only swung the ball one way and could struggle to bowl a straight ball. He was hugely succesful in second team cricket, eventually making his mark in the first team. Dave Sweeney can remember him taking 9 wickets at Annfield Plain one evening in a first team cup match against a strong batting line up.

With 38 extras Burnopfield scored 189 for 9 off their 50 overs.

Only 3 bowlers were used, Graeme Nixon 6-65, Andrew White 2-71, and Billy Wilkinson 1-31.

Smartie opened the batting with Gary Stephenson. When available Stephenson was a regular opening partner for Smartie.

Burnopfield opened the bowling with Dave Sweeney and Graham Heppell.

Sweeney made the initial breakthrough, having Stephenson caught by Allen for 14.

The right handed Graeme Dakers came in at three, he would go on to be yet another opening partner for Smartie in due course. He would also go on to have some success at Benwell and Walbottle as an opening bat.

I used to enjoy watching Dakers bat, he had a very laid back, almost horizontal manner about him, but he was an excellent timer of the cricket ball and was a graceful driver.

Today he had scored 17 when Heppell caught him off the bowling of Small.

Left hander Richie Allen batted at four, he was another opening partner for Smartie at one time, today he had scored 5 when Baxter caught him off the bowling of Small.

This brought your author, Steve Graham, to the crease at five. I can remember being in the middle when Smartie reached one of his hundreds, I'm pretty sure it was this game. I scored a creditable 24 before I became a part of Burnopfield history.

Tommy Nichols was renowned across the league and beyond as a batsman, there is a rumour that he only ever took one first team wicket......yes, that's right, he bowled me!

Pervaiz Ahmed, known to all as Peter, batted at six, scoring nought not out. Ahmed was a good wicketkeeper and would, on a number of occasions, prove to be a reliable opening batsman.

There were 13 extras in the innings.

Smartie was 117 not out. He had scored fifteen fours and five sixes in his innings. Burnopfield was not among the bigger grounds in the league and it would have been a hard shift bowling to Smartie on this ground in this kind of form.

Burnopfield had used seven bowlers to try and dislodge him.

Seaton Burn won by six wickets.

Burnopfield

P. Allen		B G. Nixon	3
M. Fishwick		B G. Nixon	0
M. Small	C G. Stephenson	B A. White	1
T. Nichols	C G. Stephenson	B G. Nixon	0
N. Hewison	C W. Wilkinson	B G. Nixon	27
D. Baxter	C W. Wilkinson	B A. White	37
G. Peacock		LBW B G. Nixon	2
K. Allen	C P. Ahmed	B G. Nixon	26
D. Sweeney		B W. Wilkinson	38
D. Quinn	Not	Out	4
G. Heppell	Not	Out	13
Extras			38
Total			189-9 Wkts

G. Nixon	A. White	W. Wilkinson
6-65	2-71	1-31

Seaton Burn

D. Smart	Not	Out	117
G. Stephenson	C P. Allen	B D. Sweeney	14
G. Dakers	C G.Heppell	B M. Small	17
R. Allan	C D. Baxter	B M. Small	5
S. Graham		B T. Nichols	24
P. Ahmed	Not	Out	0
Extras			13
Total			190-4 Wkts

D. Sweeney 1-32	G. Heppell 0-47	M. Small 2-23	K. Allen 0-42
G. Peacock 0-17	D. Quinn 0-16	T. Nichols 1-1	

Tyneside Senior League Final Table 1991

All teams play 26 matches and there were no tied games this season

	WON 5PTS	WON 4PTS	LOST 1PT	LOST 0PTS	Drawn	Tied	PTS
Felling	10	11	0	2	3	0	97
Shotley Bridge	11	8	2	3	2	0	91
Blaydon	8	9	6	1	2	0	84
South Moor	8	6	6	3	3	0	73
Sacriston	8	6	3	5	4	0	71
Lintz	7	7	5	5	2	0	70
Annfield Plain	7	6	2	8	3	0	64
Consett	7	4	7	5	3	0	61
Burnopfield	4	5	9	4	3	0	52
Swalwell	6	2	6	8	4	0	48
Ryton	4	5	3	11	3	0	46
Greenside	4	3	10	6	3	0	45
Seaton Burn	1	1	13	8	3	0	25
Reyrolles	1	2	3	16	4	0	20

League Batting Averages 1991
Qualification 500 Runs

	Runs	High Score	Comp Inns	Average
W. Thomas (Blaydon)	1165	215no	14	83.20
M. Lal (Felling)	834	102	12	69.50
S. Bhave (Ryton)	1087	117	21	51.80
S. Stokoe (Greenside)	895	107no	18	49.70
R. Marshall (Blaydon)	739	126	16	46.20
D. Thomas (South Moor)	966	184	21	46.00
D. Jackson (Annfield Plain)	1007	140	22	45.80
G. Corcoran (Reyrolle)	789	133no	18	43.80
G. Clennell (Lintz)	831	104	19	43.70
D. Smart (Seaton Burn)	849	117no	22	38.60
T. Peel (Sacriston)	728	86no	21	34.70
C. Albone (South Moor)	655	122	21	31.20
P. Shield (South Moor)	655	113	21	31.20

League Bowling Averages 1991
Qualification 50 Wickets

	Overs	Runs	Wkts	Ave
D. Brown (Shotley Bridge)	394	970	79	12.30
M. Lal (Felling)	381	878	71	12.40
S. Wilkinson (Shotley Bridge)	333	721	54	13.40
D. Thomas (South Moor)	381	1072	79	13.60
W. Thomas (Blaydon)	399	1119	81	13.80
N. Robinson (Blaydon)	330	1010	63	16.00
C. Pleasants (Felling)	413	1143	70	16.30
Dam Mccabe (Consett)	240	828	50	16.56
R. Cook (Lintz)	359	1036	53	19.50
D. Sweeney (Burnopfield)	458	1483	67	22.10

CHAPTER 16

REYROLLE

On Saturday 25th July 1992 Seaton Burn played a home league fixture against Reyrolle. Reyrolle had finished bottom of the league the previous season, with Seaton Burn second bottom. Gavin Corcoran had featured in the league batting averages with 789 runs at 43.80.

No scorebook available this time, so information is very basic, coming from scorecard only.

Long time Reyrolle player John Trotter and former Reyrolle and long time Seaton Burn player Jason Brown have kindly provided some information on the Reyrolle players.

Trotter was a right handed batsman and occasional wicketkeeper and off spin bowler. He first played cricket for Leslie's aged 15 back in the sixties, where his captain was Jack Chapman. He retired from playing aged 54 and became an umpire. He loved, and still loves his cricket. He recalls that all of the years he played he won "nowt." Finishing league runners up twice with both Leslie's and Reyrolles was as close as he came.

In 1965 he topped the Tyneside Senior League Batting Averages.

Aged 17 he scored his first hundred against Burnopfield. Colin Milburn's father Jack, was captain of Burnopfield that day and congratulated the young John Trotter on his achievement.

He also recalls taking a "five for" with his casual off spin against Ryton one day. He did bowl more when he played second team cricket. He describes himself as a very determined batsman, he never gave his wicket away, giving 100% every time he played. I remember playing second team cricket against John back in the day, this is exactly how I remember him too.

In his prime he was a good enough batsman to be selected for the league representative side at a time when they had plenty of good cricketers to choose from.

Chris Cox, describing Reyrolle earlier remembers John Trotter well, he recalls him as "the character of the team. He was an excellent wicketkeeper and forceful right hand batsman. His slight build hid an ability to smash the ball to all corners. A truly magnificent hitter!"

Jason Brown started as a junior and played a handful of second team games at South Shields. He was a right handed batsman, usually opening the batting. When he was around 21 a friend went to play for Hebburn, Jason went with him.

He says "I often got 20 or 30 and then got myself out without ever pushing on and getting the 50's that were required. I remember playing a game for Hebburn against Seaton Burn and Sheldon Fawkes and I both scored 15 or 20 each out of a total of 70 or 80.

This was in 1996 and Alan Francis somehow got wind of the fact that I was moving to Gosforth and Sheldon was there already, so it was a no brainer to move to Seaton Burn."

Jason was still playing for Seaton Burn during the pandemic season of 2020 and I saw him score an excellent 50 in one of those games.

Sheldon Fawkes emigrated to Australia within two or three years of joining the club.

Seaton Burn batted first, Smartie opening the batting with Richie Allan. Allan was now an international cricketer having represented his country in a winter tour of Australia with the British Deaf Cricket Team.

There are no bowling statistics available.

The facts of the matter, as basic as they are, Seaton Burn scored 246 for the loss of 1 wicket. Allan was caught by Michael Collins off the bowling of Kevin Hughes for 47.

Jason Brown remembers Hughes as "a right arm fast/medium paced bowler. He would invariably come on as first change but did on occasion, open the bowling. He was one of those bowlers who could take a few wickets with one or two "five fors" per season but he could go for a few as well and get himself frustrated.

As a batter he would go in around number six, he was a hitter from ball one and would never hang around with the bat. He would either get a first baller or a quick fire 30 or 40! He always played first team cricket."

Wicketkeeper Kevin Corby batted at three, scoring 13 not out.

There were 20 extras in the innings.

Smartie was 168 not out. Nothing else is known regarding the innings.

Peter Mcmahon and T.Mcpherson opened the batting for Reyrolle.

John Trotter recalls that Mcmahon didn't play much cricket. He was a left handed opening bat.

Mcmahon was a school teacher at a school in Blaydon. Trotter remembers a game when Reyrolle were playing at Blaydon and Trotter was batting. He was still there as the innings was coming to a close, facing the last over. Despite his best efforts he couldn't score a run off the first five balls of the over, he then hit the last ball for six. The next time he saw Mcmahon he told John that he knew how he had hit the last ball of the innings for six a week earlier. It turns out the young lad scoring for Blaydon that day was a pupil in Mcmahon's class and been so impressed he wrote a story about it!

Alan Francis and Graeme Nixon opened the bowling for Seaton Burn.

Francis, known to all as "Frankie," is believed to be the first professional Seaton Burn had engaged. A right arm fast bowler who the club persuaded to leave Kirkley to turn professional. He always gave his all whenever he was asked to bowl and was a very capable performer at this level. Kevin Corby describes "Frankie" as "a fine fast bowler and an outright team player."

On 21st August 1993 Francis took 9-20 against Burnopfield as they were dismissed for 35. They only had ten men, denying him the chance of all ten wickets.

I recall one of his early indoor nets at the club, I hardly knew him at the time, when I batted he bowled me a bouncer, the ball pitching "off the mat." I evaded it, but remembered it, I had my own little rule at that time, as did many fast bowlers... "if you give me one bouncer, you get two back!"

I was nowhere near the pace of "Frankie," but I was quick enough to be considered a fast bowler at second team standards of the day. "Frankie" it turned out, was at best, a lower order second team batsman. The second bouncer I bowled him "off the mat" hit him in the shoulder, it certainly hurt him as the bat was thrown down and the air turned blue!

Every time I have seen him over the intervening years he has mentioned it to me. Most recently in December 2019 I was at The George Stephenson Pub in Westmoor for the annual "Heart Attack Club Xmas Party." Who should wander in, totally at random, but "Frankie." After a brief chat and introductions to my company made, "Frankie" says to me "You, You so and so, I still haven't forgotten when you hit me in the nets!" A good hour of reminiscing and chat later and he headed off, he hadn't changed one bit in the years inbetween. It was good to see him.

The Reyrolle innings was soon in trouble.

Not neccessarily in the order the wickets fell.

Top of the innings was Peter Mcmahon, he was caught behind the wicket by Kevin Corby off the bowling of Graeme Nixon for 4.

Ian Somerville, the Blaydon Legend, remembers the wicketkeeping of Kevin Corby well. "He was possibly the best wicketkeeper I ever played against. I recall playing against Tynedale, I hadn't got off the mark yet, and I got a bat on one from Courtney Walsh, I thought it was going for four through third slip, that's where Corby caught me, third slip.........the thing was, he was keeping wicket!"

Cade Brown, who played with the bowler, Graeme Nixon, a little later in his career describes Nixon as "a terrific player and a great guy to have on your side. He was a competitor to the final ball was bowled and this shone through in the league and cup matches.

If you drew him in the single wicket competition you were always guaranteed a good tussle! He was a genuine all rounder who could open the bowling or bat in the top five, he was also a fantastic fielder which was important as we had a few who weren't!

He could always do something special to pull us out of a hole and he often did this, in particular with the bat when we were well behind in a run chase. He also lifted the average price of clothing in our side and could be relied on for shower gel!"

Fellow opener, T.Mcpherson was bowled by Francis for nought.

Harry Greaves, batting at three, scored 27 before he was caught and bowled by Nixon.

Athough he didn't play with him, Jason Brown recalls that Greaves was a left arm spin bowler but can remember nothing else!

Michael Collins batted at four and became the second duck of the innings when he was caught by Steve Hope of the bowling of Francis.

Jason Brown's memory of Collins is one of "a left handed batsman, a really good batsman actually, he was the one on the team who you hope too, expected too, score some runs for you. If he didn't the likelihood was we as a team wouldn't score many.

He was also a decent left arm spinner, he would give you a few good overs. I don't recall him being a great wicket taker but he would always chip in with a few. He was definately a first team cricketer in terms of ability."

Eddie Cavelle batted at five and he top scored the innings with 29 before he was also caught by Steve Hope off the bowling of Francis.

Kevin Hughes came in at six and he scored 17 before he was bowled by Francis.

B.Scott was batting at number seven, he made 10 before he was bowled by David Felton.

Felton would have been a teenager around this time, probably 17, a right arm fast bowler, capable of moving the ball off the pitch, even at this stage of his cricket career he could be a handful.

Kevin Corby describes Felton as "a talented seam bowler and on his good days, when he got into a rythm, he could bowl quite quickly, with the bat he could also hit the ball hard, as many a lower order batsman do!"

Cade Brown, who played with him a couple of seasons later said of Felton "the lad could play. His bowling was unbelievable in my middle season (1996) and was the equal of any professional in the league. When he had his rythmn right he was genuinely quick and would always hit high on the bat. He could swing the ball away and you always knew you were in the game at second slip. He was another one who liked to take on the big names from around the league and his banter with umpires and the opposition were almost Australian!

He had an amazing sense of humour off the field as well, there was also always a reason why his horse had finished just outside those offering a return for our money!

You could always count on Felton as a team mate, he always gave 100% effort for 100% of the time. He was a great friend of mine and his family were amazing and it was no surprise to me how successful he became in his chosen career."

Felton also took the wicket of batsman number eight, A.Powell LBW for 10.

S.Ruddock batted at nine, he was out for 15, caught and bowled by Francis.

R.Neve batting at number ten was 1 not out. Jason Brown is pretty sure this would be Alan Neve, known to all, even year's later as Rocky. Brown recalls "He was the sort of cricketer who used to fill in a lot of the time, but he did play at Hebburn nearly every week. he would keep wicket and bat in the bottom two most weeks. He was also groundsman and would go on to become an umpire. His son Johnny also played for Hebburn."

Last man, S.Hill, was bowled by Felton for nought.

9 extras in the innings.

Reyrolle 112 all out.

Francis had 5-38, Nixon 2-44 and Felton 3-26.

Seaton Burn won by 134 runs.

Seaton Burn

D. Smart	Not	Out	168
R. Allan	C M. Collins	B K. Hughes	47
K. Corby	Not	Out	13
Extras			20
Total			246-1 Wkt

Reyrolle

P. Mcmahon	C K. Corby	B G. Nixon	4
T. Mcpherson		B A. Francis	0
N. Greaves	C & B	A. Francis	22
M. Collins	C S. Hope	B A. Francis	0
E. Cavelle	C S. Hope	B A. Francis	29
K. Hughes		B A. Francis	17
B. Scott		B D. Felton	10
A. Powell		LBW B D. Felton	10
S. Ruddock	C & B	A. Francis	15
R. Neve	Not	Out	1
S. Hill		B D. Felton	0
Extras			9
Total			112-All Out

A. Francis 5-38   G. Nixon 2-44   D. Felton 3-26

Tyneside Senior League Table 1992
For the record, Whickham replaced Felling this season.

	WON 5PTS	WON 4PTS	LOST 1PT	LOST 0PTS	Drawn	Tied	PTS
Shotley Bridge	7	12	1	2	4	0	88
Lintz	11	6	3	1	5	0	87
Sacriston	11	4	1	5	4	1	78 1/2
Blaydon	6	9	3	2	5	1	78 1/2
Greenside	8	5	5	2	6	0	71
Swalwell	8	4	5	4	5	0	66
Consett	4	7	7	2	6	0	61
South Moor	7	3	4	4	8	0	59
Burnopfield	4	4	10	1	6	1	54 1/2
Seaton Burn	7	2	5	7	4	1	54 1/2
Whickham	3	4	3	11	5	0	39
Ryton	4	0	3	13	6	0	29
Annfield Plain	3	0	6	11	6	0	27
Reyrolles	0	0	4	18	4	0	8

League Batting Averages 1992
Qualification 500 Runs

	Runs	High Score	Comp Inns	Average
S. Russell (Sacriston)	1330	201	19	70.00
C. Albone (South Moor)	678	111	11	61.63
D. Smart (Seaton Burn)	1080	168no	21	51.42
R. Stokoe (Greenside)	611	80no	12	50.91
D. Brown (Shotley Bridge)	588	114	12	49.00
D. Metcalfe (Sacriston)	950	131	20	47.50
M. Fishwick (Burnopfield)	892	125no	19	46.94
P. Veitch (Blaydon)	951	120	21	45.28
W. Thomas (Blaydon)	724	89	16	45.25
G. Clennell (Lintz)	769	104no	17	45.24
D. Thomas (South Moor)	612	111	15	40.80
G. Hunter (Consett)	685	88	18	38.05
K. Corby (Seaton Burn)	670	101	18	37.22
S. Stokoe (Greenside)	515	86no	15	34.33
G. Baker (Lintz)	613	100	19	32.26
I. Somerville (Blaydon)	654	111no	21	31.14
N. Burdon (Shotley Bridge)	543	71	19	26.68
P. Dumighan (Swalwell)	507	81	19	26.68
C. Stephenson (Shotley Bridge)	549	75	23	23.86

League Bowling Averages 1992
Qualification 50 Wickets

	Overs	Runs	Wkts	Ave
F. Hilton (Sacriston)	333	700	56	12.50
D. Thomas (South Moor)	378	963	74	13.01
S. Russell (Sacriston)	413	1032	78	13.23
D. Brown (Shotley Bridge)	391	1013	76	13.32
A. Donnelly (Swalwell)	229	776	58	13.37
G. Clennell (Lintz)	374	1038	76	13.65
G. Steadman (Consett)	228	710	51	13.92
P. Carrick (Greenside)	310	983	67	14.67
D. Nevin (Lintz)	310	861	58	14.84
D. Felton (Seaton Burn)	267	799	50	15.98
W. Thomas (Blaydon)	280	863	51	16.92
I. Reid (Whickham)	317	974	52	18.73
A. Francis (SeatonBurn)	300	984	50	19.68
M. Urwin (Whickham)	380	1151	53	21.71
D. Sweeney (Burnopfield)	388	1273	57	22.33

CHAPTER 17

BURNOPFIELD

On Saturday 5th June 1993 Seaton Burn played a home league fixture against Burnopfield. Last season Burnopfield had finished ninth and Seaton Burn tenth.

Only Michael Fishwick, Club Pro last year, had featured in the league batting averages. He was plying his trade elsewhere this year, replaced by Paul Carrick.

Both Smartie, 1080 runs at an average of 51.82, and Kevin Corby, 670 runs at an average of 37.22, had featured for Seaton Burn.

Smartie had already shown a liking for Burnopfield, having scored his unbeaten double hundred and scores of 155 not out and 117 not out against them previously.

The Burnopfield team of today had four players who had played the day Smartie scored his 201, Neil Hewison, Tommy Nichols, Mickey Small and Dave Sweeney. In fact of these four, only Sweeney, who missed the 155 in 1986, hadn't played in all four games in which Smartie would score centuries against Burnopfield.

Once again Dave Sweeney has filled in the gaps with the Burnopfield players who haven't featured previously.

Only one umpire for the day, Ralph Nevin.

Burnopfield won the toss and elected to bat first. The innings commenced at 1.58pm and the batting was opened by Neil Hewison and Gregg Peacock.

Seaton Burn opened the bowling with Alan Francis and Andrew White.

Burnopfield made a slow start, after six overs they were eleven without loss. With the first ball of the seventh over, Kevin Corby caught Peacock behind the wicket off the bowling of Francis.

Robin Adams came to the crease at three. He was a native of Cumbria who came to play at Burnopfield whilst working in the north east. He was tall and elegant, usually an opening bat, he was succesful in his time with the club. He was a popular member of the team and when he returned to Cumbria he enjoyed further cricket success with Barrow Cricket Club.

The batsmen found it tough going, after fifteen overs Burnopfield were 24 for 1.

The last ball of the sixteenth over saw White bowl Hewison for 22.

Burnopfield 28 for 2 off 16 overs.

David Baxter batted at four.

Two more runs were added when Baxter was caught by David Felton off the bowling of White for a single.

Burnopfield 30 for 3 off 18 overs.

Tommy Nichols was next up. A long term Burnopfield legend and captain, he was well respected throughout the league, but today wasn't his day, he was bowled by Francis for 2.

Burnopfield now 39 for 4 from 21.4 overs.

This brought Paul Carrick to the crease. He has previously contributed to this book in respect of Greenside and has been well covered there. I think the phrase I used was "regularly a thorn in our side with bat or ball."

Dave Sweeney remembers Carrick as "a very good club cricketer, with bat and ball. He could bowl a lively pace and was a steady accumulator of runs. He was club professional this season and to this day remains involved with cricket, as the Director of Cricket at Gateshead Fell."

A bowling change was made after Francis had bowled 14 overs, his figures were 14-2-29-2. He was replaced by David Felton.

Carrick and Adams added 88 for the fifth wicket, Carrick started steadily, playing himself in and then accelerating towards the end of the innings as he got his eye in.

Adams scored 52, his only boundary being a six he hit off the bowling of White to bring up his fifty. He was caught by Graeme Dakers off the bowling of White the ball after reaching his fifty.

Burnopfield 127 for 5 off 42.2 overs.

Scott Hall batted at seven. "His family had a long association with the club. He and his brother, Damon, both came through the junior ranks to senior cricket. He was a powerful batsman and excellent fielder. His son's Lewis and Lloyd are both playing members of Burnopfield. Work commitments later curtailed his cricket and he has just retired as Assistant Chief Constable of Northumbria Police."

Hall played sensibly, scoring only in one's and two's as he supported Carrick and the pair added a further 32 for the sixth wicket.

Carrick was out from the second ball of the last over, he was caught by Shaun Stone off the bowling of Felton for 65. His innings had included eight fours.

Micky Small came in at eight and scored two not out.

Hall was unbeaten on 17.

The unused batsmen were Dave Sweeney, Ian Archbold and Keith Allen. Sweeney and Allen have already been covered elsewhere in the book.

Sweeney recalls "Ian Archbold is one of the most recognised players in the TSL and N & TSL. A wicketkeeper of the highest calibre who was highly successful at both Burnopfield and Shotley Bridge, where he still plays. A shy, quiet, retiring character he is NOT!"

Burnopfield posted a score of 166 for the loss of 6 wickets from their 50 overs, with 4 extras in the innings.

Felton had finished with 11-0-41-1.

White had bowled unchanged throughout the innings, 25-3-94-3.

At 4.53pm Smartie opened the Seaton Burn innings with John Graham.

Paul Carrick and Dave Sweeney opened the bowling for Burnopfield.

It didn't take long for the first wicket to fall, Graham was bowled for a duck by Carrick with the first ball of the third over.

Seaton Burn 9 for 1.

This brought wicketkeeper and Club Chairman, Kevin Corby to the crease to bat with his brother in law, Smartie.

Smartie, Corby and Stewart Nixon had married three sisters! Elder sister Sylvia had married Stewart, middle sister Gillian had married Smartie and youngster Julie had married Kevin!

Carrick was replaced by Keith Allen after he had bowled nine overs, 9-2-24-1.

Sweeney was replaced by Micky Small after he had bowled ten overs, 10-1-34-0

A stand of 87 was ended when Allen bowled Corby for 40.

Seaton Burn were 96 for 2 from 20.4 overs.

Graeme Dakers batted at four today.

Small was taken off after bowling just three overs, 0-16 and replaced by Peacock.

Dakers made 5 out of a stand of 33 for the third wicket before he was stumped by Archbold off the bowling of Peacock.

Seaton Burn 129 for 3 from 33.2 overs.

New batsman Steve Hope and Smartie got the scores level before the next wicket fell. Smartie was bowled by Peacock for 104.

His innings had taken 117 balls in 122 minutes. His fifty coming from 87 balls and the hundred from 114 balls. He had struck eight fours and seven sixes in the innings.

Bill Graham came to the wicket at six, he faced one ball for his nought not out.

With the second ball of the 41st over Hope hit a two off the bowling of Allen and Seaton Burn had won by six wickets with nearly ten overs to spare.

Allen finished with 11.2 -1-39-1 and Peacock with 7-0-48-2.

The innings had contained six extras.

Burnopfield

N. Hewison		B A. White	22
G. Peacock	C K. Corby	B A. Francis	1
R. Adams	C G. Dakers	B A. White	52
D. Baxter	C D. Felton	B A. White	1
T. Nichols		B A. Francis	1
P. Carrick	C S. Stone	B D. Felton	65
S. Hall	Not	Out	17
M. Small	Not	Out	2
Extras			4
Total			166-6 Wkts

A. Francis 2-49   A. White 3-94   D. Felton 1-41

Seaton Burn

D. Smart		B G. Peacock	104
J. Graham		B P. Carrick	0
K. Corby		B K. Allen	40
G. Dakers	St I. Archbold	B G. Peacock	5
S. Hope	Not	Out	10
W. Graham	Not	Out	0
Extras			9
Total			168-4 Wkts

P. Carrick 1-24   D. Sweeney 0-34   K. Allen 1-39   M. Small 0-16
G. Peacock 2-48

SBCC 1993
BACK ROW-Davie Gibson,David Felton,David Hope,Keith Ashforth,
Marcus Gilmore,David Smart,Andrew White,Peter Rippingale,Gary
Stephenson, Stephen Felton,Steve Graham,Graeme Dakers, Alistair Crease
FRONT ROW-Michael Dancer,Graeme Nixon,Bill Graham,Edgar Ridley,
Ray Cardwell, Paul Renton,Richie Allan

Tyneside Senior League Final Table 1993

For the record, Reyrolles had a name change to Hebburn for this season.

All teams play 26 matches and there were no tied games this season.

	WON 5PTS	WON 4PTS	LOST 1PT	LOST 0PTS	Drawn	Tied	PTS
Sacriston	12	12	1	1	0	0	109
Shotley Bridge	13	11	0	2	0	0	109
South Moor	10	7	3	5	1	0	82
Swalwell	9	7	6	4	0	0	79
Blaydon	3	15	1	6	1	0	77
Lintz	8	6	7	3	2	0	73
Consett	6	4	12	3	1	0	59
Greenside	2	9	10	4	1	0	57
Seaton Burn	7	2	10	7	0	0	53
Burnopfield	3	7	9	7	0	0	52
Whickham	4	5	5	12	0	0	45
Ryton	5	2	11	8	0	0	44
Annfield Plain	3	2	8	11	2	0	33
Hebburn	3	1	6	16	0	0	25

League Batting Averages 1993
Qualification 500 Runs

	Runs	High Score	Comp Inns	Average
S. Russell (Sacriston)	1084	141	17	63.76
D. Nevin (Lintz)	797	113	13	61.63
D. Jackson (Consett)	1050	117	19	55.26
I. Somerville (Blaydon)	1202	152	24	50.08
C. Glassock (Annfield Plain)	1124	114	23	48.87
D. Thomas (South Moor)	1009	173	21	48.04
M. Fishwick (Whickham)	1053	127	22	47.86
P. Collingwood (Shotley Br)	846	105	18	47.00
N. Hewison (Burnopfield)	733	88	17	43.11
D. Metcalfe (Sacriston)	896	175	21	42.67
N. Burdon (Shotley Bridge)	680	108no	16	42.50
W. Thomas (Blaydon)	530	117no	14	37.86
S. Stokoe (Greenside)	707	96no	19	37.21
P. Veitch (Blaydon)	774	100no	23	33.65
P. Dumighan (Swalwell)	796	99no	24	33.17
A. Kelly (Ryton)	751	78	23	32.65
G. Baker (Lintz)	682	111	21	32.48
D. Smart (Seaton Burn)	743	104	24	30.96

League Bowling Averages 1993
Qualification 50 Wickets

	Overs	Runs	Wkts	Ave
D. Brown (Shotley Bridge)	411	930	89	10.45
D. Thomas (South Moor)	490	1307	108	12.10
S. Russell (Sacriston)	507	1193	98	12.17
F. Hilton (Sacriston)	278	752	61	12.33
Dom Mccabe (Swalwell)	483	1238	86	14.40
D. Nevin (Lintz)	399	1101	68	16.19
A. Francis (Seaton Burn)	365	1059	63	16.81
D. Jackson (Consett)	440	1202	70	17.17
G. Corcoran (Hebburn)	337	1046	50	22.3
P. Carrick (Burnopfield)	383	1243	55	22.60

CHAPTER 18

"WELCOME CADE BROWN"

On Saturday May 20th 1995 Seaton Burn played an away league fixture at Lintz. Lintz had finished 8th last season. Going into this game they were top of the league.

They had a number of outstanding performers that season. They had five players in the league batting averages in 1994. Derek Mcconnell had scored 501 runs at an average of 35.79, including two fifties, Gordon Baker had scored 707 runs at an average of 29.88, including two hundreds and three fifties, David Storey had scored 606 runs at an average of 27.55, including one century and four fifties, Graeme Clennell had scored 500 runs at 23.81, including five fifties and Stuart Clennell had scored 523 runs at an average of 23.77, including two half centuries.

As a bowling unit in 1994, spinner Michael Edmunds had taken 45 wickets at an average of 21.11 and Graeme Clennell had taken 35 wickets at an average of 28.14.

The Seaton Burn side from 1994 had finished ninth in the league. Graeme Hallam had been club professional. He had done well enough to feature in the league batting averages with 997 runs at an average of 55.39, with two centuries and nine fifties. If memory serves me right he had decided to pursue his studies and wasn't in a position to be engaged for this season.

Also in the league batting averages for 1994 were Kevin Corby, 696 runs at an average of 38.67 including six fifties, and John Graham, 565 runs at an average of 28.25, including five fifties.

The bowling strength of the team that year had been Alan Francis, now playing as an amateur, who took 32 wickets at an average of 22.44. In 1993 Francis had 63 wickets at 16.81 each.

Seaton Burn had engaged young Australian Cade Brown as professional this season.

Cade recalls walking into the "Drift" to meet the club members and being told that they were expecting a six foot four blonde surfer. In his own words he was "clearly none of that."

I remember seeing the 18 year old Cade for the first time at a Tuesday net practise. He was small, slim built, quietly spoken and had a seemingly shy persona.

Then he went into bat for a net, it was obvious from the start he was something special, left handed, he always had plenty of time to see the ball and was an incredible timer of his strokes, he never seemed to hit the ball hard, but it still flew off the bat!

Cade's first season at Seaton Burn had been organised by Kelvin Williams through Kevin Corby. When he first got here he says he couldn't understand a word anyone said.

He came straight from an Aussie summer into a north east spring and he says the weather really knocked him around for the first month.

I also recall his first home game of the season, it was probably the first game of the season, and it was a horrible day with biting cold winds. Seaton Burn is a big field and it is relatively open, so it can be cold on a windy day.

Just to give those from outside the area an idea of how variable the north east weather is in spring, the first game of the 1981 season was scheduled for 25th April. Unfortunately Seaton Burn Welfare was under five inches of snow that day and the whole league programme was cancelled.

A couple of seasons earlier we had been given sponsored tracksuit tops, mine had never fitted me properly and I remember feeling sorry for Cade, sitting shivering in the corner of the dressing room, so I gave him my tracksuit top.

Brown says that although the weather was cold he found the people of the north east unbelievably warm. He had a Sunday dinner each week for the first month. Edgar Ridley took him along to a church service and Cade became a regular drinking with the Sunday crew, led by Kevin Hunt and Ray Cardwell.

He also recalls regular forays on a Sunday whereby, after several hours in the pub, the local tradition of "walking the pipe" across The Burn was attempted, sometimes successfully, sometimes not!

The "pipe" is a sewage pipe that stretches across "The Burn", that is Seaton Burn. It's about 20 feet of steel pipe, about six feet in circumference and goes across the width of the water plus a bit extra.

It is located a few feet west of the bridge across the Old Great North Road. At this point the water can vary in depth from a few inches at the height of summer, to a couple of feet after a storm. The drop from the top of the pipe to the "bed" of The Burn would be about five feet.

After a few beers, generally on the walk home from the Drift, you had to walk across it. Those who were fleet of foot, like Davie Gibson, would run across, the more clumsy, such as me, would tread carefully!

The most infamous failed attempt was Alan Francis. He turned up on the doorstep of Richie Allan, dripping wet, covered in mud, asking for a hot shower and a change of clothes! His failure had been witnessed by Kevin Hunt and Andrew White, so news of it spread like wildfire!

When his first accomodation fell through, Cade says he felt the quality of the North East people was on show when the Felton family took him in. They immediately made him feel like family, something he still appreciates and feels grateful for all these years later.

The other thing that made a lasting impression on the teenage Cade Brown was the love the people had for Newcastle United. Andrew White took him to a game on a cold and rainy day and he couldn't believe the passion and impact that the team had on people.

Cade Brown would play 62 league innings for Seaton Burn from 1995 to 1997 inclusive. He would be not out in eight of those innings and score 2661 runs at an average of 49.28. That included four centuries with a best of 134 not out against Annfield Plain. In his first season he had the highest aggregate run total for the season, 1234, including two centuries and ten half centuries. Five of those half centuries were in the 90's, one of those was unbeaten.

When he arrived he had no idea of what to expect in terms of the cricket, in particular how the wickets would play. He will never forget playing against Dave Jackson, the old bull versus the young bull if he ever saw it. He couldn't believe there was no sledging and that everyone walked if they nicked it behind, this was completely foreign to the way he had been brought up to play in Australia.

Cade particularly enjoyed playing against the Durham players, Neil Killeen, Colin Campbell and Paul Collingwood. He still watches what they are doing now, even though they have completed their playing careers.

He loved the fact that you could have a guy filling in from the second team, batting at nine, not bowling, but having to face up to "a mad quick like West Indian Fred Redwood." The variation in ability was something he wasn't used to in Australia but he says it somehow added to the beauty of playing in the north east.

That said, he is of the opinion that some of the local players would have held their own in Australia. Players like Ian Somerville, Biffer Marshall, Davey Love, The Dumighan Brothers, Steve Humble, Paul Veitch and others, were all exceptional players and characters who made the whole north east cricketing experience something which Cade treasures to this day.

He enjoyed a fruitful opening partnership with John Graham. Between them these two contributed 53.50 % of the teams runs that season. In the final game of the season against Greenside the pair scored 206 for the opening partnership.

Cade describes John as "an amazing player, a leader from a young age and a great friend throughout and we remain in touch to this day. There are no surprises at my end at both the level and longevity of his success at South North. He was an unbelievable player on the on side, a ball on a fourth stump line could find itself racing to either the cover or the mid wicket fence. His achievements at such a young age were remarkable and it's Durham's loss that he had all that success with South North rather than them. He had a keen eye for the game at a young age and it was a pleasure to play in the same team as him and his father.

He was awesome to watch in the field, he had great hands and he would anticipate well in advance of the play taking place. He made a couple of memorable scores against quality attacks and loved facing the pro's and the Durham players.

He was also a leader off the field, there wasn't a nightclub where he wasn't a regular and I do recall paying a pound a pint on a Tuesday night at Planet Earth!"

John Graham left Seaton Burn in 1996 to join the Durham Academy.

Brown returned to the club for the 1997 Season, also being captain for the season. This was to be his last year at the club as he returned to Sydney at the end of the season to resume his studies. As well over 2500 runs he left the club with four centuries and nineteen half centuries to his name.

Once again Graeme Clennell has provided some information on his team mates of the day.

Lintz opened the innings with Gary Innes and James Murray.

Innes was also known as "Sniper." A left handed batsman who also came through from the Lintz junior system. Graeme Clennell states that he was "a very good batsman who left the Lintz far too early, he would go on to have a good career at several clubs."

Clennell also makes the observation that Gary Innes was one of the few who came through the juniors who would leave Lintz early in their cricket career.

One of the things that struck me when writing about Lintz was how many quality players had come through their junior system and how many one club players they had.

James Murray was a right handed opening batsman. Another product of Lintz juniors. Graeme Clennell describes a batsman who "favoured the front foor, a steady batsman who settled in to play the anchor role and allow the more flamboyant batsman to play their shots. He is the most unlikely farmer I can imagine but has great taste in music and my partner at music gigs."

Alan Francis and David Felton opened the bowling for Seaton Burn.

Innes took a single off the last ball of Francis's first over and the next two overs were maidens. Seaton Burn, with Francis bowling tightly had to wait until the tenth over before they got a breakthrough, Innes being bowled by Felton for 19 with the score on 28.

This brought Stuart Clennell to the crease batting at three. He and Murray took the score to 49 before Felton got a second wicket, Murray being caught by John Graham for 19.

Graeme Clennell came to the wicket batting at four.

After 18 overs Lintz were 49 for 2.

With the first ball of the next over Francis had Stuart Clennell caught by Smartie for 10.

After 18.1 overs Lintz were 49 for 3.

Derek Mcconnell batted at five. Graeme Clennell remembers Mcconnell as "Dr Leg!" He also remembers "a right handed batsman who had started as Greenside. He represented Durham at schoolboy level, a good middle order batsman. He was excellent in both the dressing room and the bar!"

After both opening bowlers had bowled eleven overs, a double bowling change was made. Francis whose last three overs had all been maidens and included a wicket, had 11-4-18-1 was replaced by Bill Graham.

Felton, 11-4-41-2, was replaced by Andrew White.

Lintz were now 60 for 3 from 22 overs.

Bill Graham's second ball was hit for four by Clennell.

After Mcconnell hit his first ball for four, White took his wicket with his second. He was caught by Smartie for 14.

Lintz now 68 for 4 from 23.2 overs.

The new batsman was Paul Alderson. He was also known as "Aldo." Graeme Clennell describes him as "a right handed batsman who had started his career at Burnhope. He had joined Lintz from Annfield Plain. He was an attacking batsman who played some important innings in his short stay for the club."

17 runs were scored from the next 27 balls, including a six and a four from the bat of Graeme Clennell as Lintz upped their pace.

White trapped Clennell L.B.W with the last ball of his third over for 16.

Lintz 83 for 5 from 28 overs.

Paul Cameron batted at seven today. He had opened the batting during Smartie's previous hundred against Lintz in 1987.

With the first ball of the 36th over, with the score on 105, Smartie caught Cameron off the bowling of White for 13.

The new batsman was Michael Edmunds. Graeme Clennell remembers Edmunds as "another who came through the Lintz juniors, a very dangerous middle to late order bat who rescued many seemingley lost games. He was one of the best cutters I've seen, scoring his runs quickly. He captained the side for a few years and then went on to become an umpire."

The score quickly became 109 for 7 from 36.4 overs when I caught Alderson off the bowling of Bill Graham.

The game appeared to be tipping in favour of Seaton Burn as two new batsman, Edmunds at eight and Wayne Greenwell at nine tried to turn the game round.

They did a pretty good job too.

After bowling the 40th over of the innings, White, 9-0-25-3, was replaced by David Felton.

Lintz were 123 for 7 off 40 overs.

After bowling the 41st over of the innings, Bill Graham, 10-1-37-1, was replaced by Alan Francis.

The next wicket fell with the score at 142 when Edmunds was bowled by Francis for 15. His innings had contained only one boundary and ten singles as he had methodically tried to get his team a score they could bowl at.

Lintz were now 142 for 8 off 46.3 overs.

Trevor Wilson came to the crease batting number ten. As a batsman Wilson liked to lean back and hit the ball over the covers, when batting he was "pleasing on the eye but could be a bit loose."

Wilson hit a six and a further two singles were taken from Francis's last over, the 49th of the innings.

Felton had Wilson caught by Graeme Nixon with the first ball of the last over for 11.

New batsman was William Johnson. He was another who had come through from the under 13 side. A right arm slow bowler, only an occasional bowler at this level, Graeme Clennell says "a buffet bowler, brought on to buy a wicket, he had many nicknames, Mossop, Moscrop and Beach Boy Billy amongst them, but he was a real gem in the dressing room, although often the butt of many a joke! He was also an all action batsman, he got the name "Beach Boy Billy" after batting one Saturday as if he was playing on a beach. He was a good club man and is now an umpire."

Five balls left in the Lintz innings, with Greenwell on strike as the batsman had crossed whilst the catch to take the last wicket had been taken.

The next three balls were all dot balls as no runs were scored.

Greenwell took two from the fifth ball of the over.

A single was scored from the last ball of the innings.

Greenwell was 26 not out, top score for the innings, every Lintz batsman apart from number eleven, Johnson, who hadn't faced a ball for his nought not out, had scored double figures!

The innings had contained six extras.

Lintz 162 for the loss of 9 wickets from their allotted 50 overs.

Cade Brown and John Graham opened the innings for Seaton Burn.

Lintz opened the bowling with Graeme Clennell and Wayne Greenwell.

Clennell had played in the game in 1987 when Smartie had scored an earlier hundred.

Wayne Greenwell had started his cricket journey at Leadgate. He was also known as "Claud" by the Lintz lads. He would later move to Consett and play in the game when Smartie got his last hundred. He married the daughter of former Lintz captain Ralph Nevin and moved into the village. He was a talented, medium paced bowler who was a real thinker and student of the game. He bowled an accurate nagging length and line. As a batsman Graeme Clennell says that Greenwell "was a very correct batsman, a real student of the game, he should have scored more runs than he did but I think his bowling restricted his batting. His son, Ross, would also play junior cricket at Lintz."

Clennell opened proceedings with a maiden, two singles were taken from Greenwell's opening over.

With the third ball of his second over Clennell bowled Cade Brown for a single. Seaton Burn 2 for 1.

Next ball that became 2 for 2 as Kevin Corby was L.B.W first ball to Clennell. That brought Smartie to the crease on the hat trick ball.

As he walked to the crease Smartie recalls hearing Clennell talking to a team mate "He's the last **** you want to see on a hat trick ball."

Smartie took a single to avoid the hat trick and get off the mark. After 3 overs Seaton Burn were 3 for 2.

Greenwell was replaced in the bowling attack after 7-0-19-0 by Trevor Wilson.

Wilson was another product of the club under 13 side. Graeme Clennell describes him as "the man with a thousand nicknames, Waigwa, Face and Loose amongst them. He was a really good swing bowler. He first burst onto the scene by bowling out a strong Philadelphia side and he continued on through the rest of the season with his late away swing. He lost his way a bit but continued to play at Lintz for 20 years. He had a strange sense of humour that went down well in the dressing room and he was at his best in the bar!"

His figures were 6-1-21-0. He was replaced by spinner Michael Edmonds.

The next wicket fell at 161.

It was Edmonds who got the breakthrough in the 48th over. After Smartie hit him for a four and a six, with the second last ball of the over, he had Smartie caught by Wilson for 106.

The innings had contained nine fours and four sixes.

Seaton Burn were 161 for 3 wickets with 13 balls left and requiring two to win.

Richie Allan came in batting at five.

John Graham took a single off the second ball of Graeme Clennell's 25th over and Allan took a single off the last ball of the 49th over to win the game.

John Graham had carried his bat through the innings and was 53 not out. His innings had contained six fours.

Graeme Clennell bowled unchanged for throughout the innings and finished with figures of 25-5-74-2.

Edmunds figures were 11-0-47-1

Seaton Burn had taken 49 overs to score the 163 to win the match, they had lost 3 wickets in doing so, thereby winning by 7 wickets.

Lintz

G. Innes		B D. Felton	19
J. Murray	C J. Graham	B D. Felton	19
S. Clennell	C D. Smart	B A. Francis	10
G. Clennell		LBW B A. White	16
D. Mcconnell	C D. Smart	B A. White	14
P. Alderson	C S. Graham	B W. Graham	13
P. Cameron	C D. Smart	B A. White	13
M. Edmunds		B A. Francis	15
W. Greenwell	Not	Out	26
T. Wilson	C G. Nixon	B D. Felton	11
W. Johnson	Not	Out	0
Extras			6
Total			162-9 Wkts

A. Francis 2-36 D. Felton 3-60   W. Graham 1-37 A. White 3-25

Seaton Burn

C. Brown		B G. Clennell	1
J. Graham	Not	Out	53
K. Corby		LBW B G. Clennell	0
D. Smart	C T. Wilson	B M. Edmunds	106
R. Allan	Not	Out	1
Extras			2
Total			163-2 Wkts

G. Clennell 2-74 W. Greenwell 0-19 T. Wilson 0-21   M. Edmunds 1-47

8th August 2020 Andrew White still bowling for Seaton Burn first team in a game against Newcastle City

**Mid Nineties single wicket- Steve Hope keeping
wicket to Tony Wallace**

Mid Nineties single wicket sidelines- Left to Right- Darren Carr, Richie Allan, John Dixon, Alan Francis, Ray Cardwell, Kevin Hunt, Sean Smith

SBCC 1995

BACK ROW-

G.Sinton,D.Smart,S.Felton,M.Gilmore,G.Stephenson,J.Livingston,S.Graham,
K.Ashforth,D.Felton,A.Francis,G.Trick,K.Corby,D.Carr,G.Cardwell

FRONT ROW-

W.Taylor,G.Nixon,A.White,C.Brown,E.Ridley,W.Graham,J.Graham,M.Graham
G.Cardwell,S.Nixon,N.Corby

Tyneside Senior League Final Table 1995
All teams play 26 matches and there was one tied game this season

	Won	Lost	Drawn	Tie	Bonus	Points
Blaydon	17	4	5	0	36	392
Shotley Bridge	16	8	2	0	17	369
Consett	16	5	5	0	28	368
Sacriston	14	6	6	0	49	353
Annfield Plain	13	6	7	0	33	317
Ryton	12	3	11	0	46	298
Whickham	11	6	8	1	45	296
Lintz	9	6	10	1	64	275
Seaton Burn	9	4	13	0	64	260
Greenside	8	8	7	0	58	246
Burnopfield	8	7	11	0	41	229
Swalwell	5	7	14	0	53	181
Hebburn	2	5	19	0	74	134
South Moor	1	6	19	0	56	100

League Batting Averages 1995
Qualification 500 Runs

	Runs	High Score	Comp Inns	Average
D. Jackson (Consett)	1212	121no	15	80.80
C. Brown (SeatonBurn)	1243	134no	19	65.42
C. Armstrong (Annfield Plain)	658	118no	11	59.86
C. Butts (Blaydon)	841	150no	15	56.07
R. Marshall (Blaydon)	949	153no	17	55.82
J. Smith (Greenside)	856	140	16	53.50
P. Collingwood (Shotley Br)	638	88	13	49.08
D. Smart (Seaton Burn)	503	106	11	45.73
J. Graham (Seaton Burn)	912	104	20	45.60
F. Redwood (Sacriston)	831	124no	19	43.74
D. Baxter (Burnopfield)	512	134no	12	42.67
J. Dumighan (Swalwell)	923	111	22	41.96
I. Somerville (Blaydon)	927	109	23	40.30
M. Drake (Blaydon)	510	112	14	36.43
P. Dumighan (Swalwell)	687	84no	19	36.16
P. Veitch (Ryton)	785	115no	22	35.68
G. Kerry (Greenside)	588	115	17	34.59
M. Hopkinson (Sacriston)	608	130	18	33.78
S. Humble (Blaydon)	574	87	17	33.76
M. Clarke (Whickham)	604	125no	18	33.56
R. Strong (Annfield Plain)	659	75	21	31.38
S. Clennell (Lintz)	563	93	19	29.63

Qualification 30 Wickets- As the qualification was set low this season I have concentrated on those who took more than 50, the benchmark for most years, or those who have been featured elsewhere in the book, or who may be of interest due to their achievements later in their cricket career.

League Bowling Averages 1995
Qualification 30 Wickets

	Overs	Runs	Wkts	Ave
F. Redwood (Sacriston)	410.1	1115	97	11.49
P. Collingwood (Shotley Bridge)	201	483	41	11.78
L. Crozier (Ryton)	160.3	417	35	11.97
M. Urwin (Whickham)	285	756	60	12.60
D. Jackson (Consett)	417.3	1085	82	13.23
G. Angus (Shotley Bridge)	303.3	749	50	14.98
A. Francis (Seaton Burn)	266.1	806	42	19.19
C. Butts (Blaydon)	390.3	1003	52	19.39
M. Edmunds (Lintz)	172	685	31	22.10
D. Sweeney (Burnopfield)	177.2	779	32	24.34
I. Stoneman (Hebburn)	252.3	1173	30	39.10
N. Killen (Annfield Plain)	70.2	225	22	10.22
C. Campbell (Blaydon)	107	290	21	13.81
I. Jones (Sacriston)	131.5	538	23	23.39

The last three on the list were limited in appearances by commitments to Durham CCC.

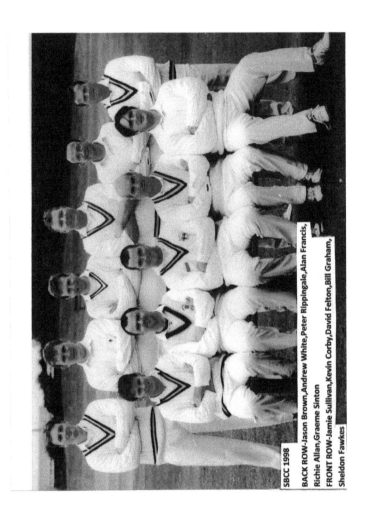

SBCC 1998

BACK ROW:-Jason Brown,Andrew White,Peter Rippingale,Alan Francis,
Richie Allan,Graeme Sinton
FRONT ROW:-Jamie Sullivan,Kevin Corby,David Felton,Bill Graham,
Sheldon Fawkes

CHAPTER 19

2003 CONSETT

On Saturday 30th August 2003 Seaton Burn played a home Northumberland and Tyneside Senior League Division A2 fixture against Consett.

The Tyneside Senior League had merged with the Northumberland County League in 1999.

Consett had finished bottom of Division A1 the previous season and been relegated. They had won just one game. Gary Hunter did appear in the league averages that season with 647 runs at 38.06. He scored six half centuries with a highest score of 95 not out.

Seaton Burn had finished third bottom of Division A2 in 2002, winning just three games. Kevin Corby featured in the league batting averages with 309 runs at 34.33 each. He scored three half centuries with a highest score of 96.

David Felton would feature in the league bowling averages in 2003 with 207.1 overs, 30 maidens, 838 runs conceded and 36 wickets taken at 23.28 each. His best bowling was 6-87.

Smartie had already started winding his career down. His last hundred had been against Lintz in 1995. He batted only thirteen times in the league that year, scoring 504 runs at an average of 45.81, with one century and three half centuries.

In 1996 he moved to Kirkley, batting fourteen times in the league. He scored 492 runs at an average of 35.14 this season. He scored one century, exactly 100, against Newcastle City and had further scores of 94 against Warkworth and 63 against Corbridge.

He also played the 1997 season at Kirkley. Batting in six league games, scoring 131 runs at an average of 21.83. His highest score was 72 against Corbridge.

He didn't play at all in 1998 and returned to Seaton Burn in 1999, playing in seven league games and batting in six. He scored 214 runs at an average of 42.80, with one half century, 94 against Lintz.

He would play just five games in 2000, 46 runs at 9.12 and a high score of 20 against Percy Main.

Only one appearance in 2001, a duck against Alnwick.

And so to the 2003 season.

According to the Daily Telegraph this was the now 51 year old Smarties first game in 4 years. Not quite true but not too far away either. Prior to the game with Consett, Smartie had scored 15 in a game against Benwell earlier this season.

No scorebook for this one, scorecard only. Dave Wilkinson has again kindly provided some memories regarding the Consett players of the day. Gordon Hunter and Ian Stoneman have featured already elsewhere.

Seaton Burn batted first. Smartie opening the innings with his nephew, Neil Corby.

Dave Wilkinson remembers Andrew (Foz) Forster dropping an easy lobbed catch at midwicket off Smartie off the bowling of Wayne Greenwell. Even "Foz" remembers all these years later that it was an "absolute bessie!" Smartie was on nought at the time, I guess you do remember those sorts of things!

Neil Corby was caught by Stephen Marshall off the bowling of Kevin Hopps for 68.

This brought Kevin Corby to the crease, father of Neil and brother in law to Smartie!

Smartie would be the second wicket to fall, run out for 104. The innings had contained thirteen fours and a six. This would be the last of the 23 League hundreds he scored for Seaton Burn.

David Felton joined Kevin Corby at the wicket and they took the score to 242 at the end of their 50 overs. Corby was unbeaten on 38 and Felton on 17.

Consett had used six bowlers. Wayne Greenwell had 0-30, Ian Stoneman 0-19, Kevin Hopps 1-83, Gordon Hunter 0-29, Philip Mellons 0-32 and Andrew Foster 0-38.

Consett opened the batting with Andrew "Bushy" Waters and Colin "Macca" Mcpherson.

Waters was a strong left handed batsman who could punish the bowling when on song. He only ever played for Consett, coming through the ranks from the juniors, seconds then reaching the firsts. He hasn't played for quite a while now due to family commitments.

Mcpherson was a right handed batsman who started out at Shotley Bridge in his early days. He was Club Treasurer until recently and still plays the odd game for the third team.

David Felton and Chris Heron opened the bowling for Seaton Burn. Heron would have been quite young at this time, probably in his late teens, he was a medium pace bowler, away swingers to the right hander.

Waters was bowled by Heron for 5.

Mcpherson was caught by Clifford Lyall off the bowling of Felton for 6.

Gordon Hunter batted at three and top scored the innings with 61 before he was caught behind the wicket by Neil Corby off the bowling of Felton.

Stephen Marshall came in at four. He was known to all as "Prud" because of where he lived, Prudhoe presumably! He was an excellent right handed bat, batting in the top five. He was still playing third team cricket in 2020, a highlight being playing with his son Will.

He scored 15 before he was caught by Peter Rippingale off the bowling of Kevin Corby.

Corby, despite spending most of his career behind the stumps, was a useful spin bowler! More than once I've seen him keep wicket then halfway through an innings take the pads off, mark out his run up and bowl right arm off spin.

Andrew Foster batted at five. He was a right hand batter and bowler. He could accelerate the score at any time. His medium pacers were useful in tight games. He is still playing in 2021. He made 9 before Felton bowled him.

John "Chappa" Chapman was next in at six. Wicketkeeper and right hand bat, he was another who could change a game very quickly with his big hitting. He scored 47 before he fell, caught by Kevin Corby off the bowling of Felton.

John Walker batted at seven. A detective by occupation, I recall playing a couple of games for Northumbria Police with him. A big hitting left handed batsman who could put bat to ball. He would often contribute important runs throughout his career. He was a useful slow left arm bowler too. He was out for 5 today, also caught by Kevin Corby off the bowling of Felton.

Ian Stoneman batting eight scored a single before he was bowled by Heron.

Kevin Hopps batted nine. He was a right handed bat and very useful opening bowler. He came through the junior ranks but stopped playing due to family commitments. He too was bowled by Heron, for 5.

Philip Mellons came in at ten. A steady right handed bat and slow bowler, he was in and out of the first team. He now plays for Shotley Bridge. He would be 4 not out.

Last man was Wayne Greenwell, known as "Wizzard". He was a right handed batsman and bowler. He was regarded as "Mr Consistent" in both areas of the game. He likes perfection. He has been with Consett for a number of years after playing for several clubs, including Lintz in 1995 when Smartie scored his last ton. He was bowled by Heron for 5.

Consett were all out for 169.

David Felton had 5-27, Chris Heron 4-39, Bill Graham 0-62 and Kevin Corby 1-33

Seaton Burn won by 73 runs.

Seaton Burn

D. Smart	Run	Out	104
N. Corby	C S. Marshall	B K. Hopps	68
K. Corby	Not	Out	38
D. Felton	Not	Out	17
Extras			15
Total			242-2 Wkts

W. Greenwell 0-30   I. Stoneman 0-19   K. Hopps 1-83   G. Hunter 0-29
P. Mellons 0-32   A. Foster 0-38

Consett

A. Walters		B C. Heron	5
C. Mcpherson	C C. Lyall	B D. Felton	6
G. Hunter	C N. Corby	B D. Felton	61
S. Marshall	C P. Rippingale	B K. Corby	15
A. Foster		B D. Felton	9
J. Chapman	C K. Corby	B D. Felton	47
J. Walker	C K. Corby	B D. Felton	5
I. Stoneman		B C. Heron	1
K. Hopps		B C. Heron	0
P. Mellons	Not	Out	4
W. Greenwell		B C. Heron	5
Extras			11
Total			169 All Out

D. Felton 5-27   C. Heron 4-39   W. Graham 0-62   K. Corby 1-33

Smartie would play one more game this season, scoring 60 against Kirkley.

He did go on to play 14 games in 2004, two half centuries, 74 and 83 as he hit 317 runs at an average of 22.64.

In 2005 he played ten league games, 185 runs at 26.42, with a highest score of 40 against Lintz.

In 2006 he played his last season, batting five times for 80 runs at 20.00. His top score was 40 not out against Alnwick.

His very last league innings was a duck against Morpeth.

CHAPTER 20

MOPPING UP THE TAIL

Smartie is still, even now, often asked why he never played at a higher level, in first class cricket. His reply is that he was too old when he became a prolific run scorer, being 28 at the time of first hundred and 33 in 1984 when he scored his next, the double hundred.

After the incredible 1984 season Smartie felt that he was "targetted wherever I played, the overseas pro's in particular would be aware of the importance of my wicket. That said, it made me all the more determined that they wouldn't get me out. I never got nervous or afraid, as a captain and opener, I always wanted to bat first, that's what I played cricket for, to bat".

He is credited with scoring 17,142 runs in The Tyneside Senior League Division "A" for Seaton Burn. Those runs included 23 centuries, with a highest score of 201 not out, and 109 half centuries. He also had two second team half centuries.

He scored two centuries in cup matches for Seaton Burn and one more league century for Kirkley. He also scored a further three half centuries for Kirkley.

He was "The Sunday Sun Cricketer of the Month for June 1984."

He also took 136 wickets for Seaton Burn in the Tyneside Senior League.

He represented the Tyneside Senior League on at least 52 occasions, scoring 12 half centuries with a highest score of 88 against the Durham County League in 1992.

He also represented Northumberland 12 times, all in friendlies, with a highest score of 52 against Durham.

Four of those games were against first class counties, with a highest score in these four matches of 44 against Essex.

His son, Ian, would also represent Seaton Burn and Northumberland, as well as a number of other clubs. He currently plays for Ponteland. A very good leg spin bowler and decent bat.

When he was a teenager, probably 14 or 15, I can recall facing him in the nets and I had never, and though long retired, never did, face anyone who could turn the ball as much from a variety of surfaces.

Ian recalls making his debut for the first team before he played a game for the second team! Aged 11 or 12 he was scoring for the first team for an away match at Sacriston. At the last minute someone cried off so Ian stepped in, he vividly remembers scoring 2 not out and batting at the end with Bill Graham against the bowling of Alan Worthy and Paul Burn, perhaps the reason he remembers it so well is that he says they didn't drop their pace for him!

I was talking to him over the Pandemic Summer of 2020 and he reminded me of his debut for the second team, I must admit, I couldn't remember the occasion, Ian could, he says I ran him out for a duck!

Whilst doing his "A" levels, aged around 18, and having gone through the Northumberland County Junior set up, he received an unexpected call up to play for the county senior side. Steve Chapman, the regular spinner in the senior county side, played for Bishop Auckland, they had a major cup final which clashed with a Northumberland game in which nothing was at stake.

So "Young Smartie" played one senior game for Northumberland, against Cambridgeshire, taking one wicket, Ian Blanchett, who later represented Middlesex, for five runs from five overs.

During his time with the Northumberland Youth set up he had played under 19 representative cricket as a 16 year old.

David and Ian Smart are one of a number of father and son duo's who played cricket for Northumberland. Kevin and Neil Corby, Mike and Ollie Youll, Allen and Matthew Thompson, Bob and Sameet Brar, Barry and Alan Evans, Stuart Tiffin Senior and Junior, Jim and Michael Thewlis, would also be on the list, with apologies to others not mentioned!

Ian went on to study at Durham University, he played a handful of games there for the third team, saying "the standard was incredible, our first team had James Foster, who would later play test cricket for England, and his Essex team mate, Will Jefferson, who had a long career in county cricket. James Bruce was also in the first team and he had a number of successful seasons at Hampshire."

He chose to play his cricket at Durham City whilst at University, mainly because the ground was a stone's throw from his accomodation.

He would go on to play senior cricket for Seaton Burn, Shotley Bridge, South North, Greenside and Ponteland. He is known as a leg spin bowler, his best senior figures being 7-20 for Greenside against Cowgate.

He fondly recalls how in his mid teen's Cade Brown taught him to bowl a "wrong un," he recalls "up until this point, my county coaches, team mates, not even my father, could teach me how to do it, Cade spent some time first of all showing me, then teaching me, then practising it with me."

His first "first" team wicket was taken in a cup match against Lintz, a batsman called Anthony Ward, who was caught by Smart Senior.

Ian now has over 300 first team wickets to his credit and he also played for the Tyneside Senior League representative side on a number of occasions.

What a lot of people, myself included, didn't know about Ian is that he is almost blind in his left eye, and has been since birth. I knew as a youngster he seemed to be wearing glasses from a young age but thought nothing of it.

As a teenager when playing for the county he would open the batting for a number of years, playing with lads like Nicky Peng and Gordon Muchall.

He recalls that as he got older and the bowling got much faster, his disability became more difficult to overcome, he simply couldn't pick up the ball outside off stump from the faster bowlers.

He did register one fifty in first team cricket, for Seaton Burn against Ryton. He says he always tried to play straight, his dad's advice being "There's nobody standing in front of the sight screen, hit it there!"

2012-13 Ian Smart bowling for Ponteland v Morpeth

Cade Brown describes Smartie Senior as follows "I have nothing but admiration and respect for Smartie, and the same for Nicola, Ian and the beautiful Gillian. He was a beauty Smartie, he had many traits that are admired here in Australia. He was so passionate about the club and he had no fear of what this meant in terms of others views. You knew where you stood with David. I saw him when he was past his best but at different times I did have the pleasure of watching him play. You could always sense the fear in the opposition when you had him in your side. The innings of years gone by were still discussed, in particular the famous double hundred. He had terrific hands in the field and you could tell he had an amazing eye. You had to earn his respect but once you did, it never went away. He was a great friend of mine and one whose feats will forever be remembered in North East cricket circles."

1981 David Smart

The above photo was taken in 1981. Given the love David had for Gillian and the influence she had on both his cricket and his life in total, I think it's appropriate that she has the final word.

A huge thank you to daughter Nicola, who sent me both the photo and the story as I was finishing the book.

Gillian had wanted a photo of Smartie in his cricket whites, but she was too shy to take it in front of the rest of the cricket lads, no doubt knowing the mickey taking that would follow. So on a non cricket day Smartie put his white's on and went to the cricket field where Gillian took the photo and no doubt treasured it for many years to come.

Because of the time cricket takes it should never be taken for granted how much family support it takes to commit to a full cricket season.

In Smartie's case, he stated earlier how marrying Gillian had changed his mental approach to the game and he credits her a lot in respect of the cricketer he was to become.

Thank you all.

CHAPTER 21

CLOSE OF PLAY

One of the things that cricket gave me over the years was quality time spent with my two boys, David and Scott. As toddlers and young boys they would attend most home games and a fair few of the away games I played. Grounds like Swalwell and Shotley meant there was plenty of room to play football or cricket around the boundary edge with the boys when we were batting.

Looking back on the fifteen or so years I played senior cricket, looking purely at the cricket, I consider myself very lucky to have netted and played with three of the very best local league cricketers the north east has ever produced in David Smart, Kevin Corby and John Graham.

I was also lucky enough to play when Cade Brown played for the club too. His first two years coincided with probably my last two, and even they were cut short by work commitments.

As a police Officer I had joined the Special Patrol Group, later renamed the Territorial Support Group, in 1993 and we policed Newcastle United matches one week and Sunderland the next, cutting both ends of the cricket season short for me, as well as the numerous major incidents we also worked.

Cade remembers me as being "someone you loved to play with because you knew he would fight until the last ball was bowled. He loved the contest, scrapping for every run, often diving to cut off those runs!

As a middle order batsman he was often in earlier than desired but would always, without fail, put a price on his wicket. Many partnerships with his great mate Kevin Corby got "the Burn" over the line, or at a minimum back in the contest.

His reflexes behind the wicket in his favourite gully position were outstanding.

He was a terrific club man and a proud dad, his two sons being seen regularly on the boundary of our beloved home ground."

There were also a good number of lads who I played second team cricket with who missed out on being mentioned in the book through the timing and the dates of Smartie's hundreds. Eddie Collins, David Hope, John Dixon, to name a few, were all people I enjoyed playing cricket with.

As someone who bounced between first and second team I also think I was fortunate to play against some truly outstanding local cricketers too. Ian Somerville and Paul Veitch at Blaydon, Bob Cook, Gordon Baker, Graeme and Stuart Clennell, Micky Edmonds, all at Lintz, Paul Burn, Dave Metcalfe and Freddie Hilton at Sacriston, Jason and Paul Dumighan at Swalwell, Stuart Wilkinson, David Love among many at Shotley. You can also add a teenage Paul Collingwood to the list too. These are just a few off what could have been a very long list.

Then there was the local lads who were good enough to be professionals, Ian Stoneman at Reyrolle, Shaun Stokoe at Greenside, Robert Stokoe at Swalwell, Dave Jackson at Annfield Plain, Donald Brown at Shotley, Paul Carrick at Ryton, again just a few from what could have been a very long list!

If you add some of the overseas professionals I played against, Qasim Omar, Wes and Dennison Thomas, Steve Russell, Clyde Butts, Mark Harper and Madan Lal.

There were others around at the time as well, who I missed playing against, Wasim Raja, Troy Cooley, Scott Styris and Wasim Akram amongst them. A pretty impressive bunch.

If you look at the players named above, you try and pick a best eleven! The standard was very, very good.

In respect of my bowling, I remember watching Jeff Thomson hammer England in 1974-75 and I think that's where my bowling action came from. I played no organised cricket until I was 13 or so and had no coaching until I was older than that and then the first thing they did was try and change my action. I think that gave me a reluctance towards coaching for a long time. I had decided, at a young age, I just wanted to get the ball from point A to Point B as fast as I could!

I do recall the season I took 67 second team wickets with a lot of pride, despite that pride I cannot for the life of me remember what year it was, I think it was 1986......or was it 1988!

That season included bowling Blaydon Seconds out opening the bowling and recording 16.4-9-20-7, and the first 8 wickets at home to Annfield Plain seconds, finishing with 8-69. I did play one game for the first team that season, and I didn't get a bowl!

My natural length was "short" of a good length. That year I only bowled "down the bank" at home games and I think the slope pushed my natural length closer to a good length and helped me to open up my action enormously.

The following season I was asked to bowl "up the bank" and I felt this pulled my natural length back to being even shorter of a good length than it was naturally. I also felt it "compressed" my action.

Instead of just getting the ball from "A to B" as fast as I could it took real effort for me to not bowl short when bowling from this end and as a result I lost pace when bowling this way.

I rarely bowled for the first team, though going through the old scorebooks I see that I took my first "first" team wicket in 1987, Davie Collingwood, LBW off a slower ball. The next two were Ronnie Platford and Shaun Stokoe of Greenside, a couple of South Moor lads then Davie Jackson of Annfield Plain. That was it for the first team that season but as i said elsewhere, I will take Davie Collingwood, Ronnie Platford, Shaun Stokoe and Davie Jackson as four of my first six anytime, especially as one was LBW and the other three bowled!

The best bowling I managed for the first team was 4-22 at South Moor, but I didn't get a bowl for six weeks after it so it obviously wasn't as impressive as it sounds!

I can still see Paul Mcelveny's leg stump going over at Blaydon on the day I took 7-20 for the second team and the full toss that landed on the bails to win the match at Swalwell. I thought Ray Cardwells description was very fair earlier in the book! I also loved bowling in the nets, always flat out!

I think the issues with my left knee started in the early nineties, I can recall doing a fitness test for work in early 1993 where I had to run a mile and a half in under eleven minutes. I did it successfully but I remember having a very unhappy knee for a few days afterwards.

Reflecting on my batting and despite the descriptions of me from my team mates, I don't think I really took it seriously enough. I had 6 or 7 first team fifties, the best coming against teams with at least one outstanding fast bowler.

On 18th July 1992, I scored exactly 50 at Blaydon, the innings contained seven fours and a six, of the 62 runs scored whilst I was at the crease, I had 50 of them, the fast bowler was Wes Thomas.

We scored 174 for 8 that day, Smartie top scoring with 57. When Blaydon batted Paul Veitch hit a stunning 107 not out, the innings included fifteen fours and a six. Ian Somerville was out for 24 and Paul Kennedy made 40 not out as Blaydon won by nine wickets.

When I scored 50 against Lintz their fast bowlers were Bob Cook and Davie Nevin.

My top score for the first team was 68 which I achieved twice.

The innings described below was against Shotley Bridge and their fast bowlers were Stuart Wilkinson and Donald Brown.

They were two very different innings.

On Saturday 30th May 1992 we played Shotley Bridge. They batted first, scoring 209 for 7 off their 50 overs. The innings included a cameo at the end, a 16 year old Paul Collingwood had an unbeaten 22 from 19 balls, including one four and two sixes.

For the first of two occasions I found myself opening the batting for the first team. I scored 68, with six fours, off 49.3 overs when I was out LBW to John Stokoe.

Peter Rippingale showed his quality in this innings, an unbeaten 56 with seven fours and a six. Seaton Burn scored 152 for 4 off our 50 overs and lost the game but we did pick up a batting point.

The best innings I played was at Swalwell on 10th July 1994. Swalwell had batted first and scored 256 for 7 off their 50 overs. I had taken 3 for 65 off 11 overs, the three were both Dumighan brothers and Michael Urwin.

When we batted our pro Graham Hallam had set the innings up with 66. Graeme Dakers, batting five, hit an unbeaten 76, with six fours and two sixes from 82 balls and I had an unbeaten 68 off 60 balls, with nine fours. I knew I was on my top score when Dakers at the other end hit a six and a four to win the game! We won with 15 balls to spare.

Looking back, the best first team innings I played were right at the end of my cricket career, perhaps I retired at the wrong time!

Through a set of unfortunate circumstances I found myself first team captain in 1990 after 3 or 4 games of the season! Looking at the league table we finished second bottom that season, winning 5 games. I did note that we picked up 13 points for not being bowled out, I would like to think that meant we fought hard for the season.

I really enjoyed fielding. In my late teens I had spent four years as a goalkeeper for Cramington Juniors and I think that helped me to become the gully fielder I was. I always felt I was in the game fielding there and I was lucky enough to have fast bowlers of the calibre of Davie Gibson, Graeme Nixon, Alan Francis, Rob Parkin, Ian Tinlin and David Felton firing away at the batsmen.

As I neared the end of writing this book I overheard a conversation between my wife, Carol, and our then 5 year old grandson, Thomas. Carol was telling him that "Grandad was writing a book about cricket," the response was "I play cricket, will I be in the book?"

Thomas at 5, thanks to the "All Stars" programme, has already had more coaching in his life than I had in mine!

More importantly, pre pandemic, when I would take him to Seaton Burn Welfare for his cricket sessions, Andrew White and Malcolm Alderson were there......with 30-40 kids! The future of cricket, and Seaton Burn Cricket, looks bright.

Thomas, or one of his pals, could be the next David Smart..... or Kevin Corby...or John Graham!

That said, they might just be lucky enough to get half the pleasure that cricket and Seaton Burn Cricket Club gave to Thomas's Grandad, if that's the case, they will have been very lucky indeed!

Grandson Thomas, aged 5, showing his grandad
how he should have done it!

ACKNOWLEDGEMENTS

In no particular order, I owe a huge thank you to the following people. I had a particular idea and those mentioned below added authenticity and content in respect of the people they played with and against, or they were record keepers, who added the detail and achievements of those mentioned.

David Smart-Seaton Burn
Ian Smart- Seaton Burn
Dave Sweeney- Burnopfield
Peter Carroll- Blaydon
Jack Chapman- Shotley Bridge/Blaydon
Joe Tyson-Felling
Ray Cardwell-Seaton Burn
Mark Graham-Seaton Burn
Kevin Corby -Seaton Burn
Cade Brown-Seaton Burn
Phil Shield-South Moor
Ossie Barrass-South Moor
Paul Carrick -Greenside
David Hickmott- Sacriston
Ian Somerville-Blaydon
Craig Johnson-Wallsend
Stuart Stanton-Ryton
Dave Wilkinson-Consett
Chris Cox- Reyrolle
John Trotter- Reyrolle
Graham Robinson-Annfield Plain
Paul Nesbit- Shotley Bridge
Graeme Clennell- Lintz
Jason Brown- Reyrolle/Seaton Burn

Credit to the unknown "Sunday Sun" photographer for the photo of Smartie on the day he scored his 201 not out!

Credit to Michael Oakes for his editing skills on both the front and rear cover.

Team photos courtesy of Bill and Mark Graham.

Credit to Kevin and Julie Smart for several of their photos

Photo of Ian Smart courtesy of Chris Barlow, Ponteland CC

APPENDIX

One Hundred Years of Blaydon Cricket Club by Jack Chapman

Cream Teas and Nutty Slack by Jack Chapman

A History of South Moor Cricket Club by Ossie Barrass

Lightning Source UK Ltd.
Milton Keynes UK
UKHW021023250721
387656UK00001B/7